RUTH PARK'S
SYDNEY

RUTH PARK'S SYDNEY

REVISED BY RUTH PARK
AND RAFE CHAMPION

DUFFY & SNELLGROVE
SYDNEY

Published by Duffy & Snellgrove in 1999
PO Box 177 Potts Point NSW 1335 Australia
info@duffyandsnellgrove.com.au

First edition 1973
Revised and expanded second edition 1999
Reprinted 2000

© Kemalde Pty Ltd. 1973
Revised edition 1999

Distrubuted by Pan Macmillan

Cover design by Alex Snellgrove
Cover illustration Australian Picture Library/Sean Davey
Maps by Sally Beech
Typeset by Go Media
Printed by Griffin Press

ISBN 1 875989 45 5

Visit our website: www.duffyandsnellgrove.com.au

CONTENTS

CHAPTER 1
Circular Quay, The Open Door   1

CHAPTER 2
The Gallows, The Rogues, The Builders   39

CHAPTER 3
Fine buildings and a Garden   69

CHAPTER 4
Farm Cove to Sydney Tower   103

CHAPTER 5
William Street to South Head   125

CHAPTER 6
How Darling Harbour became the Ent Cent   157

CHAPTER 7
Balmain to the Riverlands   169

CHAPTER 8
Middle Head to Fig Tree Bridge   195

CHAPTER 9
Here we Began   235

Acknowledgements   256

Index   257

MAPS

Circular Quay *viii*

The Rocks *38*

The City I *68*

The City II *102*

The Eastern Suburbs *124*

Darling Harbour *156*

Balmain to Hunters Hill *168*

The Lower North Shore *194*

The South-Eastern Suburbs *234*

ILLUSTRATION LIST

following page 56
Sydney Cove, 1788
Sydney, 1803
Convicts labouring
Circular Quay
The Rocks
George Street

following page 120
The Opera House
The Argyle Cut
Macquarie Street
Lord Nelson Hotel
Victoria Barracks
Paddington Terraces
The Gap
Bondi Beach

following page 184
The Botanic Gardens
Observatory Park
Mosman cupolas
Mosman Bay
Clyde Bank
Macquarie Lighthouse
Durham Hall
Sydney Harbour

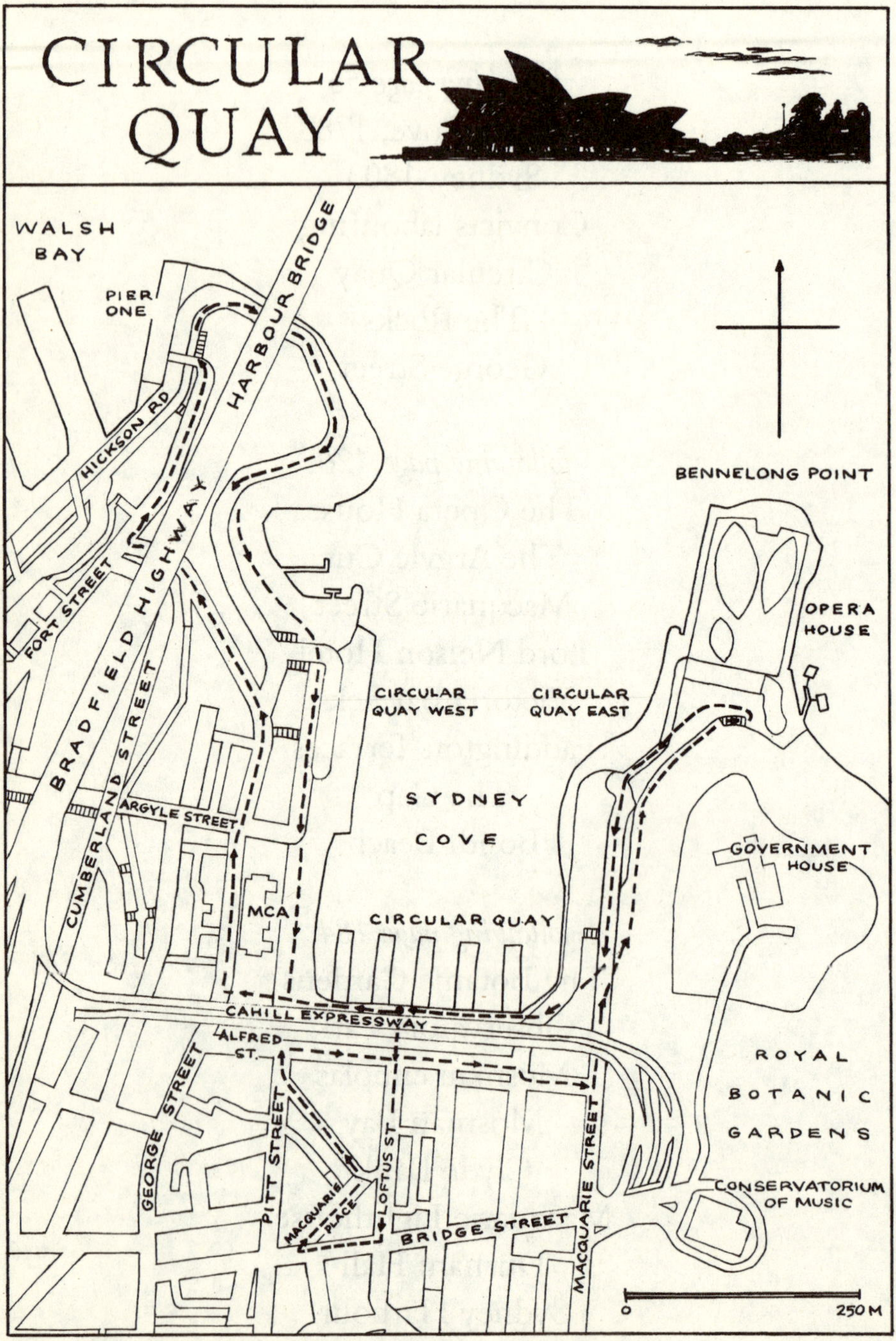
CIRCULAR
QUAY
WALSH
BAY
PIER
ONE
HARBOUR BRIDGE
HICKSON RD
FORT STREET
BRADFIELD HIGHWAY
CUMBERLAND STREET
ARGYLE STREET
CIRCULAR
QUAY WEST
CIRCULAR
QUAY EAST
SYDNEY
COVE
MCA
CIRCULAR QUAY
CAHILL EXPRESSWAY
ALFRED
ST.
GEORGE STREET
PITT STREET
MACQUARIE
PLACE
LOFTUS ST
BRIDGE STREET
MACQUARIE STREET
BENNELONG POINT
OPERA
HOUSE
GOVERNMENT
HOUSE
ROYAL
BOTANIC
GARDENS
CONSERVATORIUM
OF MUSIC
0
250 M

CHAPTER 1
CIRCULAR QUAY, THE OPEN DOOR

Captain Phillip, whom God made for Sydney – Surgeon Bowes and his abandoned wretches – Government House – the Victorian gentlemen of Bridge Street – Macquarie Place – the Sirius anchor and its lost ship, also a lost convenience – riots on the Quay, and how it was built by muddy convicts – we meet Edmund Blacket, the Tarpeian Way and the Opera House – Circular Quay West – how Sudden Solomon robbed the bank – the Rocks – murders, muggings and Chinatown – George Street north – the first hospital – one-eyed Cadman's cottage – the Argyle Cut – the great times we used to have – the Bridge – should the Opera House be on an island? – ghosts of old streets – Lower Fort Street – Dawes Point, which commemorates a virtuous young man – we meet the Campbell family – bond stores and convict bricks – ghosts along the Quay.

HERE we stand then, civilly on the doorstep. That Circular Quay is Sydney's doorstep no one can deny. At our back is one of the world's largest and finest ports, beautiful as a dream, laid upon the map like a branch of blue coral. Before us, croaking and huffing and squealing like some fabulous toad is the city, explosive in growth.

Sydney is built on a landscape littered with human bones. Indeed it might never have been born at all if England hadn't been in a pickle after the American War of Independence, finding herself without a penal destination for her stirrers and footpads, forgers and pickpockets. Thus was the town founded, the first convict settlement in the South Seas, daughter of the American Revolution, the most distant, loneliest and saddest place on earth. Or so it was planned to be.

But Sydney turned out quite otherwise. Blithe, irresponsible, slightly mad, she has air full of electric sparks, her birds shout in boys' voices, the sunshine is here more often and lasts longer. And even when the bushfire lights her domestic façades as though for some hellish *son et lumière*, you feel it's right, characteristic somehow, Sydney.

She was born not far from where we stand, in a January thunderstorm, in 1788, when Captain Phillip raised the flag for England and christened these waters Sydney Cove.

I like this little man Arthur Phillip, with his French philosopher's nose and large eighteenth century eyes, which are seen at their apotheosis in the sunny toadface of that other Pacific explorer, the Comte de la Perouse. How admirably this son of a German schoolmaster rose out of a worthy but unpublicised naval career to become the hardworking, earnest, infinitely finicky Father of a Nation. 'Upon my soul,' said one of his contemporaries, 'I do think God Almighty made Phillip on purpose for that place, for never did man know better what to do, or with more determination see it done.'

Plagued by his disorderly and slobbish charges, speared by Aborigines, suffering sorely from the stone, he returned to England after four years' governorship and six years' absence, to sink into an invalidish obscurity. In the growing history of New South Wales he was overshadowed not only by the great James Cook who went before but by those sportier governors who came after him.

He was idealistic. 'I would not wish convicts to lay the foundations of an empire. There is one [law] that I would wish to take place from the moment His Majesty's forces take possession of the country. That there can be no slavery in a free land and consequently no slaves.' And, predating G. Bernard Shaw, though not Dean Swift, he was practical, thus solving the problem of capital punishment, which he always disliked: 'I would wish to confine the criminal till an opportunity afforded of delivering him to the natives of New Zealand and let them eat him. The dread of this will operate much stronger than the fear of death.'

And how gallant was the end of life for Phillip! Ailing and alone, with life too lived-in to be longer bearable, he barrelled through a top floor window in his wheelchair. (Or so one gathers from the circumspect reports of his death at Bath.)

But on this day the forty-nine year-old Phillip's heart must have been joyful. Eighteen years before, Captain Cook had seen by afternoon's yellow light the gate to this stupendous harbour. But it had been left to him, Arthur Phillip, to make it his. Phillip, who had explored the harbour on January 23, had made up his mind as to the place of settlement, and returned at once to Botany Bay, where the fleet lay. He had been horrified to discover two French warships outside the bay. They were La Perouse's *Astrolabe* and *Boussole*, on a scientific expedition. Aware of France's intense interest in Pacific land-grabbing, Phillip must have endured anxious hours. He returned at once to Port Jackson, leaving most of the fleet to follow him. Early in the morning of January 26 he had a flagstaff erected, and 'the English flag, with all that it connoted' fluttered upon the nor'-easter.

If you now look straight across the Quay, you will see on the Loftus Street side of the Customs House a replica of the mast and flag. It is not the present British flag, but the Union Flag or Queen Anne's Flag, under which fought the British loyalists in the American War of Independence. It shows the two crosses of St George and St Andrew. The cross of St Patrick was to come later.

There has been much argument over which flag was flown on January 26, 1788. Some historians state definitely that the naval ensign with the red cross of St George on a white field was displayed – this despite the fact that the flag in Captain John Hunter's little scribble, really the only eyewitness sketch we have, shows a light cross on a dark field. Lieutenant Gidley King, writing that same day, says: 'After noon the Union Jack was hoisted on shore.' It is fact that the term Union Jack was familiarly used for the Union Flag, as it is used now for the present three-cross flag.

The first flagstaff was erected slightly above the beach, and it is said Captain Phillip stood in the shade of a huge casuarina while he read the proclamation. This tree is supposed to have lasted till 1832, but I cannot find it in any early sketch.

The eighteenth-century drawings and watercolours of virgin Sydney Cove show it to be one more of the ravishing triangular inlets that are a geological feature of the Harbour. Lying in most cases between wooded steeps or high rocks, chewed out by creeks and cascades, often bordered by mangroves, these lovely pauses in a sweeping shoreline are tidal flats which provided an abundance of easy food for the spearfishing Cadigals who first inhabited the locality. No doubt, on that first day, they were hiding in the scrub, overcome with curiosity and amazement at the extraordinary doings of the new arrivals.

The distance between us and Loftus Street indicates how much of Circular Quay is reclaimed and filled land. In fact, if we are standing outside Jetties 4 and 5, the transports *Scarborough* and *Friendship* would have been anchored broadside on just behind us. The *Sirius* and *Supply* stood like watchdogs at the head of the Cove, not far from the present Opera House. This was in case the French came nosing in.

A charming account of this great day in Sydney's history is given by James Scott, a Sergeant of Marines. He wrote: 'Saturday, January 26, 1788. At a.m. the fleet got on their way. Came to an anker at fi pt 6 o'clock in Port Jackson close to the New town which was chrisned Sydney this day and 4 vollies of small arms fired. A few mugs of porter were drunk to the colony's success and ye whole gave three cheers.'

Sergeant Scott believed that the new town was christened Sydney. But Phillip named only the cove. The settlement was going to be called Albion, and indeed it appears that way on some of the earliest maps. However, the name never took. Phillip was soon heading his dispatches 'Sydney'. The cove was named after Lord Sydney, the British Home Secretary and Phillip's immediate boss. Lord Sydney was described by his friends as a lighthearted politician, and by his enemies as a maggot-head.

The word Sydney is a corruption of St Denis. There is a haunting recollection of its origin in the way the Sydneysider often pronounces the name of his home city – Sydenie.

St Denis was that saint who converted the pagan Gauls to Christianity, and he is intimately connected with Paris where, like everyone else, he lost his head. The name Denis is a corruption of the martyr's original Athenian name, Dionysius. Thus we may say that Sydney's patron is Dionysius, which, in view of the blithe and irrepressible character of the city as it has developed, is gratifyingly suitable.

Is it possible for us to imagine Sydney Cove as it was that day? 'Every man stepped from the boat literally into a wood,' said David Collins, Captain of Marines. The female felons were not allowed ashore for nearly a fortnight. On that hot January day they must have lined the rails of the transports sniffing with fright or joy the sweet smells of the alien wood, eucalyptus, turpentine, hot rock and wet mud, most nostalgic of all after a long sea voyage. Not all of these women were debased or derelict, in spite of Surgeon Bowes's exasperated description of his female charges on the *Lady Penrhyn*: 'I may venture to say that there never was a more abandon'd set of wretches collected in one place at any period.'

But Surgeon Bowes sounds a right grizzler. Besides, he had been particularly bedevilled by a certain Ann Smith, a seven-year convict transported for stealing a pewter pint pot, value sixpence. (But she had several previous convictions for theft, and they cooked her goose.) Ann Smith always 'behaved amis' said Dr Bowes.

Among the *Lady Penrhyn's* cargo (of whom the youngest was thirteen and the eldest eighty-two) were milliners, lace-weavers, staymakers, glove-makers, barrow-women, and servants. They had almost all been transported for crimes against property, which says something for the eighteenth century's view of property. What they had in common was destitution and little hope of ever returning home.

Some of these women were wearing the remnants of the clothing in which they had left England. Others had contrived garments from the 'sacks of strong russia' (a tough linen duck) in which had been packed the cassava or tapioca loaded at Rio de Janeiro. Ann Smith had hated her russia 'slops' and thrown them on the deck, annoying Surgeon Bowes so much he wrote about it in his journal.

What the female convicts saw from the ships' rails were low hills, tawny with summer, that rolled endlessly on to vanish into hyacinth heat haze. This monotonous hillscape had a strange effect on Europeans. It 'inspired melancholy sensations, reminding one of a tempestuous sea transfixed into leaden stillness'. To the east lay a long spit like the neck of a swan outstretched on the water. It was almost entirely composed of oyster, mussel and scallop shells, a ten metre depth of bleached white shells left behind after thousands of years of Aboriginal meals on this bountiful shore. This spit was named Cattle Point, as the first stock were landed there. For fifty years it provided the little settlement with the raw material for lime burning. It is now called Bennelong Point, and the Opera House stands upon it.

To the right were the long sandstone ledges and lintels of what was to be Dawes Point, dipping down into fine deep water, the horny lizard spine of the ridge scantily clad with rufous fuzz, as though some prehistoric bushfire had flashed down the promontory and left it bare of all but wildflowers, grass trees and sea-stained scrub.

The 'run of clear water' which had made Phillip choose Sydney Cove for a settlement flowed down from the extensive swamps which lay where Hyde Park is now. We do not know what the Aborigines called this beautiful year-round stream which ran in a deep ferny gully to the cove, widening into a broad tidal estuary somewhere in the vicinity of modern Pitt Street and its western buildings. Phillip, who caused tanks to be cut in its sandstone bed in order to conserve water, called it the Tank Stream, a characteristically utilitarian name.

All round the rivulet stood a majestic forest of Sydney red gums, huge myrtles with flesh of luminous rosiness. There were mimosas (speedily renamed 'wattle' because these small flowering trees were the first to be cut down and used in wattle-and-daub huts), and there were also turpentines, ironbark, blackbutt and the strange grasstree or blackboy, lifting its lance rimmed with downy light.

In the humid recesses of the gullies grew orchids, mosses, and ferns and a battalion of immensely tall cabbage tree palms, which were cut down quick smart so that within a year not a palm remained. With equal celerity the settlers were to destroy the Tank Stream itself. Having no knowledge of semitropical water storage systems in spongy topsoil and decayed vegetation, they stripped the land bare, hoed up the shallow earth, and in no time lost that as well by erosion.

But on that first January 26, all was calm, fertile and, being January, alive with bird and insect life. Christmas beetles still flipped like tossed sovereigns into the apple gums, and the whole vale vibrated with giant cicadas playing their steely castanets till the ears rang. Flocks of waterhens scurried off to the upper reaches of the Tank Stream. Ducks left hurriedly for the tranquil Botany Swamps. The new species had arrived, and the old ones, which had been safe against the black people's scanty requirements, began to die.

The sandstone ribs of the land remain. The hills have become slighter in grade, the gullies filled, the sea driven back, a forest of steel and concrete cacti has sprung from the rind of the earth. And yet the depthless blue sky has not changed, in spite of the luxurious towers leaping for it, their dark reflective glass full of clouds, sea glitter and ghostly traffic. The shape of things is very nearly the same; Phillip would recognise it.

What is before us is a huge, almost futuristic city that in a raffish, wilful way has squeezed itself into a too small, eccentric space. Here I am, it seems to say, sea all around me, as it was meant to be, my old sandstone bones poking out of today's walls and foundations; George III coins and buttons and broken tools turning up in my sandy mud, cart track streets going every which way; hard durable inhabitants who are glad their ancestors left failing homelands and set out for the moon, which Australia might as well have been in 1788. Take me or leave me.

The elevated road rattling overhead is the Cahill Expressway. Completed in 1962, it was designed to run as a traffic distributor from the northern to eastern suburbs. At the eastern end of the Quay, it dives under the Botanic Gardens, in a quarter-kilometre tunnel, emerges, passes through the Domain and out to Woolloomooloo.

In 1962 Sydney's terrible tribe of public protesters had not yet gathered in its might, otherwise this obstruction, a kind of monstrous girder fallen across a magnificent open city space, would have been put where it should have been put, in a tunnel under the Quay. The sandstone plateau on which the city stands lends itself to tunnel making. In fact, the underside of the city resembles a worm farm, tunnels of awful decrepitude, tunnels of fabulous masonry, tunnels for mysterious reasons and no good sense. Sydneysiders have been making tunnels since the battle of Trafalgar and are still at it. So we can confidently hope that not far into the future this useful but hideous expressway will have vanished from sight.

Let us saunter across the Quay and climb Loftus Street's gentle slope. Phillip and his gentlemen would have done this, sweating in their thick uniforms. (The convicts must have been much more comfortable in their duck slops.)

Just ahead of us, past the lopsided green triangle of Macquarie Place, all that remains of the first vice-regal gardens, was Phillip's Government House. Actually, Governor Phillip brought with him a prefab canvas house bought in London at his own great expense. This grievously leaky Ur-Government House was erected on the east side of Sydney Cove. Its exact situation has not been pinpointed but one of the sketches by Captain John Hunter, second in command of the First Fleet and captain of the flagship *Sirius*, shows it standing almost under the shadow of the flag. Therefore, as we observe while standing outside the ferry buildings, it must have been very close to the present-day position of the Customs House. Captain Hunter, a well-educated Scotsman, had a notable naval career. Our earliest history is enriched by his abilities in the fields of navigation, astronomy and marine survey. He became a weak, dithery Governor (1795–1800) of what he sadly described as 'a more wicked, abandon'd and irreligious set of people [as] have never been brought together in any part of the world'.

Captain Hunter was too hard on his unruly mob of reluctant settlers. They did evil things ... pilfered food, skived on the job and were beaten for it, stole the assistant chaplain's pigs and ate them; bred hosts of illegitimate children, and ran away into the bush expecting to end up in China. Not having the skills of the Aborigines, they were brought back and put in irons. But in spite of these sins we cannot believe them criminals in our modern understanding of the word.

Through the intervening two centuries, historians have warned against our thinking of the First Fleet convicts as more sinned against than sinning. This is twaddle. A perusal of the list of their well-documented 'crimes' makes one's eyes pop. Seven years 'across the seas' for the theft of a cotton handkerchief? The same sentence passed on fourteen-year-old Mary Reiby who took a joyride on a horse in some farmer's paddock?

These severe punishments indicate clearly the terror that the landed gentry felt for the landless. The latter were the scarcely known or understood 'mob' that in France the next year would predictably rise and cut off coroneted heads. Governor Hunter, though intelligent and humane, recognised that his charges were natural subversives, but did not know how to compromise with them except by whip and hangman's rope.

How they spring out of history's pages, these first settlers – graceless, cunning, self-serving and indomitable. They despised the soldiers who guarded them, and cheated and robbed the young officers of the Marine Corps. They composed shocking broadsides about His Excellency, and later on even printed them. In these unfree and almost uncivilised men and women an inchoate sense of equality had begun to show itself.

This made uneasy every governor until the new century brought New South Wales Lieutenant-General Lachlan Macquarie.

The building of the first Government House commenced in May, 1788. It was eighteen metres above high-water mark, looking straight out on the Government Wharf, which protruded into the Cove mudflats, close to the mouth of the Tank Stream. This corner-to-be of Bridge and Loftus Streets was for a long time the focal point of early colonial society, so important that Government departments and rich settlers' mansions alike crowded around it, as Court officials clustered their mastaba tombs around the majestic resting-place of the Pharoah.

In spite of many additions, a second storey, a stone dairy, more windows, a verandah, no one loved Government House. The decaying leaking building brought querulous cries from successive governors' ladies, but it must have been rather charming, with an exquisite view over its shrubbery and vegetable garden, and the sparkling Harbour waters fenced in only by the steep bronze forests of the untouched North Shore. Mettlesome Mrs Macquarie used to walk from here, up over the hill now traversed by Macquarie Street, though the infant Botanic Gardens which she helped to design, around Farm Cove, to that comfortable sandstone outcrop still known as Mrs Macquarie's Chair. Here she would rest and look out through the Heads towards a longed-for phantom England.

Like everyone else she was homesick.

On the site of the first Government House now stands the unusual Museum of Sydney, which imaginative designers have conjured into a fantasy of historical personage and event presented experientially. A grubby New South Wales Corps soldier pops out of the wall at you, unironed uniform and all. You can sit in the dark enclosed by audial and visual reconstructions of life in the early years.

Do not skip this Museum because it is small; there are countless objects that will inform you and even touch your heart. The Stone Age tools and fish hooks of the vanished Port Jackson tribes, so crude yet so ingenious, speaking of happy feasts and splashings in the very water that laps the adjacent shore; the foundation stone of the first Government House, lost for a century and found by a workman digging a telegraph tunnel in 1899 – that's in a glass panel in the entrance lobby. Phillip dedicated it on May 15. (He became fed up with that canvas pre-fab very speedily.) In the foyer too is a glassed pit in the floor that reveals the footings and crumbly bricks of the original house.

And Macquarie's chair, motheaten wallaby hide and back emblazoned with the fist and dirk insignia that appears on other belongings of his family in the cold windswept island of Mull in the Western Isles. It reminds us poignantly of this tall serious Highlander, who drove himself almost to death in an effort to turn the tatterdemalion slummy village of Sydney into a city of which the Empire would be proud. We hope he'd be proud of us today.

Imposing government buildings indicate that Bridge Street was the most important administrative centre in the South Pacific. The grand stone buildings that survive once housed the departments of Lands, Works, Education, the Colonial Secretary, Agriculture and the Treasury. Behind the splendid facades they are now hotels, restaurants, and other worldly ventures. The Lands Department building in particular is a piece of High Victoriana, with copper domes and lovely Scottish ironwork. It speaks eloquently of the joy and pride of Empire, for every little coign contains a lion's head, and there are countless other symbols of Australia's daughterhood. The building is also generously provided with handsome niches for the statues of statesmen and explorers. But half are unoccupied. What? No eminent chaps since 1890? This is discouraging. Those who survive stand in heroic postures, radiant with hubris and perhaps dreaming of a less transient age.

The Lands Building stands on the site of the first chaplain's minute thatched cottage. The Rev. Richard Johnson, poor man, was a mild scholarly ninny, 'one of the people called Methodists', unfitted to deal with his lawless charges. He was not at all like Samuel Marsden, his successor. As for him, all you had to do was to wind him up and point him at something and he'd savage it. Parson Johnson built a church with his own hands (there's a memorial to it further up the city, at the corner of Hunter and Bligh Streets) but 'on a dark and windy evening some wicked and disaffected persons ... set fire to it'.

Johnson had already suffered many things at the hands of his unkind congregation. 'They did spit and hiccough, and His Excellency addressed me, most slightingly, as Mr Johnstone.' Also on one memorable Sunday a corporal who was overcome by Mr Johnson's endless sermon suddenly ordered the drummer to beat Retreat.

However, our first parson brought oranges to Australia. He picked up some pips at Rio de Janeiro; two of these grew in the garden of his later cottage in Market Street and he sold the fruit for a shilling a piece. Johnson's orange trees flourished until the cottage was pulled down in 1814, by which time many descendants of the Brazilian pips were growing in the colony.

Look now towards the west. It is easy to imagine how the first road began, as a red-dirt track between the marines' tents. It was divided by the Tank Stream which ran down to the sea through the deepest gully, now followed approximately by Pitt Street. Convicts and troops lived to the west of the stream, gentry and officers to the east. Over the dividing stream the first log bridge was built. Within months the crystalline rivulet, within its tangle of ericas, ferns, orchids and casuarinas, began to die. The settlers cut down its trees, ate all its waterbirds, washed their clothes and emptied their chamberpots into it.

Turn now into Macquarie Place, a quaint triangle, irregular in contour, all dips and banks under its enormous Moreton Bay fig trees. Legend says that this space, once just above the beach of Sydney Cove, was a sacred corroboree ground where the two great tribes of Port Jackson met for battles. So said Captain Phillip, but eyewitness accounts indicate that the clashes on this open ground were more in the nature of a tournament. The contestants were groomed and ornamented, carried shields, which meant that no one was severely injured, and took turns to throw spears at each other. The spectators, too, though deeply interested, showed no agitation or concern. This ritual might have been a power struggle, or even a trial of strength which decided a point of law. There is no knowing, because no matter what the curious young officers of the First Fleet wrote about the native people of Australia, it is plain they had no understanding of them at all.

Nowadays, Macquarie Place is like a peculiar little village green, very historic, containing at least two of our most important national relics. The *Sirius* bow anchor (even after 117 years' submersion in Norfolk Island waters) looks the newest thing there. It's curious to reach up and touch the pocked sun-warm iron of this huge anchor which, aside from the gun which stands nearby, is physically almost all that we have of the First Fleet. *Sirius* was one of the two escorting vessels for the six transports and three supply ships of the First Fleet; she was Captain Phillip's own command. She was a frigate about thirty metres long, as big as a small ferry. The *Sirius* first appears in history as 'ye Berwick store-ship'. Her most famous captain, Governor Hunter, says: 'She was built in the river for an east country ship, and in loading her, she took fire and burned to her wales. The Government wanting a roomy ship ... purchased her bottom.' This was in 1781. She was sent to America during the War of Independence, and 'after ye peace, to ye West Indies'.

She was re-named *Sirius* after the star which is the southern sky's most magnificent. On her first voyage she dropped anchor in Sydney Cove on January 26, 1788. Nine months later, the colony already starving, the *Sirius* flitted off before the westerlies for Cape Horn and Cape

Town, where she loaded stores for the afflicted settlers of Sydney. She was therefore the first vessel to sail from Sydney and 'run her easting down'. After loading, she continued to run before the westerlies, circumnavigating the globe in what later were known as the Roaring Forties. Thus she pioneered the great sailing ship route of the later era of commercial sail.

Sirius sailed off again in March 1790, with a cargo of convicts and marines for Norfolk Island. She was driven ashore and wrecked, though without loss of life; her anchor was recovered by divers in 1907. The gun was originally removed from the vessel and mounted at Dawes Battery, the site of which is still to be discerned near the southern pylons of the Harbour Bridge. The gun then guarded the Macquarie Lighthouse at South Head for many years. It does not have the romantic appeal of the old hand-forged anchor, which splashed into the sea at Rio de Janeiro, Table Bay and, for the last time, at Sydney. Many of the seamen who let go the *Sirius* anchor had fought in the American War of Independence.

Governor Macquarie created this tiny park from part of Government House's vegetable garden and bits and pieces of settlers' property which he swapped for other valuable lots of city real estate. The Place was much larger than it is now, surrounded by orchards and tall flat-faced houses of a style full of the golden light of the eighteenth century. Macquarie intended his formal patch of green to be the hub of administrative Sydney, and this is one reason why he erected here in 1818 the obelisk which marks the starting point of all the roads in the colony. The obelisk's convict-hewn masonry now looks like iron, but the deeply-incised legend is as clear as ever. The monument is so austere that one marvels that it was regarded as too ornate by the irate Commissioner whose criticisms in 1821 helped poor Macquarie's career to end in ruins.

Early guides to Sydney state clearly that the obelisk was erected where it is because it marks the position of the first flagstaff. Surely this must be correct. Why would Macquarie have placed his marker here, off centre and away from the Quay, if this had not been a significant site? It is, anyway, a queer old fingerpost to the past, constructed by Edward Cureton, a life sentence convict.

Cureton also built a plain but substantial water fountain designed by Francis Greenway. It supplied man and beast. The fountain also was heavily criticised as being altogether too grand for a convict settlement, and it had a sorry end in the middle of the nineteenth century by being converted into a urinal. Though I feel sure this historic fountain is still somewhere in existence in Sydney, I have not been able to trace it. I shall be gratified to hear from any gentleman who has discerned the handiwork of Greenway in, and at, his convenience.

The first street lamp in Australia stood here in Macquarie Place. Erected in 1826, it burned whale-oil, and was the only one of its kind for more than a year. Three tall graceful old gas lamps, each containing a dim yellow tassel of a pilot light, mark where it stood. These were presented by the Australian Gas Light Company in 1967. Sydney streets, incidentally, were lit with gas in 1841. Sydney was thus, as a rapturous newspaper editorial announced, 'the first city in the Asiatic world to have this beautiful art, this exquisite production of science'.

There used to be a complex of fanlike lanes angling down to the Quay on its western side. Now there are only two or three, squeezed between magnificent tourist hotels. These lanes were once occupied by important residences. Simeon Lord, the immensely wealthy emancipist merchant and trader, had his white three-storeyed mansion across the way there. A handsome dark-eyed lad, he was transported in 1790 at the age of nineteen. He died in 1840, the first manufacturer of Australian wool, the owner of whaling and pearling fleets, purveyor of South Sea Island sandalwood to the Chinese mandarins, and landlord of innumerable city frontages and pastoral properties. In spite of his own tragic boyhood, he also owned convict transports. Lord's 'wonderful house' stood until the first decade of the twentieth century. A little distance from it was the modest Georgian cottage of Captain and Mrs Mary Reiby. (The nearby lane commemorating the remarkable Mary is spelt this way. However, the name is often spelt Reibey, and one deduces from various clues that it was almost certainly pronounced Rabey.)

In Mary's cottage, which she leased to the Government in 1817, after her husband's death, the Bank of New South Wales first opened for business. The bank's first depositor was a soldier, Sergeant Jeremiah Murphy, who banked his fortune – fifty pounds. The bank was gradually successful in bringing about in Sydney the circulation of an English coinage more suitable, though less picturesque, than the astonishing array of foreign currency that was used to pay soldiers and workmen alike – Spanish dollars, Indian mohurs, Dutch guilders, rupees, pagodas, and Portuguese Johannes, not forgetting the peculiar 'holey dollar', which was a silver Spanish dollar with the middle punched out. The middle was also currency, and was called a dump, worth about fifteen cents.

The Bank of New South Wales later changed its name to Westpac.

Returning to the Quay, one might justifiably enter one of the many cafes for refreshment and rest. If it is the weekend you may watch the buskers, a happy mixture of Scottish dancers, stiltwalkers, musicians, singers, clowns and once a small chamber orchestra. On a sunny afternoon large crowds visit the Quay, just for the ferry ride, a wonderful lunch, and the entertainment. You never know what you might see. Once the writer spotted Chinese acrobats diving through the air with terrifying speed, while twenty metres away a troupe of Morris dancers pranced and circled, solemnly waving their bell-garlanded legs.

When the old seamen's pubs lined the Quay, the poet Henry Lawson frequented the early openers for a heart-starter. We are reminded of this by the poem he wrote when poor and homesick in London:

There never dawned a morning in the long and lonely days,
But I thought I saw the ferries streaming out across the bays
And as fresh and fair in fancy did the picture rise again,
As the sunrise flushed the city from Woollahra to Balmain.

The Quay was the site of many polling booth riots, and one in particular in which the standing candidate, a wealthy shipowner, restored order by bringing up reinforcements from his whalers, armed with harpoons. In another exceptionally violent riot in the 1880s, thousands of demonstrators thronged the Quay in an attempt to prevent six hundred Chinese immigrants from landing. Many of the protestors were organised bands of workmen from those trades threatened by the importation of cheap Asian labour; market growers; small merchants; seamstresses. A large number of the frail black-clad figures on the ships were tailors destined for the sweatshops so numerous in Victorian Sydney. They had already been rejected in Port Melbourne. A contemporary records:

'Surging like a human sea, the mob broke the police cordon and swept across the Quay, singing:

We don't want to fight, but by jingo if we must
We'll lick the Yellow Peril and leave it in the dust!

'The pandemonium was fearful in the extreme, stones and brickbats flew, people were trampled underfoot, carriages were overturned. By dint of great good fortune, the aged leader of his people [Sir Henry Parkes] was hustled into his carriage and away from the danger zone. Assailed by divers ruffians, your correspondent climbed a lamp post.'

Alas, such days are gone. Not even the frequent scuffles between American and Australian troops during World War II attained such drama.

It is time to resume our walk. If you have not a great deal of time, say little more than half an hour, then go towards Circular Quay East and the Opera House. An addlepated thing about the Quay is that the road which runs formally along it is Alfred Street at its west end and Albert Street at the other. We are now walking towards Albert Street. You will see that a fine square exists already in front of the Customs House.

The latter is a harmoniously proportioned building by Government Architect James Barnet who, besides many others, also designed the Lands Department building and the General Post Office. I much prefer the Customs House, which has cleaner lines. Built in 1885, it's quite huge, but hasn't that depressing air of weighing ten million deadweight tonnes common to so many Victorian buildings. The double-pillared colonnade, the wrought iron panels, are simple and dignified, and the portrait head of Queen Victoria and the massive carved coat-of-arms very fine.

Only a few decades ago, Circular Quay looked different; oldfashioned, austere and spacious, a true front door to a maritime city. It was almost entirely Victorian, except for occasional pockets of Puritan-plain early colonial government and commercial buildings. A quay, one would have said, for gas lamps and hansom cabs, and the bowsprits of famous sailing ships casting summer shadows on the roadway. How did the sylvan cove, with its wild woods and rocky terraced shores turn into this? Half a century of increasing harbour commerce had proved that Sydney's primitive wharf facilities were her greatest handicap. An experienced military engineer, Colonel George Barney, was the one who halted the haphazard development of Sydney Cove. Between 1837 and 1844 he created a highly utilitarian demilune of waterfront to be known as Semi-Circular Quay.

A brisk competent man with long engineering experience in the

West Indies, Barney tackled with vigour and imagination the colossal task of filling the Tank Stream estuary, reclaiming the mudflats, dredging and deepening the cove, and creating from the ragged shoreline the symmetrical deep Roman arch we now know. Besides his natural genius, Barney was blessed with an unlimited supply of forced labour.

For seven years the muddy hordes of convicts toiled where we now stand. The old broadsheet says:

No shoes nor stockings had they on, no hat had they to wear,
But a harden frock and linsey drawers, their feet and head were bare,
They chained them up by two and two, like horses in a team.
Their driver he stood over them with his Malacca cane.

However, contemporary drawings show them much more picturesquely dressed in old French and Spanish military uniforms, or canvas peajackets and loose trousers, scribbled all over with broad arrows and identifying letters. They wear a remarkable collection of hats, cabbage tree, battered beavers, jellybags, and peculiar felt mitres that look as though they belonged to some inconceivably deadbeat pope.

During this time the Tank Stream was buried for ever. It now debouches close to the last ferry jetty on the west side of the Quay.

During the course of work on the Quay, transportation to New South Wales ended. Circular Quay (as it rapidly became known) is thus the last and greatest convict work to be completed in the colony.

For its time, it was an almost uniquely important feat. The building of Circular Quay marked the beginning of the wonderful days of the clippers, the twenty or thirty years when the world's fastest sailing ships tied up at the Quay, and the little apprentices from warehouses and factories did indeed sit under the shadow of the bowsprits and eat their meagre luncheons. Fortunately many artists depicted this golden era. Among others, Conrad Martens, for two years artist and topographer with Darwin's *Beagle*, had settled in Sydney. He had his studio just on the Quay along here where the AMP tower now stands. He left us many felicitous watercolours and hand-tinted lithographs, so fragile they might have been painted on porcelain and then scrubbed for three weeks straight. He shows us Dawes Point dipping down ever so gently between a dense covert of stripped masts at Circular Quay, and a smaller grove of the same in Darling Harbour.

As we climb steep Albert Street we spot on the corner of Phillip Street a classic small 1854 building by Edmund Blacket. Once the Water Police headquarters and Court, it was a place one used to pass in a hurry. Successive generations of Goths had darned and patched it with hideous weatherboard adits. Even the pretty arches that Blacket designed to be flooded with northern sunlight were filled in with something chewed and crumbling, possibly asbestos board.

But now this elegant little building has been restored, and even Mr Blacket would be pleased with its renaissance, for he was a man who enjoyed a pleasurable chill scooting down the spine. It is now the Justice and Police Museum. All the gruesome relics that for over a century have been stored in cupboards in country and city police stations have now been gathered, cleaned up, annotated and deposited here – Ned Kelly's gun for instance. There are many famous guns and plenty of other horrid weapons well acquainted with murder. Most interesting, though touching in a weird way, are death masks of executed bushrangers such as Ned and Thunderbolt. They really do look quite upset.

Again and again on our strolls we will appreciate the elegant architectural taste of Edmund Blacket. In many ways Sydney is still his town. He and his wife Sarah arrived here in 1842. He was fairish and delicate, she dark with a frivolous cap. She was a dauntless sailor who liked to be roped on deck during storms, and he was seasick all the way from England. They were actually en route to New Zealand, but because of Edmund's seasickness and the harbour ('I thought I never would see so exquisite a scene,' he said) they went no further. Blacket designed many of Sydney's most famous churches, shops, banks, office buildings and some refined domestic dwellings. He was also a painter, sculptor and musician; a sweet man 'whom no unkind word ever besmirched'.

We now turn left into Macquarie Street, the sunny tail end where few of us ever go. It spindles along at the rear of all those huge new buildings which front Circular Quay East, but we can easily see how useful it must have been for providing access to the upper floors of the old warehouses and bond stores which not so long ago stood there instead. We cross Macquarie Street to the park which surrounds the walled gardens of Government House – a park usually neglected by strollers, finely green, rather English, with extremely large shapely trees. A secluded paved walk called the Tarpeian Way runs just inside the railing, and is the nicest way to see the Opera House. But first peek at the vice-regal residence.

In the last years of the twentieth century a Labor Government incontinently banished the Governor of New South Wales from his traditional residence, though the grand house is still used for ceremonial occasions. In one way this radical act benefited us all, for the house is now open for public tours, and the magnificent, formal, Versailles-style gardens can be enjoyed any time by lowly ones like you and me. Government House demonstrates those architectural features so prized by the early Victorians – a stately cloister on its northern façade, groups of ornate chimneys, battlements and turrets large and small. Its architect was Edward Blore, the young Queen Victoria's own; he never saw the sumptuous site, but really didn't do too badly. The building has a Byronic romanticism that in its time probably echoed the much older and long-demolished Fort Macquarie at the foot of the hill.

There are many fanciful Victorian paintings showing visiting ships swirling into Sydney Harbour under a dangerous load of sail, Government House and Fort Macquarie appearing ghostlike from glamorous Turneresque skies, both larger than life and extraordinarily European in style.

The Tarpeian Way, to which we now return, was named for the huge rugged sandstone outcrop which, like the spine of a dragon, lay along Bennelong Point. It was so precipitous that Phillip's officers called it the Tarpeian Rock, after that rock in ancient Rome from which traitors were tossed. It was quarried down in 1817, and some of its debris used to build sea-girt Fort Macquarie, which was manned as a garrison until 1902.

There are so many quaint forts and old gun emplacements around Sydney that one may well ask: 'Against which enemy?' Probably Russia during the Crimean War, the new United States during the 1812 conflict, and lurking French explorers any time at all. It has been suggested that Fort Macquarie was constructed to put the fear of God into mutinous convicts. But no, the guns pointed out to sea.

The Tarpeian Way, which is only a few hundred metres long, ends at the top of a nobly wide and well-proportioned flight of sandstone stairs, which once provided foot-access to the fort. From here the view of the Harbour is magnificent; little Pinchgut sitting in a lake of twinkles, like the keep of a sunken castle; the roaring Bridge just a stone's throw away. But what comes slap up against the eyeball is the Opera House. It is Pharaonic, Mayan! From this elevation the sails are well separated, the line not as fluid as one expected from photographs.

What can one say about the Opera House that hasn't been said more fully in the several good books published on this subject? The magnitude of the exterior is evident, though not as evident as it should be against the high-rise city. The great building should spread its wings against a green hill, or rise unexpectedly from the sea. You will see what I mean when you get across to Circular Quay West and view the Opera House from another angle.

There is an alarming story that once Bennelong Point was cleared of crumbling old buildings, the Minister for Public Works of the time, wanted to put the Overseas Passengers Terminal on it, but the conductor of the Sydney Symphony Orchestra, Sir Eugene Goossens, persuaded the Premier to banish the huge squat terminal to the west of the Quay, and crown Bennelong Point with an opera house instead. If you look at the terminal you can see what a tragedy was averted.

The Overseas Passenger Terminal, worthy, respectable, utilitarian, decidedly resembles some of the Opera House plans shortlisted in the competition launched by the New South Wales Government of the day. Still, we are thankful that the four judges cut loose, went off their revered heads, and unanimously chose this extravaganza from the future, the incomplete plan of which had been submitted by a youngish Danish architect who had done only domestic design. It cost a fortune and fifteen years to complete, and was financed almost entirely by lotteries.

To walk into the Opera House is to walk inside a sculpture, or perhaps a seashell, maybe an intricate, half-translucent nautilus. Morphology and the computers have composed a world of strange breathless shapes, vast, individual, quite unlike any other architecture I have ever seen. Palm ribs of steel, sea fans of concrete! And all of extraordinary height, all in harmonious dialogue one with another. The glassy declivities of the walls are almost imperceptible amber; they bring the sun into the vast structure as they bring the sky and harbour.

The immense building is a complex of entertainment areas – concert hall, opera hall, drama theatre, restaurants, cafes, viewing places. It can accommodate upwards of 6000 patrons simultaneously. In the golden concert hall, which has been described as one of the world's greatest music chambers, with perfect acoustics, stands the largest mechanical pipe organ on earth, constructed in Sydney.

You may well find yourself an ant inside the Opera House, but when you emerge you are a proud and happy ant. To think that this masterpiece came from the materialistic sixties! And the worse seventies! You go away with faith restored in humankind.

At least we are still visionary enough to create this nonesuch of a building, a white swan in a land of black swans.

Turn now into Macquarie Street, walking along its footpath which is directly beneath the sheer face of old Tarpeian Rock. It presses on one's left hand like a low cliff, blackened with soot and age, bearing a hoary network of roots and vines that have crept down from the park above. There is on this little cliff a plaque commemorating the departure of Australian troops for the Sudanese war in 1885. Not long before we reach the Cahill Expressway, we see Moore's Steps going down to the Quay. They were opened as a shortcut to Government House and the Botanic Gardens in 1868, and cover the position of Fort Macquarie's powder magazines, excavated very much earlier.

You will need an hour for a leisurely exploration of the western side of the Quay, and this does not include the Millers Point area, which I have reserved for another walk. Of course, if you have more than an hour to spare, you may branch off almost anywhere from this route to explore the quaint and endlessly interesting Rocks.

Moving west along Circular Quay, we pass the imposing Gold Fields House. Behind it is Crane Place, a dog-legged vennel among the shadows of the towering luxury hotels. Once it had a notorious grog shop of its own, the Crane and Wheel, half afloat, they said, for if the Tank Stream wasn't sloshing into its cellar the high tide was.

Not far south of this is Underwood Street, where a convict owned a shipyard. Here in 1805 was launched a 185 tonne three-masted vessel called the *King George*; she was the largest colonial-built vessel to that date. Where the slipway lay, in the Tank Stream, is now a huge handsome building, which houses the Telephone Exchange.

Near here too, in a little court now gobbled up, was the first bank robbery in Australia. The year was 1828. The Bank of Australia had been opened by wealthy and arrogant landowners as opposition to the young Bank of New South Wales. It happened to be next to a pub kept by the chief constable. This was convenient for his work as the gaol was just across George Street. One morning the bank's strongroom was opened to reveal a complete lack of money. Twenty-four thousand dollars' worth of gold had flitted, much to the amusement of conscienceless Sydney. 'It would be absurd to say that the occurrence elicited any general feeling of dismay or regret', stated the *Sydney Gazette*.

The thieves would never have been caught if an informer, engagingly called Sudden Solomon, hadn't turned them in two years later for £100, a pardon and a ticket to England. The conspirators had discovered a large drain running beneath the bank and emptying into the Tank Stream. They merely spent their Saturdays in that gloomy tunnel, pecking through the brick floor of the strongroom. Sudden Solomon did not live to return to England. Drunk as a lord, he fell into the Hyde Park swamp and was drowned.

The west side of the Quay was always more picturesque than the establishment eastern wing. Until the conversion of the muddy Sydney Cove waterfront into the Circular Quay of today, this west end was closely integrated with the eastern Rocks, which proliferated with shameless vigour on both sides of George Street North. Of course in those days there was no unbroken access from George Street to the Quay, only a tangle of alleys and 'slips' between houses.

Cross over into George Street. This was the market of the earliest days, when foreign traders began to realise that the unknown continent of the South Pacific, Australia Felix, was unknown no longer and had begun to buy and sell. The market was a loosely defined locality extending from Globe Street to Essex Street, just where the Regent Hotel is now.

Here was a droll scramble of stalls and shops, many on wheels. Cages of cockatoos and green parakeets swung at their doors, beggars and pickpockets were plentiful. The shops sold not only stolen silks and jewellery (often stolen in England), but honest and romantic sealskins, whale oil, blackish Jamaican sugar, known as custard sugar, salt and sandalwood, 'kingaroo and wallabi, prodigious high', and the rich fruits of the country, guava, loquats, mandarins and cherimoyas. Stray dogs, pigs and goats roamed among the bargainers, the dogs indeed often causing riotous spectacle. As the man about town and inexhaustible chatterbox Lieutenant Colonel Mundy writes of this Sydney of the forties, 'Many a luckless [horseman] have I seen flying along the street in a cloud of dust and dogs, fresh detachments of curs debouching upon him from every alley until they vanished together around a corner, leaving me to imagine the finish.'

Turn north now under the double-decker span of the Cahill Expressway far above. Just here was a notorious thieves' kitchen, Brown Bear Lane, half slimy cobbles, half treacherous stairs, named from its presiding demon, a sinister inn with a sign resembling a malformed wallaby. This lane, which was demolished in 1908, was famous for the murder and judicious dismemberment of a wealthy gentleman by his French valet, Jean Videll. The latter's hanging was hugely attended by an appreciative public which, then as now, dearly loved a scandal in which a nob took the starring role. The Brown Bear Lane murder sets the tone for the old Rocks badlands, until the 1850s the toughest of seaport rookeries.

From our previous spypoint at the Opera House we saw the extraordinary irregularity of this long promontory of Dawes Point. An up-and-down village it is now and a diabolically up-and-down village it must have been in its wicked years. People threw up hovels in the shadows of the huge sandstone outcrops; they occupied ledges like seagulls and penguins, or built on top of the rocks like eagles. Flights of steps, goat tracks and children's slides were all that connected them.

In some places the backyard of one house was the roof of one below. One can imagine the fights as the washtub belonging to 'them up above' came through the kitchen ceiling of 'them below'.

Sewage ran down the hillsides and piled up against housewalls. The place was always a hotbed of typhoid and dysentery as well as poxes big and small. Sailors said that you could hear the roaring of the Rocks a mile out to sea and smell it for two miles.

'There were Cheap John shops and shoemakers' hovels and no end of low publick houses. Here might always be seen the British tar and the foreign tar, as incontinently drunk as these noble mariners could desire to be. This is the land of fiddlers and brazen huzzies, of more rum and eternal spree, dancing and singing and brawling and curses and coarse revelry.'

But when Captain Phillip first saw it, Dawes Point must have looked like many another peninsula around Sydney, lying long and narrow in a summer sea, its slopes sparsely wooded with those rosy-fleshed red gums that live symbiotically with sandstone, its arid ledges and lintels alight with Christmas bells. Perhaps Aborigines were picking oysters from the rocks, or paddling around in their bark canoes. The gratified Phillip soon discovered that the characteristic flat sandstone terraces formed a natural quay dipping into five or six fathoms of water.

Glance up Globe Street as you cross it. Though the access is easier now, there used to be a flight of worn stone steps heading up to Harrington Street. There the Ragged School for the Rocks children operated for years. On the right side of Globe Street is the State Archives Office, where you can buy rather good posters and other souvenirs. However, proceed along George Street North. Opposite the Museum of Contemporary Art is the grim Victorian police station, now a craft centre. Its doorway is surmounted by the head of a lion holding some mystery between its crunchers. A bone? A police baton? Who can tell? The police station is on the site of Australia's first hospital, another of Phillip's pre-fabs. Actually, as far as health went, he didn't do at all badly with his thousand-odd convicts. Only forty-eight died on the eight months' voyage, some of those already aged or diseased. However, many arrived with scurvy and dysentery, the latter complaint speedily exacerbated by heavy labour in midsummer weather and ravenous gorgings on berries and leaves. The canvas hospital seems to have been the first building erected in Sydney, and its garden was probably the first also. George Street began at its very door, winding its way south through the convicts' tents to the marine encampment closer to Grosvenor Street.

Along the beach before this hospital were laid the 'earthen, wasted creatures' that were all that remained of the tragic cargo of the disastrous Second Fleet of 1790. Out of one thousand convicts, no fewer than 273 died en route, others died as the ships came up harbour, and others expired as they were rowed ashore. Five hundred of the survivors lay dying or convalescent under tents along the wintry beach 'and as each wretch expired, his companions fell on the body like wolves . . . prising open the stiffening jaws to snatch the half chewed plug of black Brazil tobacco from the dead man's cheek'.

The sunny, sweetly breezy First Fleet Park is no place to remember the disgusting horrors of the Second Fleet. One can imagine what the strict, conscientious Governor Phillip thought of the debacle. The arrival of British ships had been so longed for, so desperately needed to bring supplies, officer reinforcements, letters and above all orders from the Home Office, that when the first ships from the Second Fleet were discerned from the South Head lookout, almost the entire colony broke into tears and cries of emotion.

Back in England the Royal Navy had economised by contracting as transports tramp vessels of the most wretched kind. Most were owned by miserly companies and manned by discredited captains and 'pressed' crews – men of no or little sea experience drugged or banged over the head in dock taverns and kidnapped for service. Many were criminals. The captains cut down the transportees' rations to starvation point and sold the rest; they gave their crews access to the female convicts; they flogged so heavily that starved and ill men died under the lash.

The shameful covey of ships scuttled away to China and anywhere else where a cargo could be obtained, and Phillip was left with the dying detritus of the voyage, incomplete supplies of those necessities he had requested in his letters from Rio, one or two half-trained surgeons, and the desolating news that some of the mail had been left behind en route. He also had several first person accounts of the nightmare voyage from educated cabin passengers, among whom were the youthful John and Elizabeth Macarthur, later to make their considerable fortune in the colony.

Across the road, on the corner of George and Argyle Streets, is the spot believed by many historians to be the place where Captain Phillip formally proclaimed 'His Majesty's Pattent for the Establishment of the Settlement'. This significant event occurred on February 7, 1788, and is distinct from the first raising of the flag on the shore of Sydney Cove on January 26.

We know a great deal about this February 7, which many contend should be celebrated as the true Australia Day, instead of January 26. We know that it was a Thursday, that almost every white person in Australia was present, and in ceremonial dress. (Except the convicts, who had to sit on the ground and have the marines fire a volley over them three times, presumably to impress upon their minds their social position in this new world.) Captain Phillip, in full naval dress uniform, was received with colours flying and band music playing. After the inaugural ceremony, Phillip in his ear-splitting sea-captain's voice gave a speech of which we have, unluckily, few details except that we know the troops and convicts were told plainly that skulkers and loafers would not eat, the theft of even small articles of stock or provisions would be punished by death, and that he would stand no hanky panky with the women. After more volleys were fired, doubtless to the prostration of the fascinated Aboriginal onlookers in the scrub, the convicts were given a holiday, and the officers and gentlemen enjoyed a celebration dinner, though God alone knows what they ate.

But we don't know exactly where this happened.

While you are on this side of the road you may like to have a look at the Museum of Contemporary Art which is located in a foursquare dignified stone building belonging to the 1950s and not at all contemporary. You will undoubtedly chuckle at the curious design of the main doors which part in the middle to announce Museum of Con on one side and Temporary Art on the other. Actually the art is largely temporary as the exhibitions change every seven or eight weeks, coming from interstate or overseas. Above this entrance door is an impressive bas-relief of mighty convicts tossing blocks of stone around. (In fact few were mighty. Dwarfish would be the word according to our view of things.) Inside you can find arresting postmodern works. Free tours are conducted by students and artists. There's a charming shop, too, where touristy deplorables are sternly prohibited – which they are not, alas, in other parts of the Rocks. If you want an original souvenir of a visit, this is the place: unusual books, amusing jewellery, Quay and Sydney orientated rather than chains, shackles and broad arrowed shirts.

A step or two along the road is quirky little Cadman's Cottage, probably the oldest domestic building in Australia, built in 1815 for Governor Macquarie's coxswain of the vice-regal gig, John Cadman, a transportee. He was a tiny one-eyed man, so Lilliputian in fact that the doorways of this cottage are not more than 1.6 metres high. For many years it was derelict, almost a heap of stones, haunt of rats and drunks. Sometime in the 1970s it was rescued by the National Parks and Wildlife Service and restored to a clean, tidy version of what it used to be. The latter is a problem with the raffish old Rocks – everything is too clean and tidy to be quite real. However, the Parks and Wildlife people have an information centre in Cadman's Cottage, most interesting.

When little John was here the sea washed almost to the side wall. Though he lived in this house during the most notorious era of the Rocks, he must have been a contented man. He retired in 1840 at the age of seventy, and the Water Police took over his cottage. In the 1850s many Chinese settled about here; it was a little Chinatown that gave a living to the many miners who, having worked out their indentures to the Cantonese gold speculators on the Victorian diggings, elected to remain in Australia. Around the lanes and courts of the Rocks they established drinking booths, fantan lottery shops and pakapoo establishments. We are told that the fumes of opium hung in the air, accompanied by the distinctive smell of Chinese cooking. As peasant Chinese like to live loudly, the general uproar was such that one visitor commented: 'I feared I should lose my hearing by the deafening noises. Jugglers, dancers and pedlars stopped the thoroughfare, all shouting at the tops of their voices.' An outbreak of smallpox among them caused a great scare and led to some cleaning-up of the Rocks. (Chinese were almost always blamed for the outbreaks of plague, and some scholars think that this led in part to the ready acceptance of that Immigration Act popularly known as the White Australia Policy.) To see lanes as they were during the Chinese occupation, cross the road and you may retrace your steps a little to Harrington Lane, or go up broad tree-lined Argyle Street and turn down Kendall Lane on your right.

The streets about the Argyle Cut were the peculiar kingdom of the Rocks Push, for several decades paramount among the larrikin gangs of the late nineteenth century. They were Ur-bikies with no bikes, carrying on running warfare with other pushes, and harassing police and pedestrians. Petty theft, insult, assault and battery were their specialties and they used their truculent girlfriends as lures to entice wavering drunks or seamen to the shadows of the Cut for robbing and a doing-over.

We speak to an old man sitting in the sun on a stone step scooped out like a pudding spoon. He has triangular blue eyes and a bit of Christmas bush in his hatband. 'Course I don't remember the pushes. Get out! I'm only seventy. But me grandpa was one of the boys, one of Griffo's mob, you heard of Griffo? Used to tell me about the fights the mobs had, the Straw Hat Push, and the Forty Thieves from Surry Hills, and the Gibb Street Mob. Fight! Over anything, just for the love of it, yer might say. Fight with anything, fists, sticks, palings off fences, knockers ripped off doors. My old man got a clout on the nut from a stone in a sock, ruined his hat it did. All the boys wore this funny little hat, a monty, a real little lid with a narrer brim. Oh, yeah, they was lairs all right, high heels on their boots, and little mirrors on the heels, and toes inlaid with pictures of their girls. And the girls! Ostrich feathers and lace-up plush boots with "I love Albert" on them, great times they was. But even us kids had great times. They don't make times like them now.

Bonfires! You never see a good bonfire now. Queen's Birthday, Guy Fox, Regatta Day! Strewth, we'd burn everything! Matteresses … make a good smoke, matteresses … old furniture, gets rid of bugs and cockeroaches. Once we pinched Quong Kee's laundry cart, chucked it on the flames. Up it went. Quong carrying on like a yeller madman. And then the fire brigades would come. Killjoys! And everyone what was dancing around singing and having a good time would make fun of them. Names! Make yer teeth turn black. But sometimes we'd cut the hose with an axe, or turn the water on the firemen. Great times, you don't get them days now.'

You will inevitably be tempted while you are here to visit the Argyle Stores in Mary Reiby's old bond warehouse, and explore the remarkable piece of convict engineering known as the Cut. Yet, unless you have unlimited time and superb feet, it might be best if you reserved that for another time, when we can with leisure inspect the charming old buildings of the Garrison area on the other side of the Harbour Bridge. Exploring the Argyle Stores will take at least an hour, and you may have a pleasant lunch there under the ironbark rafters of the archaic warehouse.

The sound of traffic over the Bridge is loud. The sonorous roar reminds us that we are approaching the highest ridge of the Rocks, the aristocratic district of the 1850s onwards, then known as the High Rocks. Many of these streets and their fine houses were demolished in the late 1920s to make way for the approaches to the Bridge. George Street meets the narrow, serpentine end of Cumberland Street at a steep slope and steep angle, which must have caused many a wagon accident in the old days. This curious bend in George Street North marks the vanished boundary of the Government Shipyard, which stood here from 1796 to 1833.

King George V Memorial Park, which is now visible, runs in an irregular triangle right under the approaches to the Bridge. What a peaceable place it is for wandering, hardly ever seeing a soul, the grass uncommonly thick and fresh under the great Bridge's shade. The Opera House lies immediately eastwards, a handful of white butterflies at rest on the sparkling water. One sees at once why William Dobell in his enchanting picture removed the Opera House from its present position and allowed it to bloom on some imaginary island in the middle of the harbour. It is trying to float already; Dobell gave it a helping brush. One walks among the cyclopean pillars that support the Bridge, listening to the airy cries of the maintenance workers above, shouting like currawongs. Then comes the voice of the Bridge itself as an electric train rushes onto the approaches almost a kilometre back. First the hoarse roar, half pleasant, that swiftly swells to a clattering, battering clamour that swells unbearably until steel speaks to steel and all is lost in a diminishing deafening peal that has within it such woe, such lamentation it could be the sound of civilisation itself.

Here in the Memorial Park where we sit, Lower Fort Street behind us to the west, to the east the broad harbour and the city, was the High Rocks where the gentry lived, and Princes Street ran as a nobly designed carriage road from Old St Phillip's (now Lang Park). Upper Fort Street and Gloucester Street, pleasing and orderly, ran alongside. Though the murky alleys and characteristic tottering stairways ran down the steep inclines to George Street North, one may be sure that the rich, devout merchants' families never looked downhill to where the poor lived in verminous holes full of smoke and weather. (Though one does wonder about the smell in the summer when the city's prevailing wind, the nor'-easter, blew.)

The ghosts of this green park, then, are ladies with stemmy waists, always seemingly on the verge of hysterics, and immensely prosperous gentlemen with spheroidal stomachs encased in sausage skins of brown twill. Does one not get a tiny genteel whiff of eau-de-Portugal and imported brandy?

The people who lived in these two- and three-storey mansions on the High Rocks reflected in all ways the opulence of middleclass England. They were built by prosperous shrewd men who made their money from shipping, whaling, importing and large scale pastoralism, yet they reflected an older world of taxless leisure.

'No matter the semi-tropical climate,' sighed Charlotte Godley in 1853, 'the men dress just the same as in England, the black cloth coat, some light waistcoat, and the inevitable chimneypot.'

It must have been a wonderful place for a child to live in, with a crow's-nest view of Sydney, its skyline pierced with spires and Norfolk pines, its shoreline obscured by a delicate net of masts and spars. On warm afternoons the grassy sward near Dawes Battery down there on the point was dotted with nursemaids (probably flirting with redcoats) and children bowling hoops and flying kites.

In later years the children would watch the Peninsular & Oriental ships which berthed just south of Campbell's Wharf (where the Overseas Terminal is now). Their crews were mostly lascars and coolies clad in blue smocks and red caps, very foreign and astonishing.

A large number of famous men came from the High Rocks: the first Prime Minister, Edmund Barton; a lord mayor, politicians; a poet; orators. Maybe the most memorable was an army surgeon's son, David Scott Mitchell, around whose unique collection of Australiana was built the Mitchell Library. Perhaps something is to be said for high-ceilinged mansions with cedar joinery and marble mantlepieces, princely retinues of servants and cool, leisured mothers, for I can think of no famous man who came from the rookery immediately below except 'da fedder' – the scallywag Albert Griffiths who grew up to be a boxing phenomenon, Young Griffo, the greatest featherweight the world has known.

These gracious streets vanished with the building of the Bridge in the twenties and thirties of the twentieth century. So, with a flash of ghostly looking-glasses in long-vanished ballrooms, and with the faint tinkle of chandeliers in our ears, we turn towards all that is left of the High Rocks, Lower Fort Street, and its lovely terrace of three-storey houses.

This is Milton Terrace, painted dusky pink with charcoal ironwork. Though the houses were built in 1880, when architecture tended to Victorian hyperbole, they are beautifully restrained, with their London-style 'areas' leading presumably to kitchen and offices. Their bedroom windows look upon the unsurpassed view across the green and under the Bridge, but the noise from the Bridge itself must be insupportable. Beyond them are many other distinctive houses, including probably the finest classical Georgian town house in Sydney, Clyde Bank, which was built in 1824 for Robert Crawford. His contemporary, Robert Campbell, was the son of 'Merchant' Robert Campbell, whose fearless character and extraordinary business acumen finally broke the monopoly trafficking which so besmirched early colonial politics.

Robert Campbell the second was a distinguished man in his own right and before his early death in 1859 was Colonial Treasurer, and also the first representative of Sydney City in the first responsible government. He was an active campaigner for the cessation of transportation, which duly ceased some ten years before his death.

Lower Fort Street is perched on the edge of a cliff, which probably once went down by steps and stairs to the edge of Walsh Bay. There's a long flight of stairs beside the last terrace house, the Downshire Steps. Like the more famous Agar Steps, they could be made picturesque by judicious plantings of vines or flowering trees. They lead to a sequence of lower roads which used to service the wharves of Walsh Bay.

Lower Fort Street is in its way beautiful, with the immensity of the Bridge upon the right, and the iron-railed cliff on the left. If you look back now, you will see the domes of the Observatory in its high green park, and remember that this road was the access from Dawes Point and its battery to Fort Phillip, which stood where the Observatory stands now.

It is a pleasant stroll down the steep road, which appears to have no traffic at all, towards the sea. Where is everyone? Sounds of hammering, squealing of winches come from somewhere towards Darling Harbour. The sonorous sound of Sydney underlies the shout of the Bridge like a deep bass note. Oddly, two flights of old, iron-coloured stairs lead down into Dawes Point Park at the foot of the gigantic southwest pylon. Above begins the outward swing of the Bridge's arch. The park is tidy but empty, a broad green space with blooming oleanders and no one to be seen but two old winos stretched out in tousled abandon.

On the east side of the park stand cannon with big buttoned gobs; they were placed here in commemoration of Dawes Battery, knocked down in 1924 to make room for the Bridge. The first fortification in Australia, it was one more little Gothic fort with a castellated trim, named for Lieutenant William Dawes, a young Marine officer who sailed with Phillip in the *Sirius*. He had been trained as an astronomer by Dr Maskelyne, the Astronomer Royal, who had entrusted him with the duty of observing a certain comet supposed to pass through the southern skies in 1788. Dawes actually christened the rocky peninsula after Maskelyne, but the name did not take. Dawes was in command of the battery of eight naval guns in an earthen redoubt, and he set up his little observatory in a tent beside it.

The present Observatory, far behind us on the highest point of Flagstaff Hill, was built in 1858 on the site of Fort Phillip. Dawes was an interesting man, one of the first, in 1789, to try to cross the Blue Mountains. Though his observations were, expectedly, mostly geological and geographical, his heart was in astronomy, and a friend said of him 'he is so much engaged with the stars he is not always visible'. He was a humanitarian and friend of William Wilberforce, and an outspoken battler against the slave trade. He seems to have died in the West Indies in 1819.

Though this broad street, Hickson Road, was put through only in the early years of this century, it speaks plainly of an older maritime Sydney. It was excavated at the foot of the old bluffs, and these massive stones which form the embankment were carved out of the spoil. It was named after the chairman of the Sydney Harbour Trust and has scarcely changed its shape. It runs from Sydney Cove around Dawes and Miller's Points and effectively to Darling Harbour and the Entertainment Centre.

There are nostalgic glimpses of the past here, mostly at low tide, submerged loading steps, rusted iron ring bolts and bollards. Campbell's Cove is still the most beautiful of the indentations along this western shore. The long row of archaic warehouses still stands under shapely peaked roofs. In Campbell's time they were called godowns. An indigo trader from Calcutta, he brought the word from India. His grand house, Wharf House, stood over there, among romantic gardens, where many Indian and Ceylonese plants were naturalised.

The glory of Campbell's Cove today is the ravishing Park Hyatt Hotel. Built of sandstone, not too high, with a curvilinear frontage that echoes the gentle line of the historic Cove, its rooms look upon harbour views which must be among the most magnificent in the world.

Pause a moment and look towards the west. Somewhere here, between Metcalfe Bond and Gloucester Walk is the probable site of Sydney's first graveyard. The poor old bones of Australia's pioneer European settlers had many shifts, first the Rocks, then a sandy desolation away out in the southern bush, where the Town Hall now stands. Then they were shovelled up and taken by horse and dray to another sandy locality – Central Railway Station covers part of this cemetery now. Finally the bits and pieces were taken to Botany Bay, and there they will lie until Botany Bay and its riverlands and peninsulas become another great city stretching far to the south.

But this place in the Rocks in all likelihood was Sydney's first graveyard, where some of those sick of the First Fleet, for whose care Captain Phillip hurried up his portable canvas hospital, found their lonely resting-place. Others say that the first dead were buried up close to the ridge, where Harrington Street is now, but it seems unlikely that graves were dug in so rocky and precipitous a place. Here, in a patch of sandy earth, in this bay so like hundreds of others still around Sydney, a cranny of glistening cutty-grass and sparkling sea, a bay convenient to the hospital, and yet at some distance from the marine and convict camps – here surely they laid the forty-one exiles, including ten children, who died in the settlement's first five months.

Back along Circular Quay West, past Cadman's Cottage once again. When the cottage was built, Phillip had not been dead a year. When Cadman left it in 1846, Henry Parkes, the Father of Federation, was already talking about the advantages of union of the Australian colonies. Indeed, in only three years, Edmund Barton, the first Prime Minister, was to be born. One-eyed John Cadman must have enjoyed his life so close to the cove's pearly waters. He is buried not far from other waters at La Perouse.

Perhaps it is now late in the afternoon, and the crowd is spilling along the streets like a tsunami. Thousands of them hurry towards Quay trains and ferries, their faces as absorbed in innerness as the faces of the drowned. Better not join them. Sit idly in a café and drink cappuccino and consider how narrow was the escape of the idiosyncratic up-and-down old village we have just explored.

In 1971 Sydney was seized by an irresistible fit of restlessness. Times were prosperous; business expanded, ambitions went through the commercial roof. And a group of developers looked at the tumbledown tangle of lanes and stairways and downright hovels that made up the Rocks and said: 'This is the place for highrise apartments, luxury mansions with private slipways for luxury boats, maybe a tourist hotel or two. Let's pull the Rocks down.'

Some of the lanes and old factories were in fact bought. At the time there was no legislation to give even the National Trust power to protect what later became known as heritage buildings. Money was going to win.

But the wealthy developers forget that to raise marvellous new buildings you must pull the scruffy old ones down, and the secretary of the Builders' Labourers Federation, Jack Mundey, gathered his Left-wingers and refused to do it. 'We simply said we would not demolish any building the people of Sydney wanted. And we kept up the bans as required.'

Thousands of Sydneysiders joined the protests organised by the builders' labourers, not only about old colonial pockets of Sydney but also bits of wetland and bird and native animal refuges. It was a great lifesaving time for the city, and many of us have joyful memories of trees in Argyle Street in the Rocks festooned with young and old builders' labourers, hooked on like huge koalas while police tugged at their legs. Bravo!

Jack Mundey and his unionists kept at it until 1979 when the Labor Government concluded its vital program of heritage and environment protection legislation.

The Sydney Cove Redevelopment Authority has in many ways done a splendid job. The warehouses, bond stores and maritime buildings have not become museum pieces; they are beehives of bistros, craft studios and the everpresent duty free. The derelict terrace houses, so quaint with their dormer windows and banked chimneypots, have turned into offices and art galleries. Yes, it is all done well. Imagination can supply the street musicians, performing dogs, hawkers of parakeets and sellers of sparrow pies and chitterlings, foreign sailors, tattoo artists, bagpipers and Chinese magicians. Not to mention Lieutenant Mundy galloping along being pursued by regiments of stray dogs.

The crowds of homegoers are diminishing on the Quay, beautiful in the late sunset light. How good it would be to have a chat with the farsighted Merchant Campbell who would not be surprised at anything that had happened in Sydney. He was the remarkable Scotsman, younger son of the Laird of Duntroon, who by sheer resolution and business intelligence, broke the power of the officer clique.

The young adventurers of Phillip's time had long gone, and their place had been taken by arrogant toughs, as rapacious as cormorants. Theirs was the dominant place in the colony, and they used it mercilessly to extort fantastic profits from a population that had to buy from them or starve.

Robert Campbell, who came to Sydney via Calcutta, was two metres tall, with a mop of tousled brown hair, a square chin, a puritan soul and indomitable spirit. The Overseas Terminal covers the site of Campbell's Wharf (the first privately built and owned wharf in the colony), his princely home, Wharf House, and his garden where peacocks roamed. All that is left of the Campbell empire on Circular Quay West are the austere bond stores we noticed as we came past.

Campbell was married in Old St Phillip's by Samuel Marsden, and fathered a line of interesting and capable people. During his long life, that was filled with economic crises as well as achievement, he did many things besides the noble one of bringing fair trade to the infant colony under the thumb of the Rum Corps.

His stud Arabian, Hector, which had been the property of the Duke of Wellington, was the first sire of most of Australia's early racing stock. The oxen with which the Hawkesbury settlers ploughed their riverland were humped Bengalis, imported by Robert Campbell. He was a founder of The King's School, near Parramatta, encouraged his son Robert of Bligh House to fight for the abolition of transportation, steadily supported education and better housing for workmen, and experimented largely with different breeds of cattle. He had a finger in practically every colonial pie except politics and militarism. So it is ironic that his final home, called Duntroon after his childhood home in Argyle, became the nucleus for the famous military college of that name in Canberra. Part of his land grant in that area is now the federal capital.

Robert Campbell is buried in the family vault at St John's Cemetery, the historic graveyard at Parramatta.

There are many ghosts around this Quay. In the 1830s the *Beagle* came. Charles Darwin didn't enjoy Sydney. He was homesick – 'I feel inclined to keep up one steady deep growl from morning to night.' However, his friend and co-worker Thomas Huxley not only married a Sydney girl but threw out some marked hints. 'Had the University been carried out as originally proposed,' he said, 'I should certainly have become a candidate for the Natural History chair. I know no finer field of exertion for any naturalist than Sydney Harbour itself. Should such a professorship be ever established, I trust that you will jog the memory of my Australian friends on my behalf.'

Hither came the ship *Morley* in 1828, bringing with it whooping cough, which killed hundreds of people. Scarlatina came a year or two later. The introduction of almost every European disease to the fatally susceptible native-born Sydneysider came through the Quay.

Lola Montez, ex-mistress of fantastic Ludwig of Bavaria, dancer and horsewhipper of hostile editors, embarked here in gold-rush days, leaving behind both scandal and a host of creditors. A process server, sent aboard to arrest her, was thwarted simply because Lola took off all her clothes and wouldn't put them on again.

In the 1880s Young Griffo, king of the Rocks larrikins, *Sydney Morning Herald* newspaper boy, sailed away weeping to take for Australia the featherweight boxing championship of the world. He was half monkey and half demon, illiterate, terrified of ships. The first time they loaded him aboard he dived off, swam back to the Rocks and hid in a cellar. The second time they got him to America, but he never could face the voyage home. He lived in the Bowery, making a living by standing on a handkerchief and betting pub patrons they couldn't hit him, which they couldn't. He died in a snowstorm, sitting on a New York doorstep, in 1937.

In 1893 another went away, frail as a leaf, with burning black Highland eyes, and lungs afire with 'consumption'. He was Robert Louis Stevenson, who had a long happy sojourn in Sydney. He died within a year. Other famous writers came and went, Joseph Conrad, John Galsworthy, Rider Haggard, Rudyard Kipling, Jack London, who came to cover the Burns–Johnson fight in 1908, and Anthony Trollope, who was so impressed with the Harbour that he said: 'It makes a man ask himself whether it would be worthwhile to move his household goods to the eastern coast of Australia in order that he might look at it as long as he can look at anything.' And there was Mark Twain who told the reporters who met him a tall tale about a fast-swimming shark hooked in the Harbour. In its stomach was a copy of the *London Times* announcing the Franco-Prussian War. A fisherman sold the newspaper to a Sydney financier who bought up the entire wool clip, waited till the official news of the war reached Sydney uniform manufacturers, and then sold them the wool at a colossal price. 'Nothing beats inside information,' commented the original Kentucky Colonel.

And of all the famous ships, the wool clippers and the immigrant vessels, the ships of trade and commerce that made Australia, the two most beautiful ghosts are those of the *Cutty Sark* and *Thermopylae*.

Old-timers will tell you that these two famous clippers lay here at the Quay, side by side, but it's not so. *Cutty Sark* berthed at Circular Quay, pretty well in the east corner, and *Thermopylae* usually lay at Dalgety's wharf in Darling Harbour. But it's true that it was from Sydney that they flew off on their famous 1885 race to London. *Cutty Sark* was the finest ship in the wool trade, and *Thermopylae* the ace among the tea clippers from the China Seas. In this race *Cutty Sark* was queen, taking seventy-three days and beating her great rival by a week.

'All very well,' once commented someone who knew about sailing ships. 'But *Thermopylae* had a tough owner. She was badly chopped down for reasons of economy, and her skipper wasn't allowed to take chances. Different with the old *Cutty*! Her captain was allowed to take her so far south she was running through a maze of ice. And drive her! Why, half the time she looked like a halftide rock.' *Cutty's* owner was so pleased with her performance that he presented her with a golden shirt (a sark) to be made fast at the main truck.

How few, really, are the years since the *Hashemy* gave her name to yet another Circular Quay riot, when in 1849 a turbulent crowd would not allow her cargo of convicts to land. Even though it was pouring rain, their passions had been inflamed by the eloquence of Robert Campbell of Bligh House, addressing them from the open top of a horse omnibus on the anti-transportation question. *Hashemy's* visit did indeed mark the end of transportation to New South Wales.

Only sixty-one years before, the new town had been 'crisnd Sydney'.

How quiet that first night must have been, after all the confused flurry of the day. We are told that there was no sound but that of the ships' bells striking the hours, out on the dark water. Yet one imagines the stream splashing, and the frightened frogs gaining courage from the silence, and breaking it once more with their harsh vocables.

On the *Lady Penrhyn*, Ann Smith lay awake. We know nothing about her except that she was thirty, a nurse, and a most resolute woman. She landed at Sydney Cove on February 7 and absconded into the bush before February 12. She was never heard of again. Only three clues faintly indicate the future life of Ann Smith.

Almost two years later a piece of linen, supposed to have been part of her petticoat, was picked up fifty-two kilometres away in the bush. Eight years later, a fishing boat taking shelter in a bay near Port Stephens, heard from the tribesmen that a white woman was living with the Aborigines further north. And then, strangest of all in 1803, came an authentic report that on a whaler attacked by pirates in Alaskan seas, two people were killed, the helmsman and a woman from Port Jackson, named Ann Smith.

But these happenings, if they really concerned Ann Smith of the *Lady Penrhyn*, were far away from January 26, 1788. One imagines the moonpath on the water, a light fuzzing the hospital's cotton walls as a surgeon's orderly makes his rounds, a lantern moving on the slope of Bridge Street as young Lieutenant Dawes wanders off among the trees, dazzled by the arrogant brilliance of the southern constellations.

But aside from that, there is nothing but the violent darkness pressing against the camp beside the mudflats, the whole immense darkness of the unlit continent against these few feeble lights which are never to be put out again.

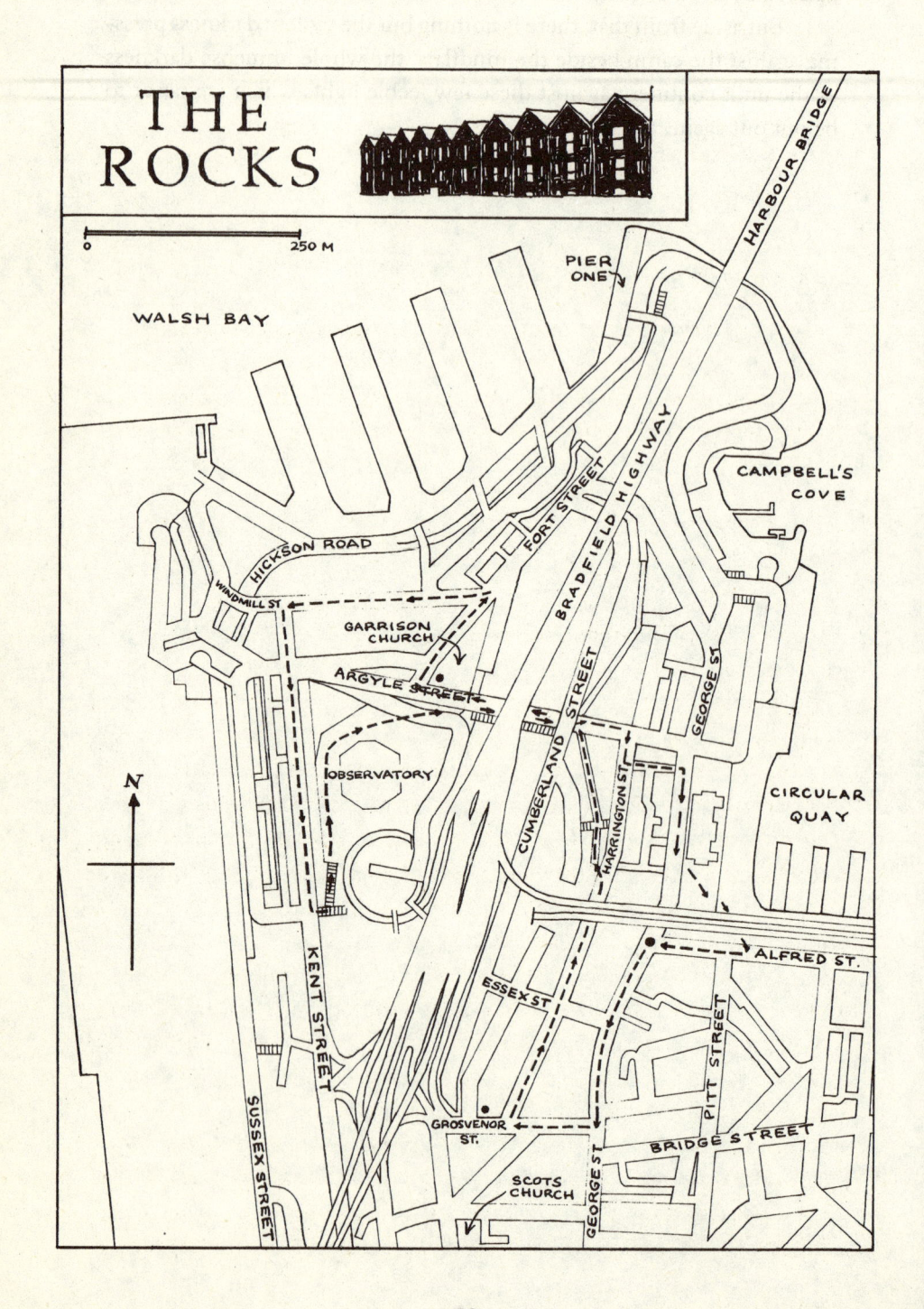

THE ROCKS

CHAPTER 2
THE GALLOWS, THE ROGUES, THE BUILDERS

The west side of Circular Quay – George Street – the first Post Office – Gallows Hill – public spectacles and the man they couldn't hang – Bridge Street – naughty orphans, floggings and the Rum Rebellion – Church Hill – the priest and the blacksmith and the two Saints Philip – Lang Park – York Street – the last of a vanished Quality Row – Harrington and Cambridge Streets – where lost souls danced – the Rocks – the Argyle Cut and how Tim Lane put it through – Windmill Street – the oldest pub in Australia – Miller's Point – Kent Street – Observatory Park – Argyle store – the admirable Mary Reiby – the Suez Canal, cut-throats' walk – George Street and back to Circular Quay.

WE begin at the corner of George Street and Alfred Street, which runs along the Quay behind us. Here is George Street, the oldest street in Australia and the Pacific. It was not always as straight as this. Time has ironed out its bumps, straightened its meandering course. Still, it follows its original plan, running from Dawes Battery on the western side of Sydney Cove to join the high road to Parramatta. George Street still meets the Parramatta Road where it used to, not far past Central Station.

When the first white men landed near here, they found themselves in Prester John's country; the sheltered, humid Vale of Sydney was full of extravagant vegetation with leaves like monstrous fans and bark as speckled as serpents. The forest was so dense that Daniel Southwell, entering the Harbour with the fleet on January 26, 1788, saw the first-comer, the *Supply*, 'seemingly up in the wood amongst the trees'.

Here where we stand was a stately grove of cabbage trees. These were felled and cut into suitable lengths for the walls of log huts, the interstices being filled with clay. Within six months not a cabbage tree remained in the Vale of Sydney. (The hard green heart of the plant's topknot was also eaten. Hence the name.) By that time Phillip had already sketched George Street, and others, on the map he was to send to Lord Sydney. 'The principal streets,' he said, 'are placed so as to admit a free circulation of air, and are two hundred feet wide.'

As he wrote, the Governor sat in a canvas house whose walls thrummed like spinnakers in the winter blast. This dwelling stood in a sea of red mud. It must have required astonishing vision to see in the infant settlement, drenched, starved and wretched, a city with streets. Yet, though it is not, and never was, sixty metres wide, George Street remains as a memorial to the Governor's dream.

In 1997–98 George Street underwent massive reconstruction, but let us look at it as it was. The pot-holed dirt track was familiarly called Spring Row and Sergeant Major's Row, but everyone knew that it was the colony's High Street. Indeed, it is under this name that George Street appears on maps until 1810 when it was officially named for King George III. Most of the buildings in George Street that year were still wattle-and-daub thatched dwellings, rather like a row of longhouses.

Upon arrival, Governor Macquarie was inexpressibly shocked to find such unmilitary sluttishness and decay in what he regarded as a British garrison town, and instantly set about rectifying the situation. Consequently, by 1810, George Street boasted some ambitious stone and brick buildings. Among these was a small but sturdy blockhouse with barred windows – the first post office run by the first postmaster, Isaac Nichols. Its location is doubtful but from a map of 1846 it appears probable that it stood where the telephone exchange is now, on the way to Bridge Street. Like so many civil officers of the times, Nichols was a convict.

This may be the place to make clear that any person of education, or indeed even common literacy and numeracy, was gratefully seized upon by the Establishment and given a post which often led not only to his eventual emancipation, but the founding of a considerable fortune.

Nichols was appointed by Lieutenant-Governor Paterson to put a stop to the felonious custom of people boarding ships and pretending to be others, so as to collect goods and mail not their own. This duty Nichols discharged faithfully. He was also allowed to charge a shilling on civilian letters and a penny on soldiers' letters. In between times he ran a general store and a grog shop. In ten years the postmaster was a wealthy man, putting his money into property on the North Shore, which was just beginning to be opened, mostly for the sake of its abundant timber. He died a rich man, directing in his will that his sons should be sent 'to England to be well and classically instructed, to qualify them for such liberal profession best suited to their genius'.

Ninety metres south of the post office, in front of a clanking windmill, was another historic office, where the city's first newspaper and Sunday paper, the *Sydney Gazette*, was published. This minute journal, which somehow continued to appear irregularly from 1803 to 1842, was written, edited, set up, printed and distributed by George Howe. As Happy George, Howe, a West Indian Creole, had been caught robbing a London drapery shop and deported to New South Wales on a life sentence. He was a gritty fellow, a spiritual ancestor of Henry Lawson's editor of the *Cambaroora Star*, who brought out the paper even if he had to print it on his shirt. Paper was especially short in the infant settlement. It was 'varied in colour, texture, size and material ... quite Protean in its appearance'. It was under these circumstances, lasting many years, that ladies going to the grocery store would provide against the want of shop paper by putting tea at one end of a stocking and sugar at the other.

Those early settlers were as quarrelsome as a handful of wasps, and it is no wonder that poor Howe, worn out by dissension, vituperation and government interference, died prematurely. His son, Robert, was even spunkier and died younger; during the eight years he ran the *Gazette*, he was horsewhipped, stabbed, brought to court for libel on several occasions, beaten up, and had lightnings cast at him from the pulpit. (Dr Dunmore Lang characteristically called him the cock of a dunghill press. But then, he had a newspaper of his own, and was not unprejudiced.) In the midst of a running quarrel with the 'arch-fiend' John Macarthur, Robert Howe tipped out of his boat near Pinchgut and was drowned. He was thirty-four. When he died in 1829, Sydney had a population of twelve thousand, and George Street south of Bridge Street was lined with wooden shanties, stables, inns and cottage gardens as far as the present Town Hall. The site of the latter was then the cemetery (already marked 'full' on the maps) and a grazing ground for cows.

Both the Howes had a pretty touch with words. Robert referred to a grand new warehouse with a corn mill on the roof as 'a frightful, lofty temple with a whirlabout thingumibob on top', while George, dutifully attending the execution of a Pennsylvanian rapist in 1804, reports:

'While the work of death was under preparation he took leave of the populace in a short harangue, warning against a life of dissipation – and then departed for an unknown region.'

Though George Street in the 1830s was struggling to turn itself into a carriageway of fine proportions, both sides bristled with alleyways, mostly of bad repute. They had haphazardly appeared on the steep slopes to east and west, as residents tramped out access to their shanties. One cul-de-sac, paved with equal amounts of garbage and cobbles, was called Redman's Court, after the Chief Constable and caretaker who lived next to that bank robbed by Sudden Solomon and his paladins, as related in the first chapter.

In Redman's Court, beside the mutton pie shop and the beaver hat factory, was a dilapidated brick print-shop where, on April 18, 1831, the *Sydney Herald* was born. It was a four-page weekly which a modern reader would vote instantly as one least likely to succeed. However, after staggering along for a decade, this little newspaper, by then a daily, was bought by Charles Kemp, one of its reporters, and a bankrupt English journalist named John Fairfax. The two young men weathered many storms and the newspaper weathered still more, for it is, of course, the present doyen of Australian dailies, the *Sydney Morning Herald*. In 1851 the newspaper was doing so well that John Fairfax was able to return to England and honourably discharge all his debts in full.

Thus by the 1830s George Street had changed greatly from its original incarnation when it was distinguished from the surrounding grass and mud only by a brace of wandering cart tracks. Perhaps some veteran emancipees, fat and prosperous, might even have looked back nostalgically to the street's romantic Spring Row days when it thronged with people lugging canvas pails of water from the Tank Stream to the hospital and their own encampments. The women's tents were further north and the male convicts just about here on our right. Their encampment was shortly replaced with a gaol made of logs and here, within six weeks of the First Fleet's arrival, a skinny seventeen-year-old, a chimney sweep's boy, was hanged for stealing food. Of course, on February 7 the felons had been very clearly warned, volleys being fired over their heads to emphasise the dread penalty for food theft, but it is pitiful that the first person to suffer capital punishment in Australia should have been someone young and hungry. His fate so intimidated the convicts that two or three weeks later an aged woman who for some extraordinary reason had stolen a flat iron and was in danger of being found out, hung herself from the ridgepole of her tent rather than face the gibbet. She was, however, cut down alive.

Now turn up Essex Street. There's still something curious about this street. It's sunny, very steep, and used to leap to each of its levels with flights of worn stone steps. Walk slowly, for this is Hangman's Hill.

During two long periods, the public gallows dominated this end of the town, until 1804 when they were moved to the corner of present Park and Castlereagh Streets. After further removes about the settlement they were permanently set in place in 1841 outside the great wall of the new prison at Darlinghurst.

Now there is nothing but sunlight in Essex Street. In its fatal days it must have been muddy, for it drained the rocky steeps of Cumberland and Gloucester Streets. On the present level between Gloucester and Harrington Streets, in the middle of the road, is a little grassy plot on a built-up embankment of random freestone. Two trees grow where the gallows stood, one a palm as tall as a ship's mast. An old woman has scrambled up somehow, and beside the palm she scrapes a horrid skilly into a rusty lid. Her pensioners await her – three wraiths of cats. She takes us for disapproving cat-haters and plops the last ort of fat down into the lid with huffy defiance. The cats flatten down to feed.

'No law agen feeding poor strays, I should hope!'

'Not at all,' we assure her. 'We just stopped to stare because this is where the gallows were in the early days.'

'Dunno about that. Cruel swine. Always doing something to somebody they were. No different now.'

She clambers down awkwardly on brittle ankles. 'Then it was people. Now it's poor cats.'

All the stonework connected with this grassy plot looks very old. Beside it run archaic gutters, stones tipped to a point, European style. Well, some queer people were turned off here, including in 1803 the wretched Joseph Samuels, 'the man they couldn't hang'. Samuels was one of four petty criminals accused of robbery and the subsequent murder of a constable who chased them. Before an immense and hostile crowd, aghast at what must have been a fearful scene, the executioners endeavoured to do their duty though the rope suspending the unfortunate Samuels broke three times.

'Some did not hesitate to declare that the invisible hand of

Providence was at work', stated the *Sydney Gazette*. The crowd was so riotous that the half-strangled and unconscious Samuels was left on the ground while the Provost-Marshal, who superintended the hanging, galloped off to see what the Governor had to say about it. The latter, the humane King, instantly reprieved the unfortunate victim. 'May the grateful remembrance of these events direct his future course!' the *Gazette* said of Samuels, who was always slightly queer in the attic afterwards. His end was odd. He was one of eight convicts who eloped from the Hunter River coalmines in 1806, stole a boat, and pushed out to sea. They were last seen driving before a storm along the north coast and were never heard of again.

It is difficult to understand authority's insistence on public executions in centuries gone by. The immense public interest, which seems to us ghoulish and brutalised, was accepted as natural, indeed praiseworthy. In 1783 Dr Johnson said: 'Sir, executions are intended to draw spectators. If they do not, they don't answer their purpose. The old method [of public execution] was most satisfactory to all parties. The public was gratified by a procession, the criminal was supported by it.'

The Golden Cob, a quite respectable pub in Essex Street, had a special viewing window for aficionados of hanging.

Admittedly, when someone was stretched at the Darlinghurst gaol in 1847 (the gallows being erected just outside the front gate) a few protests were made when it was observed that the boys from a nearby school attended in a body. Generally, however, it was a merciless age: civilian flogging was carried out under military or naval rules, the stocks were in common use for debt, drunkenness or unruly behaviour, and the hangman's rope menaced all, even the nabobs.

Essex Street now leads up to Cumberland and Harrington Streets, but rather let us return to George Street and walk along to Grosvenor Street. It's a charming street with yellow-leaved plane trees marching up the hill. Its name was once Charlotte Place, but this part has always been known as Church Hill. Near the crest, commanding the Harbour and the tidy oats and maize paddocks of the rural settlement, Governor Phillip intended to erect a suitable Government House. But he never got around to it, and on the site was built Sydney's first real church (as distinct from that wattle-and-daub construction which the convicts burned down). It was consecrated by the Rev. Samuel Marsden in 1810, and was architecturally fully in keeping with a prison colony, being an afflicting building like a brick marquee, with a battlemented tower on one end and on the other a crouching dome for all the world like a bigger version of one of Sydney's famous Victorian latrines. Mad but golden-hearted George III contributed a silver Communion service out of his privy purse, and the Anglican community purchased a small ring of bells which were known locally as The Pots, and cursed by the impious whose Sunday mornings were doomed nevermore to be restful.

The Communion plate and the Bible used in the first service are preserved in the second St Philip's, which we shall shortly visit.

(One notes that this first church was St Phillip's, called after the Governor, and the second St Philip's, dedicated to the Apostle, but at the same time bestowing a respectful backward glance at Sydney's founder. In the same way, the historic St John's of Parramatta was dedicated to the Apostle, but only because the departing Governor Hunter was also John.)

Other churches old for Sydney now stand on Church Hill: the Scots Church which is almost certainly haunted by the shade of the caustic Dr Lang, politician, editor, parson and benefactor of immigrants, yet another one of those scary Scotsmen without whom the British Empire might never have existed. There is also the gaunt Roman Catholic church of St Patrick's. St Patrick's Girls' School and the Aquinas Academy are just behind it, where William Davis, who owned the original site, had his pumpkin paddock. At the time of writing reconstruction is planned for most of these buildings.

Davis donated the site of his cottage and smithy to the Church in 1840, and the building was open for worship for the first time on St Patrick's Day, 1844. In the Catholic world, Davis is very important. An Irish rebel transported in 1799, he was a pious blacksmith who became famous in 1817 for whisking away and hiding the Rev. Jeremiah O'Flynn, an Irish priest supposedly illegally in the colony. It is hard to untangle the rights and wrongs of this now, but the Irish Catholics who were numerous among both convicts and free settlers, were not disposed to allow Father O'Flynn to be cast out, after their long years without an official chaplain. William Davis successfully hid the lively Father O'Flynn for more than a year, when the Governor pounced and deported him. Sydney legend is that this priest left the consecrated Sacrament in the cottage of William Davis, and that for many years desolate Catholics gathered there for prayers. But in fact, two years later, two

Catholic priests were officially admitted to the colony.

Before we ascend Church Hill, let us first consider Bridge Street. From the north we have already admired its High Victorian bravura as well as its breadth, unusual for Sydney. Mellow is the word for this fine street. From the corner of Grosvenor and George Streets it is not hard to imagine how things were in those years.

It is curious how, when one's imaginative reconstructions of the early colony come shimmering up from the subconscious, they are invariably set under a blazing sky. In effect they are mirages. Perhaps one thinks this way because the first diarists were so amazed and affronted by the climate of New South Wales. Indignantly they describe thunderstorms, trees and cattle crisped by lightning, and hailstones as big as plum puddings. Most of all they grumble at the insupportable heat, which they believed was caused by natives lighting bushfires. Only the likeable young Watkin Tench, one of Captain Phillip's captains of marines, intelligently speculated that the heat was carried by winds blowing over vast unknown deserts in the northwest.

Sydney today can produce summer temperatures of over 38°C. (100 F) and may keep this up for days on end. It must have been during one of these heatwaves that the bats came to Sydney. If in 1790 you had been standing in our present situation, in front of you a dusty red track that was to become George Street, you would have seen an immense flight of bats, driven by a blasting wind, suddenly filling the sky, settling on fruit and willow trees, thatches and scaffolding, blinded, scorched and swiftly dead. 'Nor did the perroquettes bear it better,' comments Tench. 'The ground was strewed with them.'

An engaging Spanish watercolour by Brambila shows Bridge Street in 1793. The Lieutenant-Governor's large verandahed house would be behind us. It became the Sydney Hotel and Coffee House in 1820. The guardhouse was on the opposing corner of Grosvenor Street. All looks grassy and rustic under a sky of doll's eye blue, Government House and a clutch of attendant cottages are at the end of the street, on the crest of a considerable hill. The Female Orphans' Asylum is on the left, pretty well where Dalley Street is now. It was set up by kindly Mrs King, the Governor's wife.

Like his predecessor, Governor Hunter, King was shocked by the moral condition of the colony: 'vice, dissipation, and a strange relaxation seems to pervade all restrictions.' The consequence of this was a small army of starveling children living in the streets and among the rocks like stray cats. 'The rising generation are abandoned to misery, prostitution and every vice of their parents.' Thus King, who had two illegitimate children by a convict woman prior to his marriage, cared for them dearly and had them educated in England.

Mrs King's Orphanage was run by a committee. The house sheltered a hundred waifs who were taught spinning, sewing, reading and sometimes writing. They were being trained to be servants. Samuel Marsden found the girls 'in the greatest order, feasting on excellent salt pork and plum pudding'. Though the protection of the girls' virtue was of serious concern to the committee, it was rumoured that many of them frequently nipped over the wall on bold forays into the world of men. When Governor Macquarie arrived, he decided that the asylum was far too close to the barracks, and lost no time in transferring his charges to the safer clime of Parramatta.

On the south side of Bridge Street, extending from the corner to the hollow of Pitt Street, where the Tank Stream ran, was the sinister Lumberyard. This was a convict workshop until 1834, when the land was cut up and sold for high prices to shopkeepers and tradesmen. Aside from the sawpits, the Lumberyard contained rows of forges, workshops for coopers, barrelmakers, harness makers and carpenters. It was also the place where the flogging triangles were set up.

Alexander Harris in his book *Settlers and Convicts* says: 'I had to go past the triangles where they had been flogging incessantly for hours. I saw a man walk across the yard with blood that had run from his lacerated back squashing out of his shoes at every step he took. A dog was licking the blood off the triangles …'. This was circa 1826.

Down Bridge Street on Anniversary Day, 1808, marched the greater part of the New South Wales Corps with fixed bayonets, determined to depose and arrest the then governor, Captain Bligh. The arrogant officer clique had been tried beyond endurance by the affronts handed out by the peppery naval martinet. Their privileges had been rescinded, their misdeeds reported to London.

And what misdeeds they were! The Rum Corps, as they had come to be tagged, might well have been on the moon for all their concern about possible retribution from Britain. They had appointed themselves the elite, beyond law except that which they made themselves. They called themselves the Pure Merinos – that is, superior persons totally outside convict culture. They exploited every money-making scheme, they met incoming ships at the Heads and commandeered their cargoes, which were then sold at exorbitant prices to the town. They paid their workmen in rum, which was supposed to be bartered to other workmen for food and services, but was too often drunk on the spot. They took advantage of free convict labour, with rations, supplied by the government, to work their splendid estates, which in most cases were government grants. Convicts also built their great mansions.

Bligh put a stop to it quick smart. He conducted a long feud with the Corps in general and John Macarthur in particular. He said disagreeable things such as suggesting that the convicts wear red coats 'as that is the only colour they are worthy to wear'. Urged on by the fire-eating Macarthur, the commander of the Corps, Major Johnston, took the step of mutiny. The officers were well wined and dined in honour of the holiday and John Macarthur rode on a gun carriage; the band played 'The British Grenadiers' and the excited citizens, promenading in the cool evening, beheld the gratifying sight of the doughty Bligh, hero of the famous mutiny and an astonishing voyage to safety in an open boat, brought forth under arrest.

Bonfires were lit on every corner, effigies of the tyrant were burned. Tales flew about – the vice-regal gentleman had been hauled forth from under a bed – he had been defended by his spirited daughter with a parasol! In actual fact, Bligh, his daughter, Mrs Mary Putland, and Merchant Campbell and his American wife had been at dinner at Government House when the hullabaloo in Bridge Street reached their astonished ears. We have a vivid version of events from Robert Campbell. Governor Bligh rushed upstairs to put on his dress uniform. He thought he was about to be hanged, and he wished to go through the ordeal in style. But Mary Putland, a tiny woman with as atrocious a temper as her father, did indeed rush to the front door past cowering servants, fling it open and lay about her with a parasol 'quite disconcerting the gentlemen'.

What an evening it was! Sydney enjoyed it tremendously.

The only casualty was a lieutenant who fell out of a loft and 'nearly dislocated his principal joints'. Poor Johnston was later removed to London for court martial, Bligh was sent off home, and the incoming Governor Macquarie restored peace. The Rum Corps was shipped back to England and a Highland regiment of less outrageous habits took its place.

The Gallows, The Rogues, The Builders

At the top of Grosvenor Street we can sit in the sun in Lang Park. With its one gas lamp, it is rather like a little village green, a somewhat neglected one, for its long grassy triangle is littered with rotting figs and tattered banana leaves. Only pigeons keep us company. There is a secretive little Gents' among the oleanders, and a shabby plinth of sandstone blocks from old St Phillip's bears a plate announcing that this was the site of the historic church. This church was cold, dark and too small, and after St James's was built in King Street in 1824 the fashionable churchgoers swiftly deserted St Phillip's. Its bricks began to crumble and it was pulled down in the mid-1850s. The new church of St Philip's was built just across York Street.

The infernal chaos of the Western Distributor, which cuts across behind and slightly north of the graceful old church, must not deter the visitor from inspecting this endearing building by my favourite architect, Edmund Blacket. St Philip's is one of those churches with a lovely smell of clean old stone, rubbed brass, and a warm equable temperature. When I first saw it, amid a perfect maelstrom of destruction and construction, the freezing wind full of dust and leaves and grit, I entered to find within a calm and humming silence. It was like being inside a seashell.

It is a modest, unadorned church, a parish church in daily use since 1856. Its walls are weathered stone, its floor of russet and brown patterned tiles. At the chancel are long, thin, stained-glass windows like strips of Hungarian braid, and the side windows are of lozenged glass with leaf shapes and trefoils in citrus colours, many agreeably random. The pulpit is white and intricately carved. Near the chancel is an interesting marble group of women and a girl child. It was erected in memory of Robert Campbell, 'youngest son of the last laird of Ashfield, cadets of Duntroon'. This is Merchant Campbell. His son, John, gave a peal of bells to the church. Outside in the porch (which faces Clarence Street) is a wee bit braggie about these bells, rung to celebrate the end of war in 1945 '... a peal of grandsire doubles, 5040 changes in 2 hours, 57 minutes'. Here also is the foundation stone from old St Phillip's, 1810.

The thirty-two metre tower bears a TV aerial on its castellated crest, and was for two generations adorned by a clock with no hands. The mechanism for the clock was stolen from the Sydney wharves on its arrival from England and for decades nothing was done to supply the deficiency. The old rectory has been replaced with a handsome building which houses a choir-practice room, the archives and museum, and the administrative office, the living quarters being on the top two floors.

Just across the road the formidable Dr Lang built his manse, across from his Scots Church, as you see. To paraphrase the football commentator, Dr Lang constantly rushed onto the field, kicking people in all directions. He had a true eighteenth-century gift for execration and his malisons boiled forth from the pulpit as well as in his shortlived papers, the *Colonist* and the *Press*. In fact he spent several months in Parramatta Gaol for libel. One of his contemporaries, John Hardwick, describes Dr Lang as having a low flat head. The question of whether this interesting physiognomy had aught to do with his diabolic temper, tempts one to speculation. However, Lang's chief interest for us was his energetic backing of a sensible immigration policy. He is credited with bringing out almost two thousand free settlers, all trained in some craft or industry needed in the settlement. Indeed, he brought out a hundred Scottish 'mechanics' and their families by his own unaided efforts, selling his own property in order to do so. The Assembly Hall now stands on the site of Lang's kirk.

Returning to Lang Park, we may rest and consider York Street. It is a fine broad street, planned to be a carriageway. In the 1840s it was a typical military road, straight as a contrail, running between Governor Macquarie's barracks and their imposing square. For their time, the barracks were the largest in the British Empire, reminding us that until 1870 Sydney was a garrison town. In those days York Street turned directly in front of us (that is to say, behind old St Phillip's) and angled away towards now-vanished Princes Street and Miller's Point.

The six hectares of valuable land, enclosed within a fortress-like wall, filled with longing anyone with a business eye in his head. Alexander Harris, newly arrived in 1825, described the situation as 'the best spot, in fact, for general commercial purposes, a spot that really ought, without further delay, be resigned to the corporation for those many important uses to which it could be applied'. But investors and town planners continued to be irked until 1847 when the new Paddington Barracks were completed, and the troops marched away to their lonely outpost amidst the scrub.

Generations of soldiers had lived in cosy contiguity with the citizenry, and all the homely joys provided by the latter. The pubs, eating houses and brothels were close at hand; the wives and concubines of the soldiers lived just behind the barracks in rows of wooden shacks in what is now Clarence Street. The troops voiced their indignation by hooting and groaning as they marched away to Paddington and the epidemics of conjunctivitis which were to be their lot in the windy sandhills. The complaint was often called 'Paddington pink-eye'.

The old barracks were demolished, and the present network of streets laid out. The later building of the Harbour Bridge gobbled up once-stately Princes Street, and nearly all of Cumberland Street. These streets were named for Queen Victoria's wicked uncles, the Duke of Cumberland being the wickedest of all. Still, one cannot help but find his street delightful. Here the visitor clearly senses the curious character of the Rocks. The hodgepodge of layers and layers of history have become a little threadbare and show through each other as in a palimpsest. The flatfaced terrace houses with tiny paned windows and modest gables originally had cedar shutters and one-storey verandahs. They were middleclass town houses. Still, here and there is a grander building. We are approaching the High Rocks, the respectable, if not upper class, area. An open court gate discloses a dilapidated coachhouse with three stalls. A Harley Davidson leans against the stone water trough.

The shy David Scott Mitchell, whose enormous collection of Australiana is the nucleus of the Mitchell Library, lived in this street in childhood, as did Edmund Barton, Australia's first primeminister. Mitchell's father was at one time surgeon-in-charge of the Military Hospital. His grant on the Hunter River included a coal seam, and the subsequent wealth of the family enabled his bibliophile son to indulge his tastes for rare maps, manuscripts and books. The Sydney legend is that D.S. Mitchell was early crossed in love and became a recluse. His quaintly respectable figure, clad in sober garments with a bowler at one end and black elastic-sided boots at the other, was familiar to booksellers for some decades. On Monday mornings he went his rounds most punctually, and was known to the drivers of the cabs he hired as 'Old Four Hours'.

Mitchell, like all book collectors, suffered torments when a rival scooped some treasure of Australiana from under his nose. Fortunately, he was able to outbid most of them. Ardently desiring the original Joseph Banks diaries, he bought the entire library of their owner, Alfred Lee, for seven thousand pounds, a fortune in the early years of this century. The late James Tyrrell, founder of a famous second-hand bookshop in George Street (later at Crows Nest), relates: 'At the appointed time next morning Lee thumped the door knocker at 17 Darlinghurst Road. The door partly opened, Mitchell's household guard and guardian angel "Old Sarah" handed out the envelope containing the cheque, said "Good morning" and closed the door.'

David Scott Mitchell was one of the first twenty-four students to be enrolled at Sydney University and graduated MA in 1859. He left the Mitchell Library 61,000 volumes and other items, together with a substantial legacy for their housing and care. In 1898 the New South Wales Government gratefully accepted Mitchell's princely gifts and then fiddle-faddled until 1905, squabbling over the building and its possible site. In that year the pioneer bookseller and publisher George Robertson of Angus and Robertson, yet another formidable Scotsman, publicly exploded in condemnation of the political numbskulls who did not realise what treasure they had in their inept hands.

'Not only books, but manuscripts, portraits, pictures, proclamations, broadsides, maps, medals, miniatures ...' thundered Robertson, and drove his point home by predicting that soon the wealthy American libraries would be turning their attention to Australiana. Privately Robertson said: 'Whenever I hear the money value of the Mitchell Collection spoken of, I am tempted to break the peace.'

How right he was. From all over the world scholars come to consult the Mitchell Library, housed in the Mitchell Wing of the State Library of New South Wales, just around the corner from Macquarie Street and open to all enquirers.

Harrington Street also runs off Grosvenor Street, and is, to my mind, the most rewarding way to enter the Rocks. For one thing, although the Authority has restored the street with housewifely care, and some splendid hotels have already discovered it, here and there are still occupied houses. Occupied, that is, by real people, ordinary residents who are just as likely to be out airing the baby in First Fleet Park or buying a nice leg of lamb at the butcher's. There are almost two thousand residents of the Rocks, says the Authority, but among the surging crowds of tourists they are as elusive as phantoms.

Some of these bijou cottages are very old. The Reynolds Cottages, 28, 29 and 30 were built in 1823 by a life convict. William Reynolds was an Irish blacksmith, a large burly man who quickly sized up his country

The Gallows, The Rogues, The Builders

of exile and grabbed every opportunity it offered him. He is a fine example of the convict who did better out of being a convict than otherwise.

You can inspect No. 28, and an eye-opener it is to anyone who is not familiar with the eighteenth and nineteenth centuries' tolerance of human beings living in mouseholes. One room up and one down, and each as big as a bedsheet, an open fire to cook on and (although glazed nowadays) tiny windows protected by oiled cotton or canvas. Seven Reynolds children were reared here, hardy brats who grew up to benefit from father William's business acumen. He left three cottages, a smith and a backyard ratting pit which must have been a goldmine. Though illegal, it would have been eagerly patronised by gamblers who bet how many rats a game terrier could kill in five minutes.

Harrington Street grew out of a track beaten out by soldiers stamping back and forth between the Barracks and Dawes Battery. They were an unhappy, dirty and scruffy lot, mostly fallen into army life for the same reasons that so many transportees fell into criminality – the dire industrial and economic distress of the British Isles. Almost all the Sydney-based British regiments were mutinous, 'disaffected' and prone to fearful fights with their traditional enemies, seamen, and, inevitably, the toughs of the Rocks. The battles that raged up and down Harrington, Gloucester and Cambridge Streets! The soldiers used as weapons their heavy leather belts, fastened with broad brass buckles, ideal for breaking heads.

Stairs go up and down in the handful of crooked streets and lanes to the west of Harrington Street. On hot days cobbles show in the road surface; these are not native stones but ballast from merchant ships, dumped here to the everlasting bafflement of future archeologists. The stairs, or steps as they are called about here, are worn and lopsided; they were the only way to defeat the dragon spines of sandstone that crumbled into cascades of boulders, around which the settlers scraped out wells, pastured their goats, grew vegetables and hung their washing. Up there was the notorious Black Dog tavern perched high on a hog's back ridge, the haunt of murderers, crimps and footpads. Residents of lower levels petitioned for its removal, lest it should collapse on top of them. Still, it survived until 1908.

And somewhere around here was another infamous hostelry, the Sheer Hulk. Alexander Harris writing for the *Saturday Evening Post* in 1858, describes the Sheer Hulk as he had seen it years before, on the night of his arrival in Sydney. He came out of a cold starry night, into a low room, clouded with tobacco smoke to suffocation. It was crowded with sailors and convicts 'free by servitude but unreformed and speculating anew in their old occupation. There danced bearded men ... amidst women the unseemliest in nature, haggard and hollow-eyed and sallow, their hair dishevelled ... smoking their pipes as they vaulted crazily hither and thither. The huge malformed negro who fiddled was capering with the rest. The candles burnt with a dim murky reddish glare ... which well they might, lighting as they did, the lost to their doom.'

There is also a marvellous story, circa 1870, of an earnest young parson who tried to preach the doctrine of hell to three old women sitting demurely outside The Young Princess. As one woman the three ladies removed their pipes from their mouths and blew 'thin blue flames' at him. They must have been totally soaked in rum, like Christmas puddings.

I always loved Cambridge Street, that is, before the Sydney Cove Authority washed its face and trimmed its hair. The tall, rather severe houses perched on their escarpment were a splendid disgrace, their feet hidden in cascades of plumbago, morning glory and dusty ivy, their dilapidated doors reached by flights of dangerous steps. And yet these houses were not old, as far as Rocks architecture goes, dating only from the turn of the century. They were built consequent upon a demolition of the leantos, pigpens, hovels and bothies that previously occupied the site. This dramatic sweeping away by authority of all that was loved as home followed the outbreak of bubonic plague in the summer of 1900. Not much is made in the history books of the fact that in the thrilling months before Federation was declared Sydney was battling an epidemic. The Rocks was not the only locality affected – Surry Hills, Redfern, Paddington, Darling Harbour, even the health resort of Manly, all were quarantined. But the first case occurred in the Rocks, a docks carter, who did however survive.

In spite of the customary political rows, shouts of corruption, incompetence and so on, an admirable architect and engineer, George McCredie, was appointed chief organiser of quarantine procedure. His reports give us a nightmare picture. 'Many things disgraceful in the extreme ... accumulations of filth ... utter disregard of sanitary arrangements – sad cases of poverty ... limewashing ... burning ... carbolic acid ... intolerable.'

The quarantined residents of the affected areas were engaged to do the work, which was undertaken with enthusiasm. The figures are staggering – over 52,000 tonnes of silt and sewage dredged from around the wharves, 1,423 dead animals taken from the Harbour, 54,000 tonnes of garbage either burned or taken out to sea and dumped and more than 44,000 rats caught. Rat fleas are of course the primary carriers of bubonic plague.

Mr McCredie brilliantly shepherded Sydney through the emergency but in most ways slum property in the city, and particularly in the Rocks, did not improve. The refusal of landlords to repair, the hostility of the terrain, the ancient tendency of dockside suburbs to become 'Alsatias', that is, areas almost impossible to police, all contributed to the Rocks's backsliding. But health inspectors were more vigilant, no more open drains and illegally narrow alleys or slypes were allowed. The so-called Suez Canal, leading to George Street, is almost the last of these. Slowly, reluctantly, the Rocks began to leave its wild colonial past.

We emerge in Argyle Street almost opposite the Argyle Steps. Time now to rest, have a meal or cup of coffee, or perhaps stroll down towards George Street and the Quay. About Argyle Street the tourists congregate, browse, shop, or if it is the weekends snoop around the picturesque open market. Every month there is something different to see or do – exhibitions, art festivals, street musicians, mime, and of course delicious things to eat everywhere. If you have a good appetite for life, try the Rocks.

However, if you have time to spare, turn left. On the other side of the great passage in the sandstone known as the Argyle Cut, there is a different world. Officially this is Miller's Point. The boundary of the Rocks is the eastern side of the Cut. But no Sydneysider will nitpick about this. We are simply entering that part of the Rocks where employment was high and stable, decent housing was built by powerful shipowners and importers, and the residents could afford self-respect.

The morning sun makes Miller's Point drowsy and nostalgic. The precipitous wall of the Cut runs with water, dark rainbow spills from Observatory Park far above.

Further on, opposite the Garrison Church, masses of greenery tumble over the rockface, with birds playing in it as they might in a waterfall. There are little scraps of parkland here and there, seats and trees. Many of the latter are European, which is almost always the case where settlement was early and English. In the old status suburbs, such as Vaucluse, fidgety rich ladies, longing for limes and chestnuts, ruthlessly dispossessed ironbarks and bloodwoods so that European replants could be made. Here, in ex-Army country stretching between the Dawes Battery and Fort Phillip up behind us where the Observatory now stands, you will find durable city trees such as planes, oaks and poplars.

Sitting here, looking across at the Garrison Church, and Argyle Place, which is so much in the style of an English green, let us consider the Cut. The earliest businessmen recognised the need for a short-cut for wheeled vehicles from the east to the west shores of the Rocks, but it was not until 1843 that work commenced as part of George Barney's vigorous plan for the reclamation of Circular Quay.

The fearful task was undertaken by convict gangs, marched down four abreast from the Hyde Park Barracks, their coarse jackets stamped HPB to mark their origin. As stonework, like roadwork, was the severest sentence outside of hanging, many of the men were convicted of grave crimes, and were chained as well. They were under the ungentle supervision of an outrageous bully, Tim Lane, whose cry was: 'By the help of God and the strong arm of the flogger, you'll get fifty before breakfast tomorrow!' It was pick and hammer work, very slow and arduous. Most of the sandstone removed from the Cut went to form sea walls around the Quay, and the rubble was used as fill on the mudflats. After many years of delay, the project was finally completed with free labour in 1864. Thus both ends of the excavation are convict-hewn, and the middle of the Cut severed by paid stoneworkers. It was originally bridged by wood, and then stone. It is now spanned by an arch which carries traffic to the Harbour Bridge.

We cross over to Holy Trinity Church, or as it is familiarly known, the Garrison Church. I like it best when I'm by myself, for that's the kind of church it is, a constantly-used, not too well-endowed parish church, Gothic in style, with flags and regimental shields on the pillars, a wine-glass pulpit of red cedar, and a delightful east window, glittering like enamel in the gentle gloom.

The foundation stone was laid in 1840, and the church built from stone quarried out of the cliff behind. It was built by free men, but convicts carted away the rubble and did other heavy labour. It became the

Sydney, 1788

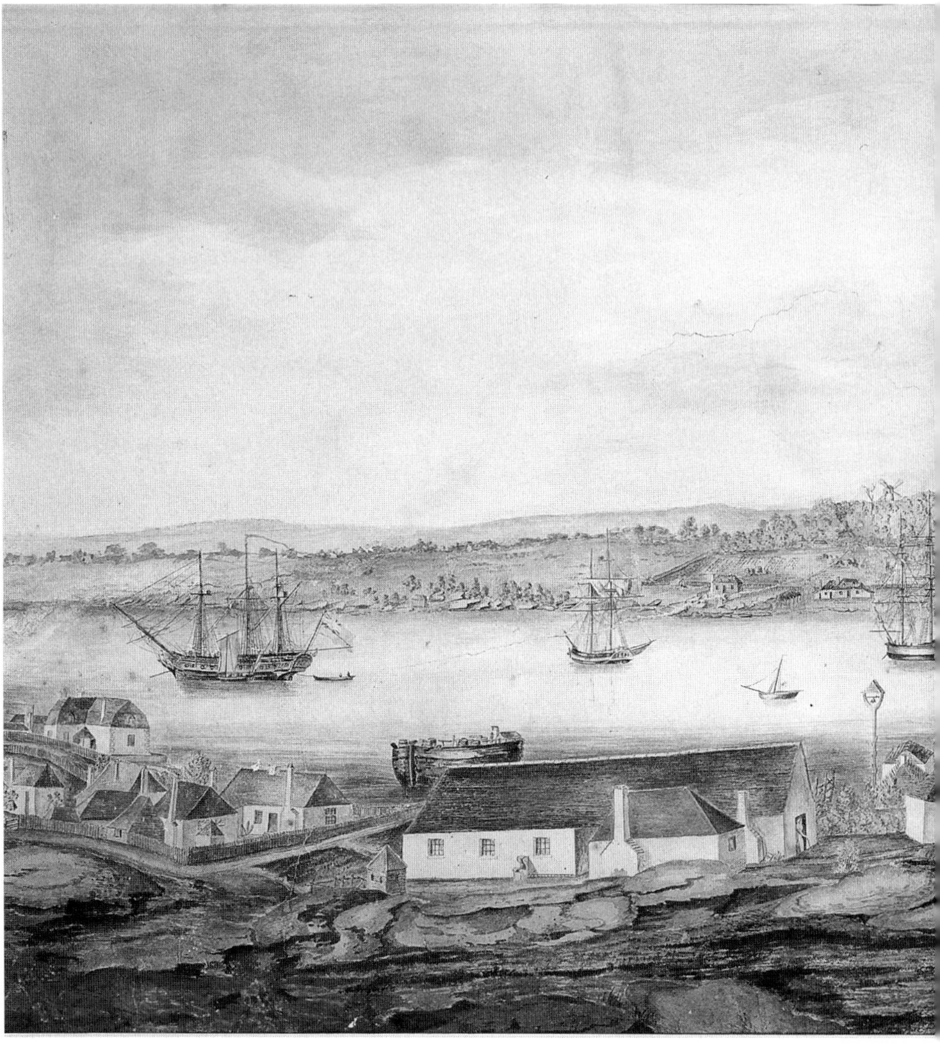

Sydney, 1803

The convicts despised the soldiers who guarded them, and composed shocking broadsides about His Excellency ... In these unfree and almost uncivilised men and women, an inchoate sense of equality had begun to show itself.

During the course of work on the Quay (1837 - 1844), transportation to New South Wales ended. Circular Quay is thus the last and greatest convict work to be completed in the colony.

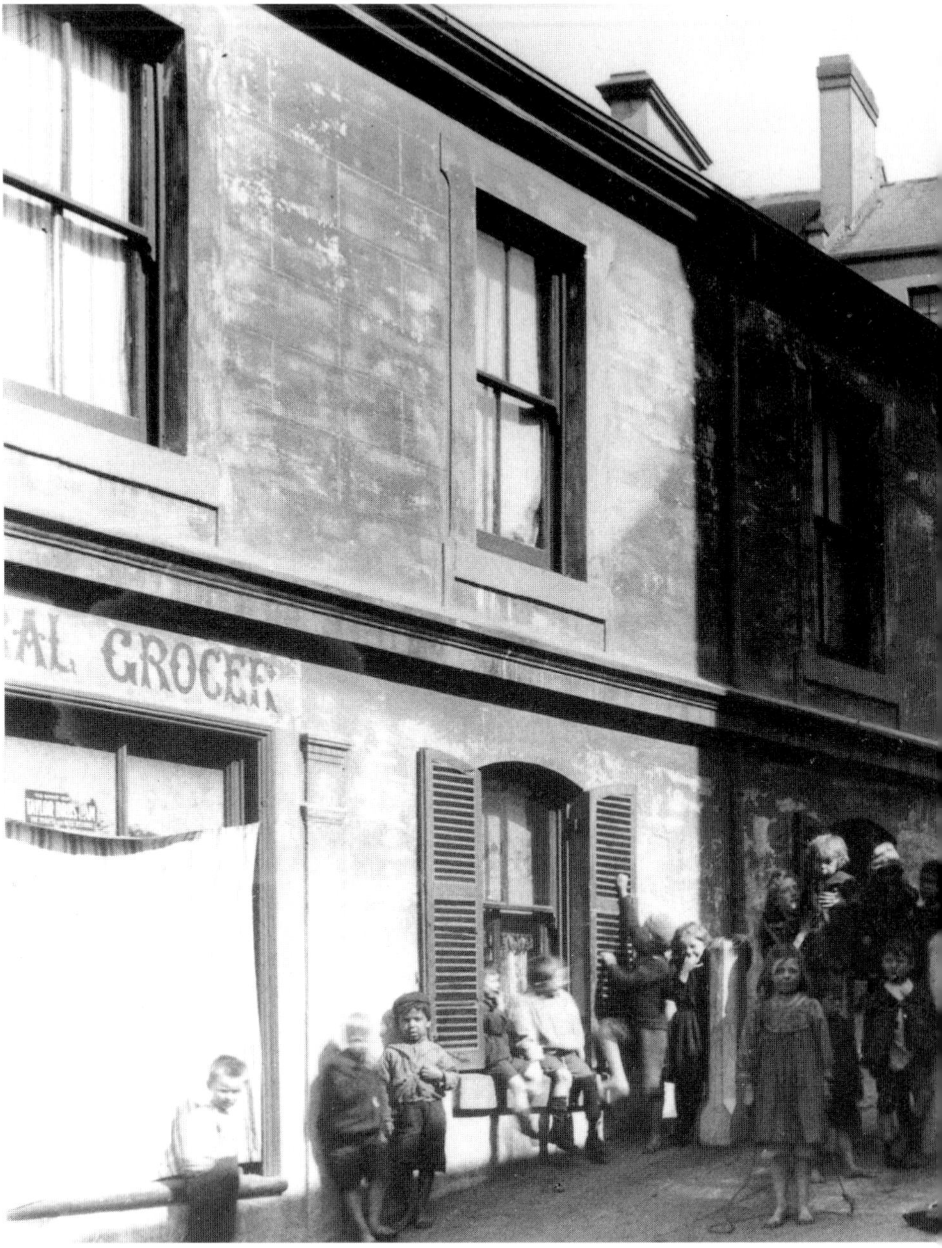
AL GROCER

Cumberland Place, the Rocks.

George Street, the oldest street in Australia and the Pacific.

first official Garrison Church of the colony. It is easy to imagine these dark pews filled with redcoats, marched up from Dawes Battery for morning prayer. In spite of many generous gifts, Holy Trinity was not rich, and for some time its windows were made of oiled canvas, medieval style. By 1878 the church had been enlarged and in some ways altered by the architect Edmund Blacket. Before this the eastern window was donated by book-collector David Scott Mitchell's mother.

Argyle Place has a sunny openness. Its houses are dapperly kept. Their paint shines, their garret windows glitter, their chimneypots are like soldiers at attention. They are a fanciful compendium of the several styles characteristic of Sydney's domestic design from 1830. The cottage in the centre, No. 50 Argyle Place, displaying iron lace, tall cedar shutters and wooden gingerbread, is very engaging. This house is now in the care of the National Trust and one day may be open for inspection. It is said that more than twenty patterns of iron lace can be counted in Argyle Place, some no longer in existence elsewhere.

Topographically, Argyle Place is somewhat of a curiosity. It is almost entirely enclosed. With the amber leaves drifting down from the English trees, no one to be seen but one housewife with a baby in a stroller, the air full of sunshine that seems to hang and quiver, it might well be the bottom of a bowl, or the bed of a dry lagoon. The houses fringe the north bank, and along the south rises the scarp of Aboriginal rock, topped with green Observatory Park and many Moreton Bay figs like enormous parasols. It is a true village within a city, and as far as possible has been preserved as such by the Sydney Cove Authority.

As we stroll along Lower Fort Street towards Windmill Street, we look towards Clyde Bank and those fine terraces we admired on our first Circular Quay walk. On the corner of Windmill Street stands the Hero of Waterloo, severe and dignified. Some claim that this is the oldest hotel in Sydney. Below it are detention cells with barred windows, either for convict servants or rowdy drunks. It was almost certainly licensed by 1818. Opposite it is an old grocer's shop which in 1842 was licensed as The Young Princess. This name was in honour of Queen Victoria's eldest daughter, Victoria of Prussia and mother of Kaiser Bill.

Windmill Street probably still holds the same level as it did when 'it led from one windmill to another'. Both belonged to Jack Leighton, the miller of Miller's Point. In 1838, the commentator Maclehose stated: 'In Windmill Street a number of respectable dwelling houses have lately been erected, and are mostly occupied by opulent persons ... it is probably one of the best neighbourhoods in Sydney.' There were also numbers of respectable taverns, some with splendid names; Hit and Miss, Live and Let Live, and The Old Cheshire Cheese.

The north side of the street was for almost a century occupied by the fortress-like warehouse of Parbury Bond, the major place of employment for the men of Miller's Point. At the time of writing, this huge, priceless site was marked for development. On the other side of Windmill Street is a long tidy row of workmen's cottages trimmed in creme de menthe, with flowerpots and sleeping cats in their sunny tiled porches. At the end of this street, where Windmill Street meets Kent Street, there is a steep flight of steps down to Hickson Road and Walsh Bay. This part of Kent Street was known as Scotch Row, because of the many Scottish 'mechanics' settled here by John Dunmore Lang at his own expense. (A mechanic was a fully qualified tradesman.)

Turning up Kent Street we see on a corner the austere Georgian Lord Nelson which proclaims it is the oldest hotel and private brewery in Sydney. Sadly the customer can no longer buy the reputedly knock-em-dead Nelson's Blood Stout, but there are available beers that require respect if not reverence, including the one brewed on site by mine host, a genial New Zealander. The Lord Nelson looked exactly the same from the time it was licensed in 1838 until 1998 when it was renovated. Its builder and original landlord was an emancipee Billy Wells. It is probable he fought at Trafalgar. Sydney is rich in Peninsular War names and judging by the great collection of Trafalgar and Nelson memorabilia displayed by this hotel, Landlord Wells had a close connection. The Lord Nelson has a popular restaurant and, at the time of writing, a limited number of charming bedrooms behind those small-paned windows on the top floors.

Behind the hotel the ground falls away abruptly towards the Harbour. The terraces run downhill like a pack of cards.

Now back in Argyle Street, we pass a few homely village shops, a butcher's shop, a little café. The Palisades Hotel, magnificently nineteenth century, famous for its restaurant, perches upon the escarpment opposite now unneeded wharves, marked for demolition. Time has moved on, and Sydney is no longer the great shipping port it was for so long.

A bridge passes over Hickson Road, which rumbles with a constant rush of heavily loaded trucks. Beyond the bridge is a perfect maze of uneven little streets and lanes, which have crept right out to the edge of a high lump of sandstone. They are up and down and roundabout, sunny, without a soul to be seen; no cats, kids or housewives. The houses have odd chimneypots, balconies big enough for brownies, sometimes steps down to the footpath. They have not changed since riggers, boatbuilders and 'stout labourers for six shilluns a week, found' dwelt here and enjoyed the sun, and the salty smell from the hillocks of shells dumped by the Pittwater boats for the limeburners just below.

In the far western corner of Miller's Point the narrow lanes are like a tangle of grass, existing where they could find space between godowns, flights of iron steps, slipways and huts. In Roden's Lane, I once found a blacksmith's shop which occupied a cave in the sandstone, two walls being sootstained cliff. A smith was working there, making handforged firedogs and brackets and domestic ironware. He had taken over the smithy from the last of the Rhodens, the fifth generation of the family that had worked in that fantastic cranny.

I have a fancy that just about here stood Jack the Miller's largest windmill. To the citizens of Balmain, across Darling Harbour, it was like a watchtower. He was a larky fellow, who is said to have turned down a grant of the whole of Miller's Point because the Governor of the day required him to put a fence across the promontory. He erected his first mill on this clifftop about 1795. The grain was wheat and maize from the Hawkesbury and it was landed at the foot of the cliff and hoisted up with block and tackle. In 1826, Jack tumbled from the top of a very long ladder and died. He was drunk. By the thirties, the steam mills had taken over from the wind.

We return to Kent Street, which was named for Queen Victoria's dissolute papa. It runs straight as a die, right through to Liverpool Street, and once was the city's most important wagon-road. It is a road that seems only a metre or so above sea level, and was probably mudflats once upon a time. You can see its future upon it already, for the handsome hotels are creeping along from the city centre. For the time being life has flowed away from it, but the new century promises that old Kent Street will be a noble boulevard.

Narrow cobbled alleys serve the back areas of the substantial yellow stone houses that remain. These houses, which appear to have been built in the 1870s, stand in the lee of the escarpment below Observatory

Park. This cliff is the remains of a hill of solid stone, sliced through by convict labour to allow the construction of the road. This part of Kent Street was then called the Quarries, and many of the buildings are built of the spoil.

Not far away can be seen Richmond Villa, designed and constructed in 1850 by the Colonial Architect of the time, Mortimer Lewis. What a bow-windowed charmer it is, and how odd to recall that it was built in quite another place as part of a handsome town house terrace that stood behind the Parliamentary buildings in Macquarie Street, nicely positioned so that it and its fellows could look out on the tranquil Domain. It was brought to its present location more or less stone by stone in the latter part of the twentieth century.

A building that has never been moved, and looks as if it will hold its place for at least another century, is nearby – the amusing house No. 126 Kent Street, standing all by itself on an elevated island of stone. Dating from 1818, this dwelling was one of a terrace of three built by stonemason Thomas Glover on a grant given him by Governor Macquarie. This terrace is reliably believed to have been the first built in Australia. Of the three, one house collapsed, and the other was demolished. When the hill was quarried down, the surviving cottage was left like the marooned Noah's Ark on Mt Ararat. It is indeed known locally as the Ark. Plain as a pot, indestructible, its stonework is genuine jumblychook, a mosaic of odd-sized blocks, a memento of Glover's skill.

The simple, unpretentious domestic buildings of Miller's Point must have been like those on the High Rocks swept away long ago. They were the homes of middleclass, comfortable people, ship builders, solicitors, doctors, who used carriages to carry them into the city and probably the Agar Steps to take them up to the high meadow of Observatory Park. From there the Blue Mountains can still sometimes be seen; they must have been constant companions to Miller's Point children and nursemaids out for an airing.

The Agar Steps have been much painted and photographed during their long history. Their Italianate character lends a strangely romantic note to the maritime atmosphere of Miller's Point and Walsh Bay. From the top of the steps we catch a glimpse of the neo-classical, rather beautiful building which for 120 years was Fort Street High School. It stands very much to attention, this building, and so it should, for it was built in

1815 for Governor Macquarie as a military hospital for the accommodation of a hundred patients. It was designed by John Watts, who had architectural training before he joined the army during the Napoleonic Wars. Later he became Macquarie's aide-de-camp. The clever young Irishman followed the construction of the Military Hospital with many more buildings – some still fortunately existing. They include Government House, the towers of St John's Church, and the Lancer Barracks, all at Parramatta. He also superintended the making of the Parramatta Road.

The double row of arched windows was added at a later date by Mortimer Lewis, a specialist in graceful façades. The old hospital is as useful as ever, being the headquarters of the New South Wales branch of the National Trust. The building just behind – once an isolation ward – is the S. H. Ervin Gallery of Australian Art and Architecture.

Observatory Park is one of my favourite places, and it's a pity it's not other people's as well. If you see one old man snoozing in the benevolent sunshine, or one council employee somnolently sweeping leaves, you're fortunate. The whole park is elevated on a high sandstone bluff that was, as we have seen, carved away into a cliff at the western side. There's a tall iron fence along the edge of this cliff, a fortress-like palisade, and through it you may look down into the backyards of the Kent Street houses and inspect the poinsettias, frangipani and washing.

There is a surfy sound of traffic from the spider-grey Bridge, and a great view all around, sometimes so bright that the water dazzles, and there's a faint down of light around the three TV masts on the far northern shore. Other times smog works its magic, and the whole world is seen through an opal haze, faint and flower-tinted, so that docks, ships' masts, wooded headlands, monster buildings with cranes scissoring the sky assume the mysterious beauty of a mirage.

There are vast Moreton Bay figs around the Observatory, each in its fallen garland of mummified fruit. Sparrows play among their shiny leaves, seagulls squabble around the old popgun which stands near the Boer War monument. There are no other birds. The older buildings of the Observatory are of rain-stained stone. They have low, faded green domes, and look their age. As we know, young Lieutenant Dawes built a tinpot observatory close to his Battery, down there on Dawes Point. At that time, this hill was called Flagstaff Hill. Later, Fort Phillip was built here, and still later an important windmill rose upon its highest point.

The present Observatory was erected in 1855. Thriftily, the builders used the peculiar octagonal foundation of Fort Phillip, which can be observed from the air. In the Observatory are preserved some of the earliest astronomical instruments brought to Australia, including those used by Governor Brisbane in his private observatory at Parramatta. This latter building is long demolished, but you will see an obelisk marking its site not far from Old Government House in Parramatta.

Now let us sit on one of the ramshackle seats beneath the eastern fortress wall of the Observatory. We are almost opposite the Bridge toll-gates. One of these days you will want to walk over the Bridge, but here is a peaceful spot from which we can consider its immensity. The Harbour Bridge is the visible sign of Sydney's resolutely bilateral development. From the beginning, the Harbour, which brought such swift industrial and commercial growth to the infant settlement, meant laborious travel to those who lived along its shores. For instance, before the ferries, Manly was 113 kilometres from Sydney Cove, and that by a bullock-track haunted by bushrangers.

A harbour bridge was a dream constant throughout Sydney's early days. (There was also a vociferous tunnel party.) Macquarie's architect, Francis Greenway, said: 'In the event of a bridge being thrown across from Dawes Battery to the North Shore, a town would be built on that shore, and would have formed with these buildings a grand whole that would have indeed surprised anyone on entering the Harbour, and have given an idea of strength and magnificence that would have reflected credit, and glory on the colony.'

In the 1880s, Henry Parkes used as an election slogan the words: 'Oh, who will stand at my right hand, and build the Bridge with me?' When, after his accession to the Premiership, the Bridge did not eventuate, an acid editorial commented: 'Someone must be standing on his right hand.'

All varieties of bridge were suggested through the years, truss' suspension and even floating. In 1900 the minister for works invited competitive designs and tenders for a bridge. Twenty-four were submitted, but the project was shelved. Not until 1922, after considerable parliamentary shuffling, was official approval given to the plan submitted by J. J. C. Bradfield, chief engineer of the Metropolitan Railway construction department.

The Gallows, The Rogues, The Builders

In effect the Bridge as we see it is completely Bradfield's. (Some slight structural modifications were asked for by Dorman Long and Co., the British firm whose tender for construction was the successful one.) The enormous demolition, which on Dawes Point as we have seen, demanded the complete sweeping away of palatial Princes Street, most of Cumberland Street, and a whole complex of alleys which cross-hatched the Rocks, caused similar displacement on Milson's Point, the site of the northern Bridge approach. In addition to the resumption of much commercial property, four hundred families or more were dispossessed from the north shore promontory. Materials from demolished houses were sold at fantastically low rates. One house, for example, fetched ten pounds. It is characteristic of Sydney's happy-go-lucky methods of doing things that this extraordinary engineering project was embarked upon when the approaching Depression must surely have cast a prophetic gloom over the future. It is to the credit of the government of that time that work on the Bridge went on, from 1923, when the unemployed percentage of the workforce fell slightly short of ten per cent, to 1932, when the Australian unemployed totalled close to thirty per cent of the workforce.

During these terrible years, the Bridge was known as the Iron Lung, for it kept so many people breathing. It gave work to a fairly constant number of 1,400 men on the site, as well as many thousands more in the steel, cement, sand and stone trades which supplied the immense quantities of materials. To a city bogged down in the demoralisation of worklessness, the great steel pincers nearing each other from the opposing shores must have seemed symbols of a prosperity that would one day come again.

Ex-Premier J. T. Lang, writing of those times, says: 'Sydney was ringed by soup kitchens ... every night thousands slept in the parks, on railway stations and in odd shelters. Sydney became a city of beggars.' It was these shabby people, haggard with hardship and hopelessness, who stood in their thousands on an autumn day so many years ago to see the Bridge opened. They were surprised and amused to see a joker in the pack, an oddball named de Groot, whip in and cut the ribbon before the premier could wave his scissors. Here are some figures concerning the Harbour Bridge. Its total length is 3,480 metres. Its main arch span is exactly the width of the water between Dawes and Milson's Points, 1,520 metres. The height of the crown of the arch is 404 metres above sea level.

The estimated life of this colossal structure is five hundred years. One idly wonders why it is not blue, like the waters across which it humps like a giant anaconda, or the bronze-green of the summer hills of the northern shore. The grey becomes delicate and spooky when illuminated at night, crowned with a solitary rubicelle. But why grey?

A spokesman for the Department of Main Roads answers: 'When the Bridge was completed in 1932, grey was the only paint on the market that was functionally suitable and in sufficient quantities.' Thus the colour of the Bridge recalls again the deprivations of the Depression. Still, it could have been black.

Far northern suburbs have odd glimpses of the Bridge, down the valleys and between highrisers. Out at sea, it can be seen like a subsiding bubble, long after the rest of the continent has become invisible or indistinct. It hangs there, like the ghost of the Wheel of Fate, in a sky brindled with sunset, until darkness comes and vanishes away this distinctive shape which is above all things the sign of Sydney.

Though Sydneysiders in exasperated moments often cry: 'I've a good mind to jump off the Bridge,' there have been only thirty-nine leapers to the date of writing. Of these six have lived. The parapet is so protected with netting and barbed wire that only a determined and agile person could reach it. Would-be suicides usually take wire-cutters with them. How does it feel to jump? Here is the statement of one who survived. 'I was not frightened, just sad. Then I jumped. It's a strange feeling to go flying through the air. It must be like skydiving. The wind just whistles past and the water keeps rushing up to you. As I went down I did a few somersaults and turns. Subconsciously I guess I was trying to slow down my fall. I remember seeing the water very near and then everything was dark. People have told me that I hit the water and came up swimming, but I don't remember. I don't remember being picked up out of the water. I woke up in hospital later in the day.' This man's only injuries after falling almost sixty metres were bruises and a black eye.

On the northeastern corner of Observatory Park, the Bridge Stairs go off to Cumberland Street through a somewhat sinister, ill-lit tunnel. Now cross the road. Behind the Glenmore Hotel are a series of steep descents which turn out to be the Argyle Steps. These will take us out close to the Argyle Cut and almost opposite Cambridge Street. The steps, though repaired and broadened in Victorian times, are very old, dating from Macquarie's rule.

If you prefer, you may saunter down the long gentle slope of Watson Road which runs ramplike down to Argyle Street. Turn left now down Argyle Street, and enter the high arched stone doorway of Mary Reiby's old kingdom, the Old Argyle Bond, now the Argyle Store. Built in 1828, this is the oldest part of the warehouse where Mary Reiby ran her varied businesses, always accompanied by her servant and bodyguard, a giant Fijian woman named Feefoo. The carriageway is rutted, the courtyard within is cobbled with the original stones. Off this courtyard are cellars, and in the cellars are the dark cubbyholes where assigned convicts were confined if they were obstreperous.

Across the spacious courtyard is the Argyle Store proper, built of Italian bricks. The colour of sour cream, they were imported in the late 1870s for a hospital and never used. The date over the doorway is 1881, and the word IVES refers to the Lord Mayor of the time, Isaac Ives. This was a famous rum store until it was taken over about 1968 by the Authority, and indeed one still often gets an elevating whiff of Old Harry. The interior is whitewashed, with barred windows that cast zebra shadows, and adzed ironbark beams that look as though they will outlast the Pyramids.

Here and there in the Rocks you may buy pictures of Mary Reiby. These are copies of the painting in the Mitchell Library. It also appears on the $20 note. What a nice old granny! She has a snub nose, small oval glasses, a widow's cap and what someone has described as a pussycat expression. No pussycat was Mary, however. Transported as a child of thirteen or fourteen, for sneaking a ride on a farmer's horse, she arrived in 1792, not a good year.

The first thing she did was to write a letter to her aunt, who had been her guardian, to say that she had arrived safely. The second thing seems to have been her betrothal to Thomas Reiby, a young ship's officer from the *Royal Admiral* on which they had travelled.

Thomas plainly had a business head, for he had brought with him various trading goods. The young couple (they married in 1794) opened a small shop in the Rocks. Mary looked after it and her growing family, and Thomas went on trading voyages, bringing back astonishing things – cedar, sandalwood, sealskins, spices, sugar, silk, chamberpots, china, rice, waistcoats, corsets, tea. Nine years later the Reibys were prosperous enough to build a commodious house in Reiby Place, the house that was later leased to the newly-created Bank of New South Wales.

Sadly, in 1811, when this industrious, enterprising couple were wealthy, owning schooners and brigs, houses and farms, Thomas died of sunstroke. Mary had seven children. Forty-four years of widowhood lay before her. She was a shrewd bargainer, a person of astonishing foresight. She built up her family's fortunes to a degree equalled only by Robert Campbell and Simeon Lord. She travelled widely, even returning to England in 1820, perhaps intending to settle. But her family was Australian, and she sailed back to Sydney, this time in comparative luxury.

Mary Reiby is a brilliant example of the convict for whom transportation meant opportunity. One of her grandsons became Premier of Tasmania. Mary Reiby does not haunt the Rocks – she would be too sensible to waste her time.

Instead of returning to George Street by Argyle Street, preferably walk along Harrington Street, which joins Argyle Street. Not very far along, you will see a herring-gutted passageway, a true 'slip' between high walls, diving down towards George Street. This is called Harrington Lane, but it is the infamous Suez Canal, a sort of Sweeney Todd alley, into which passers-by were dragged and robbed. Not far from here in Harrington Street was a Ragged School, a free school for the Rocks urchins, conducted more or less on the lines of a modern public school, but with a distinct air of self-conscious Victorian patronage about it.

The Suez Canal, which was so noisome that some early writers thought it an open drain, is now quite clean. It is barely a metre wide at the George Street end, so it is no wonder that most passers-by miss it. About halfway down was a blind court which seems always to have been unnamed, but was notorious as the abode of half-savage women who would rip the clothes from your back and the gold from your teeth. Even in 1908, someone inspecting the demolition after the plague scare unwarily wandered in here. He said, 'A man with a diabolical countenance resented my intrusion, and I was glad to get away.'

It is now a sunny little backwater, a shortcut to George Street. Who would guess how it used to be, the cobbles running with rain and sewage, the dark houses lit only by the swooping light of a tallow dip, and the half-mad harpies descending on the unwary passers-by like a flock of crows on a cast sheep.

Having delivered you to George Street, with Circular Quay directly in front of you, I bid you au revoir.

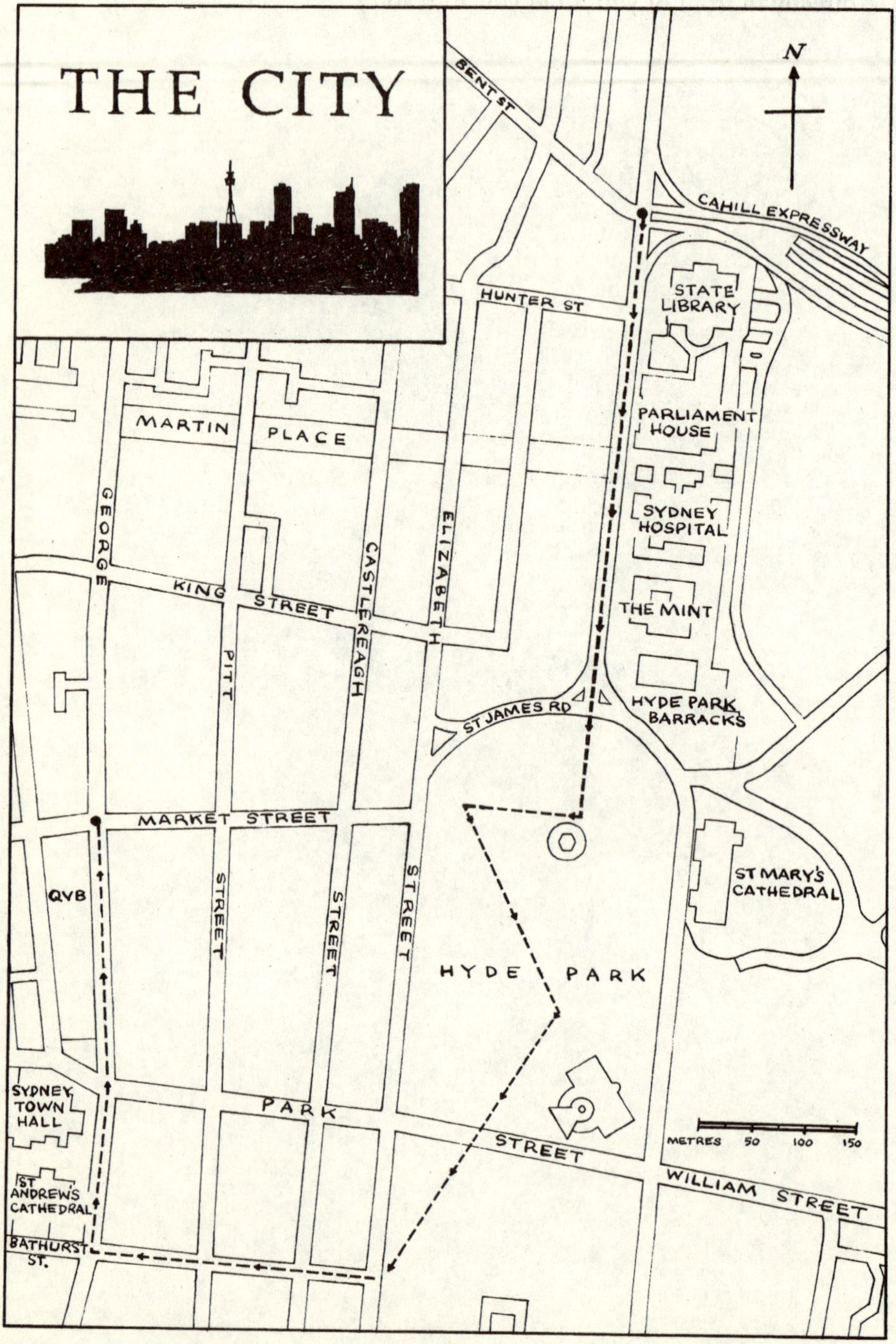
THE CITY
N
BENT ST
CAHILL EXPRESSWAY
HUNTER ST
STATE LIBRARY
MARTIN PLACE
PARLIAMENT HOUSE
GEORGE
ELIZABETH
CASTLEREAGH
SYDNEY HOSPITAL
KING STREET
THE MINT
PITT
ST JAMES RD
HYDE PARK BARRACKS
MARKET STREET
QVB
STREET
STREET
STREET
ST MARY'S CATHEDRAL
HYDE PARK
SYDNEY TOWN HALL
PARK
STREET
METRES 50 100 150
ST ANDREWS CATHEDRAL
WILLIAM STREET
BATHURST ST.

CHAPTER 3

FINE BUILDINGS AND A GARDEN

A fine day in Macquarie Street – the Botanic Gardens – the Palace goes up in flames – music in a stable – in praise of horses – Mitchell Library – the Governor's Rum Hospital – Nightingale nurses – Parliament House – the Old Mint and Hyde Park Barracks – how not to sleep in a hammock – racecourse to city oasis – Mayor Thornton's smelling bottle – the Great Synagogue – stocks and market days – Queen Victoria's Building saved for posterity – Brickfield Hill and two horrid ghosts – Haymarket now and then.

TODAY we shall look at some fine buildings and a garden. The Garden is the Botanic, up the hill alongside Macquarie Street. We leave Circular Quay somewhat reluctantly for it is blowing its own trumpet as usual – ferries tooting, flags slapping, the Bridge speaking up sonorously. A square-rigged sailing vessel slides around Dawes Point. The spinnaker sails of the Opera House, close at hand, show the faintest silken perturbation like a mirage. Sydney Cove itself brims like a saucer of milky blue, under a huge joyful sky.

Up Macquarie Street now, recalling that this was yet another high bony ridge, for a long time occupied only by three or four windmills and bandicoot-infested scrub. Eventually it was commandeered by authority to be the grand street of the infant colony, a high place from which the posh could look down upon the rabble. Governor Macquarie designed it. He allowed the wealthy citizens to build on the west side but reserved the east for public buildings, particularly the capacious well-run hospital he had always wanted. Where the stately Mitchell Library now stands he built long brick barracks for his Light Horse. It fell into disuse after Macquarie's departure and the building was turned into a School of Industry for Indigent Girls. Oh, the dreariness of it, the meagre life those poor pinafored orphans must have endured, though a succeeding governor publicly congratulated himself that they had the finest view in the civilised world.

The Romanesque style of the library complements that of the Art Gallery, seen across the Domain, but it is of more harmonious proportions. It has a pastoral view of trees, meadowland and Harbour and we shall have a closer look at it on the way back from the Botanic Gardens.

We begin in Shakespeare Place, which links Bent Street with the Cahill Expressway. The roaring highway divides like a stream in spate around a marooned group of statuary, Shakespeare reassuring Hamlet, Falstaff and Romeo and Juliet that the cars aren't going to get them. The group was sculpted by Bertram Mackennal, who also did the Cenotaph in Martin Place. In India he perpetrated many of the insufferable statues of Queen Victoria and her viceroys that the crowds hauled down and beheaded after the departure of the British Raj.

Entering the tall gates on the north side of the expressway, we find ourselves in what is still called the Palace Garden. And here, on the site of the long-vanished Garden Palace, is Achille Simonetti's grandiose and pretentious statue of Captain Phillip, posed among allegorical figures and meek waterspouts. Wretched Victorians! We have learned to love their ornate buildings, spiked as crabs, their tombstones armoured with urn and angel against the fell blows of Time, but there is nothing of the tough, sensible Phillip in this statue at all.

We have a description by Captain Landman, whose father was a friend of Phillip. Landman himself was one of Phillip's midshipmen, but his family would not allow him to undertake the venturesome voyage to New Holland. Here is Phillip in a small boat: 'Well I remember his little figure smothered up in his brown camlet cloak lined with green baize, his face shrivelled, and thin aquiline nose under a large cocked hat, gathered up into a heap, his chin between his knees, sitting under the lee of the mainmast, his sharp and powerful voice exclaiming: "I cannot bear this, I am as sick as a dog!" '

Sydney should have a memorial to Phillip as he really was. I find it intriguing that although he was 170 centimetres, a respectable height for those times, most of those who knew him call him 'little'. He must have been exceptionally slight and wiry in build. Where this mendacious statue preens stood the Garden Palace, which from 1879 to 1882 dominated every sketch of the city's western aspect. Dwarfing the Gothic pile of Government House, reducing the castellated Fort Macquarie to a dilapidated something from the Northwest Frontier, it rides its high ridge like the pavilions of Kubla Khan – cupolas, domes and towers all adorned with pennants rigid in a permanent nor'-easterly.

The Garden Palace was largely constructed of timber. It was built for Australia's first International Exhibition, opened in September 1879. The exhibition was the greatest success, and all Sydney attended, high and low. The low were blamed for the litter. A French visitor reported: 'These lawns so fresh, so green, are completely unrecognisable under the mounds of paper which carpet them. Everywhere, sitting on the grass, there are workmen in their Sunday best with their wives and children, scattering around chicken and shin bones ... all these people drink, eat and enjoy themselves, all with the greatest gravity.'

After the conclusion of the Exhibition, the Garden Palace was used for concerts. Government departments began to shift their files into the storage basements. Among these were the records of a lifetime's work by the famous geologist, the Rev. William Branwhite Clarke, who died in 1878. There were also many irreplaceable documents of the convict era. All these were lost when the Garden Palace, in a spectacular fire, burned to the ground in September 1882. The dome collapsed with the roar of cannon at sea and the charred debris was blown as far as Potts Point. Sheets of corrugated iron hurtled across Macquarie Street, then at its social height, and shattered windows and even walls of the fashionable town houses. These latter are described in the 1870s: 'View them on a summer's evening, when the drawing rooms are in a blaze of light. Beautiful ladies, dressed in white ... lounging on magnificent couches, partially concealed by rich crimson curtains, in drawing rooms which display all the luxurious comforts ... of the East, intermingled with the elegant utilities of the West.'

We stroll on down through the Gardens, observing Victorian marble and stone statues lurking here and there. Legend says that these are but a fraction of the allegorical marble population that once infested the Gardens. Where have they all gone? In fact, municipal councils have secret graveyards in which they inter expensive and unsaleable objects outgrown by the city.

If you look at the map, you will see that the entire green area south of the Botanic Gardens, the Domain, and Hyde, Phillip and Cook Parks are related. They are all part of old Government House's original demesne and farm. We are really in Macquarie country here, since it is a fairly firm tradition that the Gardens were laid out mostly by Mrs Macquarie. But this was cultivated land long before her time, from the earliest days of the settlement, when Governor Phillip and his butler-cum-agricultural adviser, Henry Dodd, debated where they would sow the seed brought from England, Rio and the Cape of Good Hope.

The most historic part is the Middle Garden where the first furrows were ploughed in 1788. We will see a small obelisk and plaque to mark the spot, close by the teahouse. The Gardens are lovely, flourishing and well-cared for. Little changed through the years, they are still a perfect background for the genteel Sydneysiders we see in old watercolours and pen drawings, top-hatted gentlemen with their coats fastened only at the top button, escorting bustled ladies with straight fronts and parasols, and small pinafored and sailor-hatted children with hoops and skipping ropes. Is it not an echo of the everpresent homesickness of the Australians of last century that these gardens contain one of the world's largest collections of non-Australian plants?

The Gardens have had some famous directors, including the first, Charles Fraser, the explorer who was appointed by Macquarie as Colonial Botanist in 1816. Poor man, he was speared to death by Aborigines while gathering plant specimens in the countryside. There were also the two Cunninghams, of whom the second, Allan, was a renowned explorer. He spent five years on the *Mermaid* when she was surveying the Australian coast, and many of the thousands of rare plants then collected by Cunningham were first domesticated in the Gardens. An obelisk commemorating Allan Cunningham stands in the Gardens; his ashes are in a casket within this small memorial.

Everyone has his pet dawdling spot in the Gardens. The Spring Walk, now well over a century old, is exquisite, with many interesting old-fashioned specimens of azaleas that one rarely sees nowadays. Close by this close-set display of rosy colours are the remains of the ponderous Macquarie's Wall, and in one place where it has crumbled away is the Wishing Tree, a seedling of the original Norfolk Island pine which was planted by Mrs Macquarie. Elizabeth Macquarie's tree lived for 120 years, exceptional for a Norfolk pine.

The orchid house is worth seeing, every Australian species being represented here, and the herbarium should not be missed by student botanists; it has a fine library, and exhibits specimens gathered by most famous botanists in the Australasian area back to Solander and Joseph Banks.

My favourite place is the palmery, a moist jungly little vale full of warmth and shadows, reminding one of how strange the first European explorers found our palms, and how curiously they drew them, with leaves like kelp and stems brindled like sea monsters; vegetation from Xanadu. It is said that the Botanic Gardens have the greatest collection of palms in the world. One recognises old Sydney friends, the feathery bangalow, the phoenix, and cabbage tree (hats from its fanlike leaves used to be made and worn in many coastal towns), and the towering kentia, which I had always thought to be a house pet. The little brook, running along a fretted stone channel, often half-hidden behind papyrus and bamboo, is the domesticated tail end of a creek which drained the high spongy slopes on the north side of William Street.

From time to time we see through the treetops a white sugar plum of a building, not Government House but a lesser piece of confectionery. This is the Conservatorium of Music, surely the only one in the world to be built in a stable. It was erected by Governor Macquarie from a Greenway design, and was intended to be the impressive stables for a future Government House worthy of the Empire. Poor Macquarie had a fearful rap over the knuckles from King's Commissioner Bigge, who came to the colony in 1819 to stickybeak into the settlement's affairs. He carped: '[The stables are] in a style of magnificence far exceeding the wants or allowance of any Governor!' He further considered that Sydney would have done better with a new gaol.

However, the building continued to be used as a stable until 1914, when the central courtyard was roofed over as a concert hall, and the edifice converted into the Conservatorium. It has been extensively added to since then, but its whimsical Gothic façade on Macquarie Street and the Cahill Expressway is close to Greenway's original.

At the time of writing the Conservatorium is undergoing extensive alterations so we might not be able to see it closely. On another day we shall visit Farm Cove, appropriately with a picnic (though with no shin bones). Now is the time to cross the road, obedient to the lights, and have a peep at the Mitchell.

First linger at the entrance to the Gardens and read the touching memorial plaque to the gallant horses of the Australian Desert Mounted

Corps, 'who carried them over the Sinai Desert into Palestine, 1914–1918. They suffered wounds, thirst, hunger and weariness almost beyond endurance, but never failed. They did not come home.' High Command forced the Australian troops to abandon their horses in Egypt, a wrong never forgiven.

The Mitchell, the treasured old wing of the State Library, should not be missed. On the glass entrance doors are etched pictures of the great Pacific explorers' tiny ships. On the floor of the lofty atrium is a dazzling representation of Abel Tasman's curious map of New Holland, worked in brass and marble by Melocco Brothers, the craftsmen who also created the glittering mosaic in the crypt of St Mary's Cathedral.

The northwest wing of the Library was first and specifically built to house the priceless Australiana collection given to the Library by the wealthy recluse, David Scott Mitchell. (More about him in the Rocks section.) The original total bequests from Mitchell, comprising 61,000 items (books, maps, manuscripts, pictures) together with a fund for their housing and upkeep, have been so added to by purchases, legacies and gifts from other collectors, that we have here the world's greatest collection of Australiana. Among the Mitchell treasures are the original journals of James Cook and Joseph Banks, Captain Bligh's *Bounty* log and valuable manuscripts relating to the seventeenth century explorations of Abel Tasman, de Quiros, and Torres.

Another shy bachelor collector, Sir William Dixson, collected objects of Pacific interest; maps, coins, portraits, and memorabilia of the early settlement. By an extraordinary stroke of good fortune Dixson, who died in 1952, took up collecting almost where David Scott Mitchell left off. Between them they covered very nearly a century of collecting. Sir William's bequest to the Library included more than 20,000 items, as well as investments worth more than a quarter of a million dollars. The income is devoted to the reproduction of historical manuscripts, translations of non-English books of Australian interest, and the reprinting of rare books.

The Shakespeare Memorial Library contains some two thousand volumes, some rare, such as the 1623 First Folio. It also has numbers of rare editions of other Elizabethan literary works.

Libraries have always been associated with Macquarie Street, the first, scant, over-used and unendowed, being housed nearby in a metal pre-fabricated building of dire appearance, brought from Scotland by devout Presbyterians, and commonly known as the Tin Church. How different from the superb white State Library, just around the corner from the Mitchell, and dating from 1988. Technologically on the crest of the latest wave, it is still an impressive library to which people flock in droves. Will we seek a seat in the Glasshouse, its airy café? Perhaps just to have a coffee and a sandwich and a brief rumination on Governor Macquarie's so-called Rum Hospital, that once in its entirety occupied the entire eastern side of the street.

And yes, it was indeed a Rum Hospital. To get it built, Macquarie had to revert to the evil customs of earlier times and effectively pay in spirits. Smack in the middle of the old Rum Hospital site now stands Sydney Hospital, an ill-tempered looking khaki pile that displays all the faults of a degenerate Victorian architectural style. It occupies the site of the centre block of the historic Hospital and dates from 1894.

The vanished centre block resembled the others, except for a characteristic central peaked gable bearing the letters G.R. It accommodated some 300 sick convicts. Out-of-town assigned servants were admitted if their masters provided their rations. The north and south wings were barracks for the surgeons, their staffs and apothecaries. The whole was enclosed with a stone wall more than three metres high, over which, it was presumed, the patients would not be able to escape.

In the early nineteenth century Sydney desperately needed a new hospital. The existing hospitals at Parramatta and at George Street North were overcrowded and dilapidated, occupied not only by the sick but by old or infirm convicts, for whom the Government was responsible. The urgency of the matter forced the Governor to agree to the conditions of a triumvirate who submitted a tender for the hospital's erection. In return, surgeon D'Arcy Wentworth, Garnham Blaxcell and Alexander King were given a rum monopoly for three years, during which time they were permitted to import 170,325 litres. They were allowed the free use of twenty convicts and twenty working bullocks, and rations for both. It is said that each contractor made £10,000 from this deal.

In January 1816, a Victory Ball was held in one of the unfinished wards. It celebrated Waterloo, news of which had just reached Sydney, seven months after the battle. Hurriedly-gathered greenery 'hung in graceful festoons ... forming a scene rivalling those Arcadian bowers so celebrated in the pages of poetry', reported the *Gazette*. The Governor and his lady entertained more than 120 ladies and gentlemen of the colony to supper, while the tiny staff of the of the *Gazette* worked all night setting up Wellington's somewhat overdue dispatches from the battlefield.

Patients were transferred the same year from the decaying building in George Street North. D'Arcy Wentworth was Surgeon-in-Charge for three years. During this time 'a gloomy disorder prevailed, and hell itself could not hope to rival the melancholy torments of the helpless sick'. In short, the shameless exploitation of those not at liberty to retaliate, proceeded as was usual in the early nineteenth century.

The place, as described by J. F. Watson in his *History of Sydney Hospital*, sounds nightmarish. Patients received the common ration of 250 grams of salt beef and 250 grams of flour daily. They stole this from each other and sold it to passers-by from the hospital verandah. Those who could eat cooked noxious messes in the wards, amid the ravings of delirious patients and the screams of amputees. The privies were out in the yard, so the corridors were full of dysentery patients crawling back and forth on hands and knees. The kitchen was the deadhouse. (It was said that when the building was eventually demolished in the 1870s, many bones, possibly of amputated limbs, were found buried beneath its floor.) The nurses and wardsmen were convicts 'depraved and drunken, delinquent, ravenous wretches that stole the patients' food and peddled the very rags away from them'. These ghouls were locked up with the patients in the wards from sunset to sunrise.

A constable had to be stationed at the entrance to the female wards, but he could be bribed with food, rum or the patients' rations. Visitors took away anything detachable, even the patients' sheets, if they were so lucky as to have them. Treatment was of the most ruthless: bleedings; purgatives; starvings; cold douches. Yet some survived to be convalescent, and they joined the merry horde of sheet-snatchers and ration-floggers.

In other parts of our history D'Arcy Wentworth is spoken of with sincere praise and admiration. His handling of Sydney Hospital during its first years could scarcely be worse. Not until 1819 when a capable Englishman, Dr James Bowman, was appointed as Surgeon-in-Charge, was this hellhole cleaned up.

After the cessation of transportation the hospital ceased to be a convict infirmary, and in the late 1840s became a public hospital under its present name. It was still no fun to be a patient. 'Patients were mustered every evening by the overseer, who locked them into the wards at sundown. There they remained until the following morning at six.' The nursing staff, too, fully fitted Florence Nightingale's description: 'The women who embraced the office of nurse were generally too old, too weak, too drunk, too dirty or too bad to do anything else.' Among the matrons in those days was a gentlewoman possessing probably the most picturesque name in our history. She was Mrs Bathsheba Ghost, matron from 1852 to 1866. What Charles Dickens might have done with that name! Bathsheba, who died in 1868, the same year that Florence Nightingale-trained nurses arrived to take over the hospital, lies in St Stephen's graveyard at Camperdown. Even in death she is colourful – her tombstone is between the Dunbar Walk and the Straight and Narrow.

Miss Lucy Osburn headed the six Nightingale nurses who arrived in answer to Premier Henry Parkes's request to the invalid but still vigorous Miss Nightingale. Matron Osburn, a dark-haired pretty creature, looked upon nursing as the highest female employment. She was, we are told, 'an exceptional woman, well-read, having an absolute fascination of manner and a most indomitable will'. With Lucy Osburn began the reformation of nursing and hospital administration. Her long Australian service ended in 1891. During this time she had experienced what Florence Nightingale had suffered before her – obstructive behaviour from the medical profession. Doctors' tactics included withholding of information about the medical condition of gravely-ill patients, and the locking of nursing staff out of rooms where post-operative cases had been left without attention. Gradually this prejudice was overcome in the early 1880s, the first decade which showed any improvement in the social status of women in Sydney. More and more women were allowed out of the sweatshops and the poorly-paid domestic labour market to work in shops and factories. In 1881 the University, against extraordinary opposition, granted admission to women. The old Rum Hospital had already been a training hospital for some time.

Meantime the more graceful remnants of the Rum Hospital stayed in use. The north wing has been Parliament House since 1829. The south building, more interesting than the north, is one of the iron prefabs often used in early Sydney. It had originally been designed in Victoria as barracks for goldseekers on their way to the diggings, and was a bargain for £1,800.

There have been many attempts to house more fittingly the Australian Mother of Parliaments. But somehow Parliament has gone on sitting in this huggermugger of Georgian, early Victorian and later structures. It has seen every hard-fought step towards self-government since 1823 when the Governor was 'an unhampered tyrant, responsible only to the Home Office in a city [London] unknown to the majority and half-forgotten by the rest'.

The building has resounded to the roars of rough, tough politicians and their hatchetmen in those robust days when gentlemen did not mince words; when, to quote one of them, 'they stood face to face like men and did not crawl about the face of the earth like those who now beslime it with their unsightly and unclean carcases'. This was Henry Parkes in 1880. The same day Parkes copped his from W. P. Crick (one of the few ministers ever charged with corruption – Crick was finally booted out for taking a bribe). His description of Parkes was 'You could not blacken the devil and for that reason you could not hurt the character of Parkes'. He also called the government of the day 'a set of robbers and hounds who ought to be prosecuted for robbing the Treasury'.

Newspapers entered the lists. In 1858 the *Sydney Morning Herald* described Charles Cowper, one of the first Premiers under responsible government as 'weak and treacherous, full of subterfuge and artifice ... never trusted'. How profoundly one regrets the virile journalism of the early days! Ours is a weary and colourless age.

When Macquarie went home in early 1822, together with his family, his servants, his old horse Sultan, seven pet kangaroos, five emus, seven black swans and the favourite cow Fortune, the street which is his major memorial in Sydney had not changed greatly from the wandering track he had carved from the scrub along the high dragon-back to the east of Government House.

Governor Brisbane later complained of the bushrangers and runaways who lurked in the scrub. Yet civilisation soon came to Macquarie Street, and in the words of Michael Massey Robinson, Sydney's own Topaz McGonigall:

'... *where the dark fantastic forest grew*
Aspiring structures meet the wond'ring eye
Trophies of art, of taste and industry!'

A big improvement, he thought, on earlier times when

'... *yon repulsive mountain's brow*
Sullen, o'erhung the craggy wastes below
Where the gigantic members of the wood
Had long in venerable silence stood'.

By the 1840s Macquarie Street was the West End of Sydney. The doctors had gone there because of the hospital, the fashionable people because of new Government House. The houses were described as Italianate, with flights of graceful steps and light airy verandahs. Not many of the old town houses remain. The best-known is No. 145, now owned and restored by the Royal Australasian College of General Practitioners. This house was one of a terrace, two of which were occupied by the young proprietors of the *Sydney Morning Herald*, Charles Kemp and John Fairfax.

In due course the south wing of the Rum Hospital became the Mint, the first branch of the Royal Mint outside England. This is a building you must investigate; the Mint Museum is a charmer, and children adore it. The gold discoveries in the early 1850s threw the Establishment into a panic, and for excellent reasons. Industry almost closed down; boarded up shops and factories bore the sign 'Gone to the Goldfields'. A new and bolder breed of bushranger appeared, bailing up gold convoys; there was even piracy when the authorities tried to send some of the astonishing flood of gold to safety to Britain. They appealed urgently to the Home Office for permission to establish a local mint and coining factory.

The Mint operated until 1927. The buildings then were so fallen into decay it was thought nothing more could be done with them. However, like other Macquarie buildings, they had their renaissance in the 1970s. If the rich gleam of gold fascinates you, this is your place – wonderful collections; much of the original machinery; an extraordinary golden curtain in the museum shop; an opportunity to 'mint' your own personal medallion on a coining press, and for the kids, an invitation to crack a safe. Also a peaceful old courtyard and a little restaurant.

And now we come to the writer's favourite Sydney building, one of classic simplicity and confidence in a job well done. In every line this treasure shouts 'Greenway'. Hardy Wilson, in his excellent work *Old*

Colonial Architecture in New South Wales and Tasmania comments on the cranky little redheaded ex-convict who designed it: 'With the barest means and economy in execution he produced architecture which never has been excelled in this land. His bigness of scale, rarest excellence in his art is nowhere better expressed than in the Hyde Park Barracks.'

For a long time, a 130 neglectful years, the condition of this building was a hissing and a weeping. Only the centre building, a portion of a cell block, the gate piers, and some fragments of wall remained. The central building, like the vanished portions constructed of soft red brick, bore the well-known triangular pediment, ornamented by a crown, a large clock, and the words *L. Macquarie, Esq., Governor 1817*. Some hideous appendage obscured the arched, tiny-paned window on the left, a splayed porch hid the fanlighted doorway. Corrugated iron had replaced the split wood shingles of the original roof. But these sins were as nothing to the wartish proliferations of additions and partitions which sprouted in every direction. Some seemed merely sheds attached tumour-like to the old walls.

Repeated public protest demanded that the barracks should be pulled down and a genteel block of government offices erected there instead. The building reminded respectable people of convicts, floggings, chain gangs – not nice at all. No one wished to remember that there was a small possibility that 'an unfortunate person' wearing brown and yellow garments had been an ancestor. Now, of course, things are quite different and if you have a First Fleeter in your family tree, you are envied by those who have only Earls and politicians in their backgrounds.

Poor Greenway, though disorganised and prone to tears and tantrums, had done very little to deserve transportation. A bankrupt back home, he altered a clause in a business contract so that he had the chance of retaining a little of the money owed him. No luck. But then he wore ill luck like an old shirt, that man. Swiftly he fell into disfavour after the departure of Macquarie. The things that happened to him! His eldest son was drowned, dogs bit him, footpads bashed and robbed him, his wife died, he was driven from his house. Ruined and miserable, he died in 1837 in East Maitland, and is buried in a grave now forgotten. His one memorial aside from the mutilated remains of his buildings is a tablet in the north porch of St James's church.

Folklore says that Greenway died of a broken heart, and we may believe it. Yet, as we look at this tenderly restored building, his great feeling for beauty strikes us anew. On a poorhouse budget he achieved not only his usual excellence of proportion, but graceful ornamentation within the limits of the few materials available to him – the pretty red rubbing bricks of the arches and window heads, the base course and string-courses of finely-worked stone. This building looks its best when the western sun strikes between tall buildings. Then the upper air, its pollution visible, is full of spinning detritus like disintegrating tinsel, and the faintly-veiled light lies upon the Hyde Park Barracks like the reflection from a fire.

When Macquarie came to Sydney, the inhumane law was that the felons were fed and employed by government, but not lodged. Many were assigned as servants and lived in; others with some small financial resources built slab shanties. But the homeless, after their day's work was finished, slept in the open or begged for the privilege of sleeping in someone's henhouse or stable. The ill-lit or pitch-dark streets, thus inhabited with crowds of vagrant 'depraved creatures that knew not God nor the patronage of Mammon', were nightly the scene of robberies, brawls and murders. These homeless convicts are the ones we see in early drawings, tousled, unwashed, clad in garments of fantastic filth and variety wandering off to their jobs in gravel pits, lumberyards and brickworks after bell-ring every morning. Hyde Park Barracks were designed as a male convict dormitory. They were built in two years, and from 1822 were occupied by up to nine hundred convicts. Although the men were fed, clothed and sheltered, they didn't like communal living, and it became a privilege to sleep out. Those so permitted were men of fair character, and were called out-of-barracks men.

There were twelve well ventilated wards, each in charge of a watchman who had to summon the guard if fighting or sodomy took place. The men slept in hammocks, and were called at sunrise to a nourishing breakfast of porridge, which they hated. We are told 'a generous quantity generally remains'. They were, after a while, put into dreary uniform of yellowish grey canvas, branded HBP from the place of their origin, and marched off to work, some of the recalcitrant wearing leg-irons. At noon they marched back to dine on a meal 'not insufficient to dispel the quirks and crochets of a moderate appetite'. The dish was a sort of soupy stew of salt beef and vegetables, served in small tubs, one for each mess of six men. The men had an hour for lunch, worked the rest of the afternoon until sunset, and retired to rest at 6.00 pm. (It is noticeable how early colonial routine-planners were obsessed by this nursery hour. Even hospital patients were locked up for the night at 6.00 pm.)

Macquarie reported that street robberies and fights dropped to one-tenth shortly after the Barracks were occupied. At first floggings were to a great extent replaced by a few days on hard tack and water in the solitary confinement cells. But under later governors this was not so, and Hyde Park Barracks had as bloody a reputation as had the sinister Lumberyard of Bridge Street in earlier times. From 1836 to 1843, when he was forced to resign, the superintendent of the barracks was that Timothy Lane whom we have already met flogging his chain gangs to complete work on the Argyle Cut. The corpulent, drunken Irishman revelled in the abuse of his defenceless charges. He liked to have his armchair dragged out into the court so that he could watch the floggings. Here is an eyewitness account of him:

'Watch the joy-beaming countenance ... your ears will be delightfully regaled by his exclamations of: "Scourger, do your duty!" and as the poor wretch writhes and moans under each infliction of the lash, a half-inward, heartfelt chuckling laugh – "Ah, he feels it now! There, tip it to him on the raw!" And though we live in the nineteenth century you will be convinced that there is still such an abortion existing as a Vampire revelling in Human Blood.'

In 1848, as a result of constant complaints from Sydney citizens about the now notorious convict barracks in the middle of the town, the remaining male convicts were transferred to Cockatoo Island. The building then entered upon the most picturesque part of its existence, when it was a staging-camp for thousands of newly-arrived immigrants.

Immigrants came to the colony in waves. From 1838 to 1841 there arrived almost 50,000. Assisted immigration rose to a high peak during the 1850s, when each year brought more than 10,000 British settlers, predominantly Irish. The ships were often crowded: 'There were twenty-two of us huddled into a space of about 18 by 8 feet, having a space in the centre of about six by seven as an entrance into our berths.' Passengers cooked their own food in relays with consequent warfare: 'Mrs Watson (a quarrelsome Liverpool wife) lost a pudding, and got in exchange one that might have been thrown over the top of the mainmast, without the least danger of its separating, and dreadful lamentation she made. She hawked it about the deck for nearly an hour, but no one would own it.'

The ships anchored off Dawes Point, and employers rowed out to engage male immigrants. After Mrs Caroline Chisholm interested herself in the often calamitous colonial experience of single female immigrants, these were taken immediately to the Hyde Park Barracks, where hirers could interview them under supervision. Mrs Chisholm, an Indian Army wife of extremely good sense and inflexible will, founded the Family Colonisation Society, an easy-instalment plan of paying passage money. She interested herself particularly in improved ship accommodation, supervised working conditions, and the placing of unaccompanied girls in suitable domestic jobs. (In 1841 she placed eleven children under thirteen years of age in situations paying from £2.10 to £7 annually.)

The Barracks are a wonderful place to visit. All memories of the well-intentioned but meagre housing for the single female immigrants, the even more meagre furnishings for the elderly indigent women who occupied the old building after the immigrants, and the law courts and judges' chambers that were accommodated there after the old women moved out – all have been removed. The building has been restored to its original spartan but well proportioned interior appearance. Plenty to see and hear, too – guided tours, access to the convict record database, archeological exhibits from the history of the Barracks themselves.

But everyone finds the dormitory loft most fascinating, the cavernous, well-ventilated chamber, and the rough timber frames supporting rows of swinging hammocks. Climb into one – it's permitted – and immediately be engulfed in a variety of sausage skin. This is discomfort raised to an art form. Nevertheless, you may wish to spend a night there. Can you believe this is the most booked-ahead form of accommodation in Sydney? Such a night of torture is followed by a convict breakfast ... can it be the skilly which the original tenants disliked so much they preferred an empty belly? Then off you go for a brief cruise on a sailing ship. This time-travelling venture is so popular the Barracks don't have to advertise it.

Underground passages lead from the Barracks to both St James's Church and the law courts. Willing convicts apparently were permitted to attend divine service, and unwilling ones were hauled along to the courts when they deserved it.

The charming open space of Queen's Square is directly before Hyde Park Barracks and very close to Hyde Park itself. The pug-faced statue of the old Queen is by E. J. Bohemia, and was erected in the year of New South Wales' Centennial, 1888. St James's Church is a quiet, sweet old building, again by Greenway. It was intended by Macquarie and the architect to be a court house but the Governor was bullyragged by Commissioner Bigge into turning the half-built structure 'with a portico 40 feet high like that of the Temple of Minerva' into a church. St James's was consecrated in 1824, though the senior chaplain had preached its first sermon in 1822. Although the Greenway design has been altered, the church restored and restored again, all these changes have been done sympathetically and so St James's retains considerable charm.

The fashionable congregation quickly deserted mouldering Old St Phillip's on Church Hill, and St James's became 'the favourite resort for the more aristocratical amongst the votaries of Hymen'. However, it is not bells but knells which have made St James's particularly interesting for history students. The memorials include many to founding fathers familiar to most of us. Among the most interesting is that to the hotheaded barrister, Dr Robert Wardell. With W. C. Wentworth, he edited the crusading *Australian*, stamping on many toes in the process, including those of Governor Darling, who sued him for criminal libel and lost. In 1834, three runaway convicts murdered Dr Wardell; on his memorial plaque appears the first Latinisation of the local word 'bushranger'. It reads: *A LATRONE, VAGANTE OCCISO*. Another commemorates the north Queensland explorer Edmund Kennedy and his faithful companion the Aborigine Jacky-Jacky, who tried to defend Kennedy during the fatal attack by wild natives.

St James's is otherwise connected with early exploration. Its parsonage is on the site of John Oxley's town house. Surveyor-General Oxley led unsuccessful parties in 1817 and 1818 to discover the mouths of the Lachlan and Macquarie Rivers, missing the as yet unknown Murrumbidgee, and returning to Sydney with the discouraging news that 'the centre of Australia is a vast inland sea, uninhabitable for all purposes of civilised man'.

St James's is a lovely example of the pure, plain old Georgian style. Once its slender spire was a landmark to ships entering the Harbour – can one imagine that nowadays? The spire is sheathed in copper and it is said that each sheet is engraved with broad arrows. (It is popularly believed that broad arrows have something to do with the situation of being a prisoner, but what the symbol means is 'this man, this shovel, this copper sheet belongs to the Government'.)

If the opportunity comes your way, find out about the chamber music and the solo recitals often given in St James's. And a place of delight, if you are looking for your ancestors, is the monument room in the crypt where there are countless ledgers that hold the records of marriages, funerals and baptisms held in the church.

Hyde Park at lunchtime has that enchanted air that light diffused through tree canopies knows all about. There are many European trees, curdy green in spring, and the gardeners tend to grow arum lilies and cannas, which add to the English atmosphere. Phillip would be pleased with the park. He very quickly designated all this locality as 'a common, never to be granted or leased', but allowed residents to pasture stock there. By the time Governor Macquarie came along, this western side of the common had already assumed a rough oval shape and was known to the citizens as the Racecourse.

Macquarie bowed to popular demand and set his Scots troopers to clearing and levelling the ground. It was he who called it Hyde Park. A racetrack of just over a kilometre length was laid out, and a proclamation of nearly the same extent was posted all over the town. 'No Gaming, Drunkenness, Swearing, Quarrelling, Boxing, Cows or Goats Pastured, no Pie Selling, no erection of Booths for the sale of Liquor.' A troop of auxiliary constables was mustered to arrest and carry off offenders.

The first race meeting was in October 1810, the original Spring Racing Carnival in effect, and lasted three days. The jockeys mounted at a squawk from a bugle and set off to a musket shot. The prizes were excellent, for instance, fifty guineas for the Ladies' Cup. (This would have been two years' pay for an average worker.) Surgeon D'Arcy Wentworth – he who made a fortune with the rum monopoly paid for the erection of Sydney Hospital – won three times with his bay Gig, his son William – later to be the Father of the Constitution – aboard. Gig was stabled at Mr Wentworth's country property, Homebush, better known to us as the current Olympic site.

After the races concluded a grand ball was held and went on to all hours, or until, as the *Gazette* poetically put it, 'the Rosy Deity assumed his preeminence and chased pale Cynthia down into the western world'.

There were giants among journalists in those days. The winning post was in front of what is now David Jones's eastern window display, and the race was run clockwise as is still the tradition in New South Wales and Queensland. The latter state was for a long time part of New South Wales.

After ruminating on the enviable times they had in early colonial days, we seek tranquillity approaching what we think is a Japanese fountain near the northwest corner of the park. But alas, it is an unimaginative stairway of concrete saucers and soupy trickles, the kind that needs a gnome with a fishing rod to make it complete. The fountain is a memorial to Busby's Bore, Sydney's first real water supply. The bore was a two kilometre tunnel planned to drain water from the lagoons and spongy lowlands of what is now Centennial Park. A huge reservoir to hold almost 60 million litres was to be dug in the middle of Hyde Park, which by 1827 had more or less reverted to being a common.

Busby's Bore was admired as the second most stupendous engineering achievement in the colony, the Argyle Cut being the first. The man in charge, John Busby, was a mining engineer sent out from England to survey coal deposits around present-day Newcastle, then the Coal River Settlement. He lived until age ninety-two so we have some photographs of him, furiously sidewhiskered and looking most offended. After many mishaps here he was sent to New Zealand to suppress the Maoris, but they called him the man-o'-war without guns and shamed him terribly. However, he did indirectly start the winemaking industry in Australia, at his estate on the Hunter River.

The building of the Bore was fraught with difficulties. Busby's calculations were often erroneous, the terrain was unpredictable, and his convict workmen mutinous and unskilled. Toiling crookbacked in the lamplit twilight of the narrow tunnel (less than two metres wide and 1.5 metres high), they removed more than 10,000 cubic metres of spoil. In June 1827, after ten years of this torture, the conduit reached Hyde Park, and water began to flow at the rate of more than a million litres a day. The reservoir was not built; instead water carts filled up at the standpipe near the corner of Park Street. By 1860, with steam-pumped water coming through from the Botany swamps, and much of Sydney by then using a reticulated water supply, the old tunnel was no longer used.

Throughout the years, sneaky people have used the Bore as a useful place for dumping rubbish. In 1849 a carter was fined for dumping 200 tonnes of nightsoil, and in 1916, rebellious soldiers dropped their rifles down a handy shaft. The tunnel and its several side drives have often been explored, but the water level is unpredictable and there is risk of drowning. Now it is just one of the dozens of tunnels under Sydney and by no means remarkable.

Traditionally, Hyde Park is used for two-up games on Anzac Day, when the police turn a blind eye on the several rings from the Archibald Fountain to the Anzac War Memorial. The old soldiers squat in the sunshine beside the glistening pool of reflections before the Memorial and baffled migrants look on as the coins flash in air. No one looks at the Memorial with its sad figure of sacrificed youth, the 120,000 stars which stud the ceiling of the dome, each star representing a voluntary enlistment in World War I. And indeed why should they? Most war memorials are personal.

We leave Hyde Park for Elizabeth Street. Look now down Bathurst Street. What can that curious column be? It is an obelisk, with lacy metal crown and couchant sphinxes. I have never yet met a Sydney resident who knew what it is. Actually, it blocks the footpath, and its cryptic inscription 'Erected 1867 by George Thornton, Mayor' can be read only from passing buses. This is the 'Hyde Park Scent Bottle' (or, sometimes, 'George Thornton's Smelling Bottle'). Its erection was an experiment in sewer-ventilation made in 1857 during one of the mayoral terms of the indefatigable Mr Thornton. Fortunately for Sydney, he had just completed one of his several world tours. Thornton had been impressed with the Egyptian obelisks souvenired and re-erected in Rome, and thus Sydney was blessed with this majestic flue.

Until 1880, when new sewerage and drainage works were started, Sydney literally smelt like a drain. The old sewerage system, laid down mostly in Mayor Thornton's time, was breaking down, and even the city's water supply had become 'so contaminated that the idea of drinking it is nauseating'. Fetid vapours, it was said, floated on every wind. Typhoid was almost endemic, and twelve per cent of all children under a year old died. The five main outfalls, carrying both sewage and floodwater, discharged into the Harbour, which was 'polluted beyond either human or piscatory powers of endurance'. These outfalls were cosily close to the city, at Darling Harbour, Farm Cove, Fort Macquarie, Woolloomooloo Bay and Blackwattle Bay. The shallow, spongy ground above the latter, now occupied by Wentworth Park, was said to be a steaming bog of sewage and refuse from the factories and breweries of Glebe.

The new sewers, which discharged into the ocean, were claimed as being the best in the world. In 1903, when this boast was made, the ocean had not today's habit of casting back that which was given. But then Sydney still had not quite a million inhabitants.

Not far from the Hyde Park Scent Bottle on Elizabeth Street is one of Sydney's most unusual buildings. The Great Synagogue, sumptuously Eastern, looks across to the green sward and the cascading flowerbaskets of Hyde Park. We peer through its tall wrought-iron gates – magnificent gates worthy of more ancient and more famous temples of Jewry. The wheel-window repeats the design of the gates and is considered one of the finest in Sydney. Under the broad shallow porch arches, all in opulently-worked stone, one observes the details of that portico which architect Thomas Rowe considered the 'most gorgeous and ornate' he had ever designed.

The Synagogue is crushed cruelly between two towering modern buildings which brutally indicate the disparity in taste between our age and that of the 1870s, when this fascinating little Byzantine structure was erected. It is classified by the National Trust as a historic building.

The Jewish community, which is still somewhat small, began with the First Fleet, when James Larra arrived on the *Scarborough*. He became a prosperous hotel keeper in Parramatta. In 1817 twenty members of the Jewish faith formed a society for the burial of their dead, and a small portion of the Town Hall graveyard was given over to them. Divine worship according to the Hebrew rites was officially performed in 1828, and the first Rabbi arrived in 1830. The original synagogue, opened in 1844, was on the western side of York Street behind what is now the Queen Victoria building. It, too, was a building of alien architecture, described as Egyptian, and indeed resembling the plinth of some Pharaonic structure, with immense tall thin windows, and three stumpy towers.

The interior of the Synagogue is fabulously beautiful. Even though the word has been debased, fabulous is what it is – its architecture rich and symbolic, its ceiling starry. There are guided tours every Tuesday and Thursday about midday, which somehow combine the spectacular and the intimate.

We cross Pitt Street, and as we enter George Street we see

St Andrew's, which must be one of the very few back-to-front cathedrals. Especially do I like St Andrew's in spring. Then its attendant jacarandas are smudges of blue, so frail and insubstantial that one suffers uneasy intimations of mortality. But behind these spectral blooms one sees the fortress walls of the oldest cathedral in Australia, the citadel of Anglicanism, surely built to stand a thousand years. Thus one is made comfortable once more.

St Andrew's looks very fine at night. It is illuminated with considerable skill (as indeed are many of Sydney's buildings) so that massive blocks of darkness support faintly-limned arches, and the quaint tick-tack-toed spires spindle imperceptibly into the night sky. The church is built in Perpendicular Gothic style, and it is indeed a tall thin building, with much dark timber and carving, and massy pillars like close-knit banyan trees. There is a delicate west window of clustered apostles and disciples, and one wonders if this is the window painted by the youthful Edmund Blacket as his first job after he arrived in Sydney in 1842.

The original architect of St Andrew's was James Hume, who commenced building in 1837. Two years later the finances of the colonial Church were already tottering before the onslaught of the Great Depression of the 1840s. Banks restricted credit, wool prices fell from 3/6 to 1/- per pound; valuable flocks were boiled down for tallow in order to keep the sheepowner and his family alive. Six hundred shopkeepers went bankrupt in 1842. 'Amongst the mercantile class several acts of self-murder were committed; many of them poisoned themselves by ... continuous drinking. Respectable merchants expired under the influence of delirium tremens.'

The rich flockmasters and speculators, who had dashed around the city in 'real London-built chariots, brilliant in paint and varnish and complete in every luxury, with a coachman attired something like worthy Sam Weller' cried out: 'What is to become of the colony? Where is all the money gone to?' An editorial of 1844 commented: 'Everything is struck with a kind of paralysis. The banks narrowed their discounts, and smash went the whole of our prosperity ... and vanished like the dream of a drunkard.'

The gold discoveries resurrected New South Wales from this coma of ruin. Capital flooded in, thousands of new settlers followed, but the old order, whose prosperity had depended almost entirely upon the prosperity of the landowners and agriculturalists – 'the squirearchy' –

had changed for ever. Already the great industrialists, such as Thomas Sutcliffe Mort, stood half-recognised in the near future.

During the Depression the Anglican congregation, too numerous for St James's and St Phillip's, overflowed into a storeroom in the brewery owned by John Terry Hughes, the wealthy nephew of 'the Botany Bay Rothschild', the diabolic old millionaire Sam Terry. Hughes's Albion Brewery is commemorated by Albion Street. Hughes himself crashed in the Great Depression, after a career of 'fraud, folly and roguery'. In Sydney folklore his beer is remembered for superlative flavour and muscle, these virtues being attributed to the water used in brewing. It came from the creeks which drained the nearby Devonshire Street burial ground, now the site of Central Station.

In 1846, the vagrant congregation took heart when work on the new cathedral was recommenced, this time under the control of the still youthful Edmund Blacket, who was appointed diocesan architect. His design is thought to be closely related to that of St Mary's in Oxford. He concluded his association with the church in 1874, when he designed and executed the two western towers, these being regarded as among his finest work. To the left of St Andrew's altar you will find a modest plaque to Edmund and his loved wife Sarah, indicating that their ashes are buried nearby.

St Andrew's has the decidedly military atmosphere of so many Anglican establishments, displaying tattered flags and a flock of regimental crests. There are some touching little mementoes of England – a stone boss from the House of Commons 'destroyed in the Blitz', a copy of Thomas Cromwell's Great Bible of 1539. The pavement of the chapel on the north side is recent and rather good. It is of marble from St Paul's in London.

However, the church is in no way an ecclesiastical museum. There are always people in the pews, praying or meditating in the warm near-silence. There are many interesting things to look at, the decoratively tiled floor, the carved altar, very mediaeval, with figures in high relief. The altar is adorned with flowers, and one recalls with a smile blunt Samuel Marsden's description of the cathedral's distinguished Bishop Broughton: 'The Archdeacon ... is a very high churchman, though not inimical to the Gospel.'

Sitting here in this tranquil place, we think of the genesis of this quiet cathedral in the minds of Governor Macquarie and his ambitious architect, the odd little forger Greenway. Some of Greenway's ideas were wonderfully grand, and one cannot help but be sorry they never came to be reality. I do rather yearn after the castle on Observatory Hill and the majestic Bernini-like colonnade which was to form an enormous pillared portico around a reconstructed Circular Quay. But the original St Andrew's, which Greenway sketched in obedience to the Governor's request for a noble church in a noble square at the very centre of the town, was a fine lofty structure. Macquarie actually laid the foundation stone for this building in his imaginary square. It was out in the middle of George Street, but now is safely within the present St Andrew's, being relaid by good Governor Bourke in 1837.

The viperous Commissioner Bigge, who so ruthlessly destroyed many of Macquarie's schemes, nipped both church and square in the bud. This is a great shame; Sydney could have done with a Place de la Concorde. As it is, while standing outside St Andrew's, we can detect the ghost of an aborted plaza in this open space which, for chaos, congestion and architectural disunity is second only to what is charitably called Railway Square. The sad thing is that hindsight may justly infer that Commissioner Bigge's hostility towards Macquarie was exacerbated by disapproval of the Governor's liberal attitude towards emancipists. If only kindly Macquarie hadn't invited those discharged felons to partake of port and Madeira at Government House we might have had our noble square.

The cathedral originally turned its back on George Street. Strangely, its massive front doors opened on a tiny lane running off Bathurst Street. This west end was for ages completely blocked off by St Andrew's Cathedral School, a dreary unstylish pile. The church was re-orientated in 1941, and the main doorway now opens hospitably on George Street.

In the 1960s and 1970s St Andrew's began falling to bits to the alarm of clergy and parishioners. The church liaised with the Sydney City Council, creating a strategic plan for this significant part of the city. Tatty old buildings between and behind St Andrew's and the Town Hall were demolished and there is now a small square between the two massive buildings. Sydney Square it is called. It is not La Place de la Concorde, and Greenway would undoubtedly have a fit of hysterics but it is pleasant and leafy and a nice place to rest while we psych ourselves up to cope with the Town Hall.

As with most ponderous buildings, it is best to view the Town Hall from a distance, say from the corner of Park and George Streets. From this point we may have a meditative gawk at this extravagantly tiddly-winked massif, which (as we are informed by the Town Hall's own Public Relations Department) is considered one of the noblest civic structures in the southern hemisphere.

Civic structure indeed. From the air it looks like a thumping great hippo. Even walking around it you are uneasily aware of dropsical protuberances and swellings which shouldn't be there. They offend an eye perhaps put out by the gaunt pale simplicities of Georgian style. We cannot altogether put the infelicities of the Town Hall down to the Victorian age in which it was created, but rather attribute them to the succession of architects of differing ages, schools and intents who struggled with this building from 1868 to the 1930s.

The Town Hall, because of certain scandals and charges of corruption during its construction, has been called the graveyard of reputations. It is in fact built on a graveyard, Sydney's second. It must have been a great eyesore; half-wild pigs roamed among the graves, as did bad characters who lit picnic fires with paling fences and bivouacked within broken vaults. The *Gazette* thundered: 'Dastard must be the living spirit that would thus pollute the mansions of the dead with wanton and unprofitable crime.'

The City Council first applied for the site in 1843. The Corporation of Sydney had been formed in 1841 after a ten-year running battle between the Patriotic Association, the members mostly wealthy emancipists or emancipist descendants, and the Pure Merinos, whom we met back in archfiend John Macarthur's day, who demanded that no transportee or transportee's son should ever have a vote. This was a class struggle. Great donnybrooks raged around the hustings and heads were broken, as the *Gazette* gravely records. One candidate, obviously a patriot, brought a mob of sealers with him, armed with pikes. The Pure Merinos lost the day and indeed are not much heard of now except in the social pages during Race Week.

Being municipal property, the derelict Old Burial Ground was resumed in 1869, and the bones of the earliest settlers, both free and unfree, were carted out to The Sandhills (Devonshire Street Cemetery) from which they were moved once more when Central Railway took over. It is thought that a number of coffins remain beneath the Town

Hall. Certainly in 1904, when electric cables were being put down close to the footpath beside the south gate, a lead coffin was exposed. A bottle containing a note of the occasion, and the day's newspaper, were placed inside, and the casket was re-cemented under the pavement.

While St Andrew's and the Town Hall were being built, all kinds of itinerant vendors pitched little ragbag stalls against the wooden fences that walled off the constructions from George Street. Many of these sold books and overseas newspapers which were obtained by the proprietors by rowing out to incoming ships (sometimes as far as ten kilometres, we are credibly told) and buying up every last line of reading matter on board. The Australian Subscription Library (later to become the Sydney Free Library) was started in 1826, but could not allay the book-hunger of a rapidly-growing population. The most famous of these secondhand booksellers was Jerry Moore, who later opened Moore's Bookshop in George Street and published that curiosity, *Old Moore's Almanac*.

Where we stand is close to the site of two celebrated taverns of the 1850s onwards, the Emu, run by a family called Easy, and the oddly-named Swan with Two Necks. Both were much frequented by radicals, and the Swan has been described as the birthplace of the Associated Trade Unions. Outside the Emu about the same time the last of the Kuring-gai or Cadigal tribe, which Captain Phillip had found so numerous, sat begging, quarrelling and shivering within their government issue blankets.

Their leader, Old Gooseberry (traditionally the last member of the Cadigal to survive), had been the 'queen' of the intrepid and intelligent Bungaree, who had twice circumnavigated Australia and was Governor Macquarie's friend. Here then sat the homeless, landless remnants of Bungaree's people, who had been so perfectly adapted to their life, and so completely without defence against civilisation.

The Town Hall foundation stone was laid by the Duke of Edinburgh, that royal 'Affie' whom some earnest anarchist endeavoured to bowl over at the picnic races at Clontarf in 1868.

The Town Hall is a huge structure, occupying the best part of a hectare, its external dimensions being one hundred metres long, sixty metres wide, and its height to the main parapet almost thirty metres. The tower is close to sixty metres high, and there is a flagpole on top of that. The architectural style is pure Bondi Renaissance, and if you are a collector of columns you can find every variety known to the mind of man. Still, as in most Victorian architecture, there are areas of beauty. The lovable naiveté gets to you in the end.

The vestibule, which is one of the older parts of the building, is very stylish with its interesting skylighted dome, ornate vaulted ceiling and superb chandelier. The Centennial Hall, also, with impressive galleries and spacious orchestral platform, is enriched with an unusual ceiling of panelled and coffered zinc. Metal in fact is used surprisingly often around this Victorian building. The striking large domes on the exterior roof are of polished steel and some of the clerestory windows have sashes of wrought iron.

The Centennial Hall, before the erection of the Opera House, was the scene of almost all important concerts. It can seat 2,535 persons and it is supposed to be the world's largest entertainment hall built in conjunction with a city hall. However, its acoustic properties are often carped at. At the western end of the Centennial Hall is the Great Organ, a historic instrument regarded for many years as the best example of its kind in the world. It has 8,672 pipes ranging in length from a centimetre to twenty metres. The façade of this mighty instrument itself looks like the façade of a rundown fairy castle. It is possible to see over parts of the Town Hall during certain hours.

Now strolling north along George Street we come to one of the most remarkable and anomalous buildings in Sydney, the mighty Queen Victoria Building, which fills a whole block between York and George Streets, its south and north ends being bounded by Druitt and Market Streets.

For almost fifty years important people threatened to take dynamite and the wrecking-ball to it, and other important folk swore to commit suicide at its main entrance if they did. It was described as a neglected, tatty and derelict barn, the catacombs of Rome infested by rats, the biggest eyesore south of the line. During the long municipal battle to decide its fate, its admirers spoke ardently of its 'dazzling romanticism', its air of 'something cast adrift from Xanadu'. And after its 1971 reprieve from demolition, the humorist Barry Humphries, who had been a vigorous defender of the abused building, triumphed:

> They've reprieved you with wisdom and vision,
> A brave solemn pledge.
> Let us pray that this Mayoral decision's

FINE BUILDINGS AND A GARDEN

The thin end of the wedge.

To me the Queen Victoria Building, even in its decline, was always one of the great sights of architectural Sydney, something conjured up by Aladdin's lamp, sign and symbol of the innocent pomp of an age whose prime article of faith was that the Empire would last forever, that prosperity (though it was absent at the time) was bound to come back, and the dignity of Great Britain must be upheld even on Australia's coral strand.

It was no use telling me and many other writers and artists that it was a senile hunk of Victoriana. We raised our piping voices in every radical journal and gained several reprieves. For us the QVB was derelict because of outrageous neglect by successive municipal authorities without foresight or imagination. We were among those who planned harakiri on the doorstep because we saw that the doomed building was a majestic example of its kind. Where the Town Hall is lubberly, the Queen Victoria is noble, all because of proportion, perhaps. Like the Town Hall, it is ornate, but whereas the former is prinked, pranked and bedizened, the ornaments worn by the Queen Victoria Building are as unaffectedly splendid as those of a moth or a seashell. Even in those days of its humiliation, it had a recherché beauty.

As with other sandstone buildings, sunshine gave back the QVB a little of its ancient glory. It drew out the foxy hues of the fine-grained Waverley stone even though that was ravaged by a near century of undisturbed soot. It struck an antique green from the tarnished copper domes, and spilled lustre over the Italian marble figures with their snail-shell coiffures and scrolly garments where the city pigeons nestled in garlands of soiled feathers.

The German stained glass, though in perfect condition, was encrusted with dirt as thick as felt, inimical to the light for which it was created. The writer was fortunate to be allowed to explore the QVB while it was more or less on death row, the Council offices which occupied some of its cavernous interior in the process of being packed up. It was a haunting few hours, that expedition, marked by inexplicable glimpses of pretty tesselated marble showing through dry-rotted timber over-flooring; wrought iron spiral stairs twining upwards to reach galleries no longer in existence; doors that opened on space. In the corridors were fragments of extravagantly embossed ceilings, an air vent concealed in a fragile spindled contraption like a chandelier, a marble bust of a dignitary, yellow as wax and now wearing sunglasses. There was a dank cockroachy smell and much of the building was pitch dark. The neglect was shameful.

Well, that was an old battle triumphantly won. The restored Queen Victoria Building is spectacular, a phoenix. One cannot imagine anything like it ever being built again anywhere. The dimensions, which stupefied little Victorian Sydney, are impressive today. The length from Market to Druitt Streets is almost 200 metres roofed by a majestic glass barrel vault. The Scottish architect George McRae who designed it was regarded as dangerously progressive in his time. He was also stubborn. The Council wanted Byzantine, he said, they were going to get Romanesque. The result is sui generis, fantastically detailed, the QVB style.

You will find over 200 boutique shops there, and many other things including cafés. It would be a good idea, seeing we have walked so far today, to sit there among drifting music and the quiet hum of conversation and ponder the long association of this part of the town with buying and selling. Market Street was not called that for nothing.

There are many references to a mid-city market in newspapers and memoirs. Indeed, four long low rows of ramshackle market sheds stood nearby after 1810, on a square laid out by Governor Macquarie. In 1828 the produce seemed exclusively rural – grain, green forage, live fowl, vealers and sucking pigs and homemade butter and cheese 'sold by freckled girls of majestic stature'. But by 1846 the shopper could buy colonial tobacco – 'hell hath not such a stench' – tropical fruit, local wine, pugs, poodles, monkeys, flying foxes and emus. Customers drank freely and ate what seems to have been the old English pease pudding, oysters and blood sausage.

On market days all was enlivened by the presence of the stocks and pillory which stood at the Druitt Street end of the markets. The populace, happily supplied with vegetable detritus from the latter, pelted and abused the prisoners. The stocks, always much beloved by rowdy crowds, seem mainly to have been used to restrain drunks, who could ransom themselves by paying five shillings. Even after the markets were removed elsewhere, and a disagreeable crouching Police Office was erected on the site, the stocks remained until 1837, their abolition being one of the last acts of William IV's reign, and much resented by fun-seekers.

In 1841 the Police Office was besieged by a furious crowd of British tars on leave from the man-o'-war *Favourite*. Some of their number had been arrested after causing a brawl in the Royal Victoria Theatre, and rescue was the probable motivation of one of the noisiest riots Sydney has seen. The Governor took charge of the Police Office, and armed troops stood at the ready around it. The mob, swollen by excited sightseers and organised bands of louts from the Rocks, were thrown into disorder by a volley fired over their heads. Instantly 'out rushed the constables with their staves and fell promiscuously upon all and sundry ... between fifty and sixty persons, men, women and children, were indiscriminately assaulted and knocked down'.

The Navy hastily withdrew its men from shore leave, and the *Favourite* fled Sydney Harbour in a hurry, leaving Sydney characteristically describing the beleaguered police as 'cruel and ruffianly' and the unruly sailors as 'jolly jacks'.

At that time the population of Sydney was about 45,000. To keep them in order the City Police mustered a force of four inspectors, twelve sergeants and seventy-six constables, all clad in the familiar bobby uniform of the London Police Force.

At the time of writing, George Street is pulling itself to pieces yet again. If one could but have time-lapse photography of history! One would see such elderly highways twitching, shrinking, expanding, inexplicably bursting over and through obstructions and forgetting their very existence, cutting corners, plunging through swamps and over corduroy logs.

It is plain that from earliest times, officialdom hugged the north end around the Quay, and commerce, trade and robust entertainment flowed towards the south and the Haymarket. From Bathurst Street, then an important access road to the docks and the growing maritime industries, George Street was known familiarly as Brickfield Hill. Parts were very steep, the low areas filled with dangerous quagmires which in summer were petrified into rutted concrete by the raging sun. The road was a cart track, which wound through charred stumps and the bark huts that sprang up in squalid disorder among the kilns and claypits. Here from the earliest days were dug and baked the bricks which built a city now almost gone. The brick carts, each loaded with 700 tiles or 350 bricks, were drawn by teams of twelve convicts, accompanied by an overseer with a bullock whip. Each team had to accomplish in a day four loads of bricks or five of tiles. The load was dragged from the bottom of Brickfield Hill as far as George Street North, by men not only three-quarters starved but suffering almost incessantly from dysentery and various other diseases of malnutrition. We read of great cruelty.

'He said: "I'm done for, boys," and all in a flash there was the blood foaming from his mouth and nose like he was a horse with a broke heart. Overseer comes along, gives him a kick, and says: "Well, one less for rations."'

Though no wraith of these wretched convicts seems to haunt this graceless district, the downtown end of George Street used to have (and may still have) two resident phantoms. They belong to Private and Mrs Jones, a redcoat and his wife, who in 1798 took an axe and 'knocked all to pieces' an English missionary who had been kind enough to lend them money and incautious enough to ask for its return. Having accomplished a drawn-out messy slaughter, they and their accomplice, Elbray, tossed the body in a nearby flooded sawpit and had a drunken singsong to celebrate. So far this was not unusual for the Sydney of those times. The tale of the uneasy shades of the two horridest of the 'three horrid unregenerate monsters' arose rather from the manner of their end.

After their prompt apprehension, trial and condemnation, Governor Hunter, always prone to righteous indignation, sent a party of troopers to burn down the murder house, a bark shanty on the southwest corner of George and Goulburn Streets. Amid the ashes an exceptionally high gibbet was erected, and here, before the massed inhabitants of Sydney, Mr and Mrs Jones and their unhappy assistant were turned off, Mrs Jones properly wearing the canvas bloomers which the era's sense of womanly decency required. For a long time the mummified tatters of Jones and Elbray hung there in nets of chains, but Mrs Jones was handed over to the surgeons for dissection.

Oddly, the ghost of Elbray does not seem to have joined his friends on this haunted corner, where for decades into the nineteenth century the spirits of the redcoat and his bonneted wife were occasionally reported moaning and whimpering amid the weeds and rubbish which filled the shunned, empty, and unbuilt-on block where their shack had stood. This corner is now marked for an impressive redevelopment – unhaunted we hope.

At the bottom of Brickfield Hill, even with its greatly modified incline, we can plainly see where the old swamps lay, and the sea crept in from Blackwattle Bay and Cockle Bay to create the complex of salt fens, creeks and freshwater ponds that stretched from the Blackwattle Swamps (now Wentworth Park) to meet the many creeks that tumbled down from the rocky heights of Surry Hills into Dickens's Pond at the foot of Hay Street.

Dickens's Pond was an ancient nesting place for ducks, swans and migratory waterbirds. Men caught geese there, and built fishtraps and speared mud eels. The hay and wool wagons coming in from Parramatta travelled over a causeway which sometimes was washed away at high tide. Dickens's Pond was filled in with the spoil from Brickfield Hill. Almost a million cubic metres of solid rock was removed by pick and shovel, and transported down the hill to the valley. In the more enlightened days of 1827, the carts were dragged by bullocks rather than men.

The district still called the Haymarket thus took on the shape familiar to us today and, until the railway was opened in the 1850s, it was the custom for the woolbrokers to meet the wagoners in the Haymarket inns and over the local ale bargain for the commodities already becoming New South Wales's greatest wealth.

The wagoners and countrymen rarely got beyond the slope of Brickfield Hill. Their Sydney was bounded by Bathurst Street. For some sixty years every entertainment such a man would want was to be found either in downtown George Street or its attendant alleys – ratpits, dogfights, cockfights, prize fights, betting games of all kinds, brothels, dance halls, and countless pubs, many of which indicate by their names their habitual clientele – the Woolpack Inn, the Fleece, the Plough, the Squatter's Arms.

There are some delightful descriptions of the Saturday night "mechanics' promenade" from the Haymarket to King Street. So if you can, imagine a gaslit George Street, eight o'clock on a summer's night, people everywhere: country boys wearing moleskins with red sashes, and soft felt hats entwined with blue or green veils; bashful Aborigines brought to town by some squatter with 'strict advice how not to get lost'; blind fiddlers, darting newsboys, many foreign seamen; persons from Bombay and Madras selling filigree, ivory walking sticks, monkeys and curious bright shawls. At ten this lively crowd thins; at eleven when the hotels close and the theatres empty, the shops close and become dark. By midnight the city is empty save for the echoing footfall of the policeman on his beat as he marches along trying the shop doors, flashing his lantern over singing drunken homegoers, and admonishing them to get along to bed.

The waterbirds are long gone, the purveyors of tripe and shinbones unheard of, the royal teams of Clydesdales laid to rest. Darling Harbour where the Cadigals speared mud eels among the mangroves and later white settlers dug cockles and trapped crabs to sell to Sydneysiders all alive-oh – the same Darling Harbour that for a century and a half was the shipping and industrial heart of the colony, its shores lined with wharves, its southern extremity the railway workshops and shunting yards – all this has vanished.

In the mid-1980s more than a billion dollars was spent on Darling Harbour, a good deal of these funds multinational. By 1988, the Bicentennial year, the 54 hectare site had become the nucleus of a famous entertainment centre. It's touristy, yes, and why not? There are fine things to do and see and we shall visit them on another day.

THE CITY II

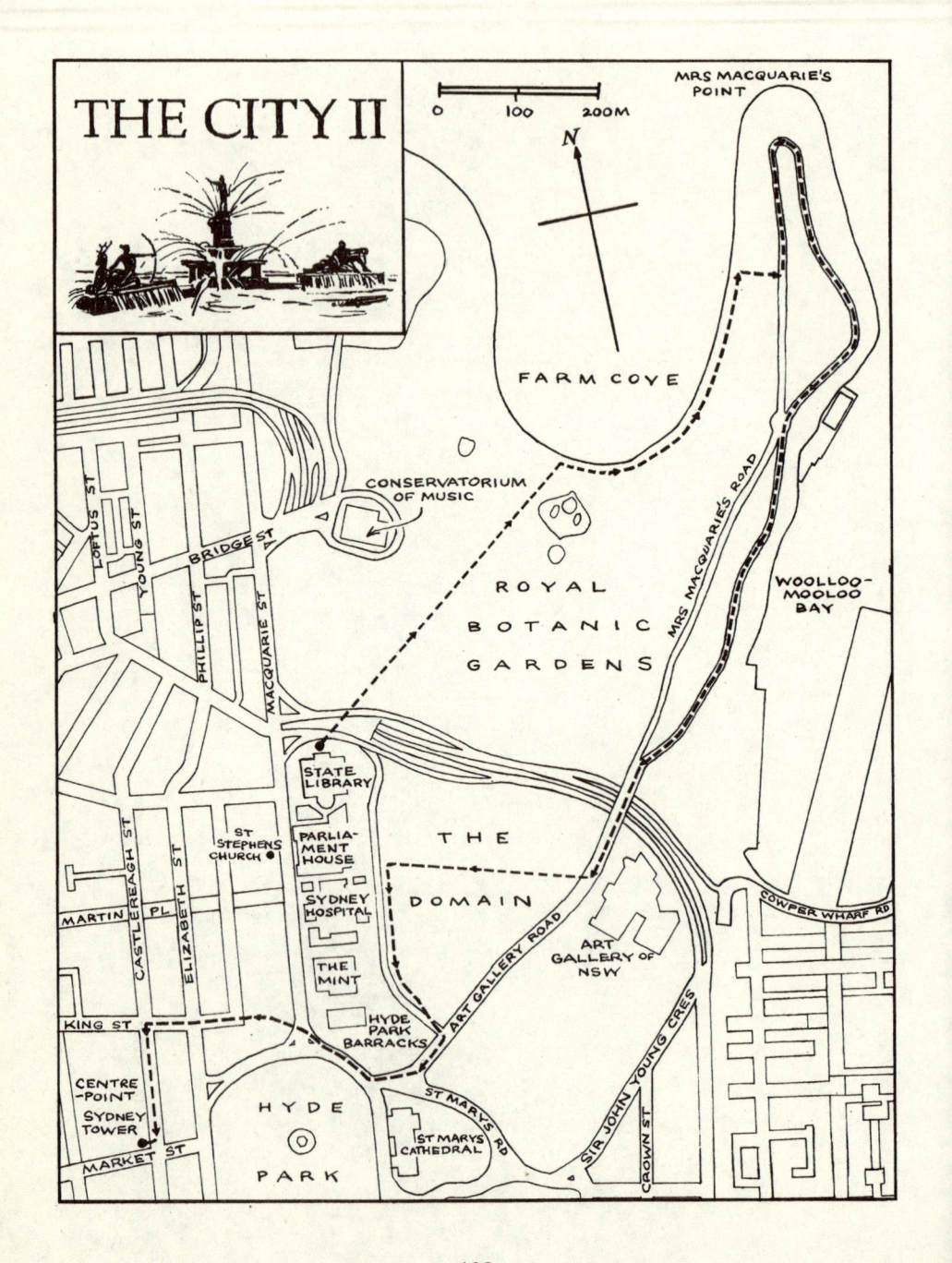

CHAPTER 4

FARM COVE TO SYDNEY TOWER

Lunch at Farm Cove – Governor Phillip's legacy – Elizabeth Macquarie and her famous chair – hanging on Pinchgut – the first cabbages – adventurous Bungaree – Woolloomooloo past and present – Jacky Palmer and his grand house – the Domain baths and past heroes – Henry Lawson in love – the Art Gallery and dazzling Aboriginal paintings – the Domain and what went on there – sad story of a balloon ascent – St Mary's Cathedral and a unique mosaic – Hyde Park and the remarkable Sydney Tower.

TODAY we shall have that picnic at Farm Cove which we promised ourselves days ago. What a day it is, flags snapping, water flashing in the wake of skimming sailboard riders, gulls tossing. Sandwiches and a bottle of wine purchased at the Quay and we're away through the Botanic Gardens and down to the shore. Of course a more sedate lunch can be had at the Gardens restaurant but who wants to be sedate on a summer's day?

Away to the right a tall hotel at King's Cross floats in the faint gilded haze like Fata Morgana's topmost spire. The battlements of Government House are half concealed by the thick curdly green of European trees. Can there be a large brash city just behind us? We hear nothing but a distant beelike hum.

What a miracle it was that this heavenly cove and its eastern promontory were preserved for us intact, if not in their original state. Man has made it symmetrical, but has not ruined it. We must thank Governor Phillip for that. One of his last administrative acts before he returned to England late in 1792 was to order that no ground within the boundary should ever be granted or leased. Flow-on laws from this original decision have preserved it for us, with but slight alteration, in perpetuity. The one major exception was Major Grose's later grant of forty hectares to John Palmer, Commissary-General of the colony and former purser of the *Sirius*. If this had not been made, the scrambled and crowded dockside district of Woolloomooloo would never have existed. We would instead have that once romantic vale as part of the Domain.

Farm Cove's native name was Yurong, its soil was sandy and covered with the sharp-edged cutty-grass so common to low-lying beaches. The present name comes from the Governor's farm. Here, over nearly four hectares of shallow cultivation, English wheat and corn were sown for the first time on the continent. The foreshore was filled and levelled, and the seawall built between the years 1848 and 1878, under the direction of Charles Moore, who was master of the Gardens for forty-eight years.

The Farm Cove anchorages are reserved for naval use. To our left we see the Man-o'-War jetty, originally giving access to Government House and Fort Macquarie, which stood where the Opera House is now. Foreign ships used to anchor in Farm Cove, and we have a lively picture of those busier times, the cove 'alive with officers in uniform landing or departing in longboats manned by blue-jacketed sailors or with consuls going on board to pay their respects, and foreign warships leaving with some festive demonstration in return for kindness received'. There's a little plinth near Man-o'-War Steps marking the occasion when Queen Elizabeth II stepped ashore in February in 1954, the first time a reigning monarch had set foot on Australian soil.

We will now walk around to Mrs Macquarie's Chair, often called Lady Macquarie's Chair. Part of the way we shall walk along the foreshore, observing the sandstone outcrops, possibly the low cliffs of earlier times. They are incised here and there with crumbling stone stairways, now leading nowhere in particular. We ascend the Fleet Steps to Mrs Macquarie's Road, continuing to go north towards the end of the point.

Mrs Macquarie's Road is almost five kilometres long; it was built by her husband, extending from Government House to the point named for her. Here she liked to rest. The road now runs right around the west side of Woolloomooloo Bay in a long loop, but the portion that connected with Bridge Street seems to have been swallowed up by the Cahill Expressway. It is said that Mrs Macquarie loved to walk along this road, but in fact the earliest records call it a carriage road.

As we stroll along to the enormous sandstone 'chair' where she used to sit, let us ponder on Elizabeth Macquarie who married (though candidly informed that his heart was in the grave of his first wife) Sydney's most human and interesting governor. Lachlan Macquarie was born in 1761, in a freakish January in which 'birds nested and strawberries ripened'. On another January in 1810, when he was nearly forty-nine, he arrived in Sydney to take control of the colony from the mutinous leaders of the Rum Rebellion who had deposed Governor Bligh. Macquarie was a man of long military experience, mostly in India. He had typical Scots family pride, though that family had long been ruinously poor. He was a grand sight of a man in his red uniform, very tall, with aquiline face and greying hair. In his portrait his eyes appear to be Highland black, but his wife tells us they were fine and grey.

His wife was a Jane Austen lady, slight, pretty and accomplished, the compleat gentlewoman, privately endowed with considerable pawky humour. She was a woman of Napoleonic times, for a good deal of her life had been lived under the shadow of impending French invasion. In the year she arrived in Sydney, the Duke of Wellington was having adventures in Spain, Napoleon divorced Josephine, George III was out of his mind again, and the hated Prince of Wales was hissed and pelted by yet another crowd.

Mrs Macquarie came into a ramshackle town where all the windows were tiny-paned because the colonists couldn't get glass of any other size, and the roof shingles were painted blue because that was the only colour paint that could be purchased. A third of the population wore military or naval uniform, and the rest, if female, were in tattered brown serge jackets and petticoats, and if male, in summer-issue dark frocks over canvas pantaloons, or the ragged remnants of gaudy uniforms salvaged from prisoners taken in England's many wars. Nearly all commerce was in the hands of New South Wales Corps officers, a set of bullyboys and tearaways. The women of Mrs Macquarie's own social class were mostly toadies of horrid Mary Putland, deposed Governor Bligh's daughter, or disagreeable proud ladies who were against everyone and everything. Everyone who could write dispatched poisonous, tattling, malcontent letters to influential friends at Home.

No wonder Mrs Macquarie went for long walks, usually accompanied only by an aide-de-camp, and George, the Governor's black servant, whom he and his first wife, the consumptive Jane, had bought as a child in India for 85 rupees. George was the Governor's faithful companion all his life, and was present at his death in miserable lodgings in London. Although the British Government treated Macquarie with shameful stinginess, and Elizabeth was poorly-off after his death, she set up the Macquarie Trust to look after the descendants of George, who married while in Sydney. In spite of frequent ill-health, Elizabeth was Macquarie's almost constant companion during his energetic governorship. She seems to have had some gynaecological disorder, and suffered at least six miscarriages before the birth of their one child, the frail Lachlan.

Macquarie left a Sydney which was the direct ancestor of our own. His buildings and his ideas are everywhere. It was his desire for appropriate and expensive buildings that eventually caused his recall to England. The most important are still standing in Macquarie Street, as we have already seen on another expedition.

Some people criticise Macquarie for his habit of naming geographical sites after himself. Thank heaven he did. We have no memorial raised to this man in Sydney. William Charles Wentworth was a faithful friend of Macquarie's and after the old man's departure tried to raise a subscription for a monument. But for all his vigour and influence he failed. I call this scandalous. With the common people who lamented the departure of Macquarie, I say, 'Bring back the Old Viceroy!' even if only in marble.

Mrs Macquarie's Chair is under cover of a huge Moreton Bay fig. It is a place where one can fall into a reverie. Was she homesick, poor Elizabeth, who, as her husband wrote, 'never troubled my heart with a complaint or tear'? Her return home was not to be happy for long. Macquarie died in 1824 while he was in London trying to obtain official recognition for his long service.

Mrs Macquarie's Chair used to be a fashionable picnic place. A naive Grandma Moses type picture of an early Victorian picnic at Mrs Macquarie's Chair hangs in Old Government House, Parramatta. It is crammed with slightly misshapen people doing things, lolling, eating, flirting, selling pies, skipping rope, slapping children – everything but looking at the scenery.

Pinchgut Island lies 400 metres off Mrs Macquarie's Point. I've seen that little isle with its low stone walls and martello tower ride stormy seas like a warship. But now, with the mist blowing away, and the sea immaculate, it is a floating top hat with its replica upside down in the water beside it. The correct name is Fort Denison, but who calls it anything but Pinchgut? Naval legend says that its colourful name has nothing to do with convicts or guts, but that the islet was called that by some early surveyor, possibly Captain Hunter, who did the first harbour survey. 'Pinchgut', they say, is a nautical term for the point at which a channel narrows.

Pinchgut didn't always look like that. It was originally a reef with a tall steeple rock, and even a little ruff of vegetation. The Aborigines loved to fish there, paddling out in their canoes which were, as Watkin Tench says, 'nothing more than a large piece of bark tied up at both ends with vines'. Sometimes these canoes carried little fires, on beds of earth, for cooking the catch immediately. But after 1797, when a gibbet was erected on Pinchgut, and the murderer Morgan hanged there in chains, the natives took fright, and would not go near the place again. There Morgan clanked, blackened and sun-dried, for three years. Both before and after this, recalcitrant convicts seem to have been marooned on Pinchgut with a ration of ship's biscuit and a bucket of water, so the familiar name may have a double-barrelled meaning.

The original lofty pinnacle must have been an impressive sight standing alone in the Harbour as it did – twenty-five metres high, on a pedestal barely a fifth of a hectare in extent. How curious that someone didn't say: 'Providence has sent us a flagpole!' and proceed to hitch a Union Jack to its crest. Many admired it; during the first century of settlement various ideas for erecting statues of a monumental Miss Liberty nature were mulled over. But defence of the colony was of necessity always uppermost in the minds of those in charge.

Sydney's defenceless condition was demonstrated when two American Navy sloops arriving at the heads before dawn in December 1839, simply quietly sailed in and dropped anchor in Sydney Cove. No one had heard or seen a thing. The American consul made things worse by announcing that if Britain and the States had been at war, the ships could have reduced Sydney to ashes and sailed out again in perfect safety. Public shame was total.

In 1840 consequently, Governor Gipps ordered that Pinchgut be quarried to sea level and a fort be built. The 10,000 tonnes of stone taken from the island were used by Colonel George Barney in the construction of Circular Quay. The Rev. Dunmore Lang who had something to say about everything, complained: 'This natural ornament of the Harbour, this remarkable work of God, which has stood like a sentinel for thousands of years, was at length destroyed by the folly of man. I can never pass the island without feeling indignant.'

The fort was constructed much later, during the Russian scare at the time of the Crimean War; the present structure was built of sandstone quarried from Kurraba Point at Neutral Bay. But the guns were never fired in anger. The remaining three 32 pounders were installed in the tower before the top was put on and cannot he removed without wrecking the fort. Pinchgut was once shelled, however, when a US ship hit it by mistake during target practice in World War II.

Pinchgut is a wonderful place to take holidaying children. About twenty thousand people visit the archaic little fort annually, so you will be well advised to book in advance. There is a museum, cell-like powder rooms, cannonballs and all their paraphernalia, gunpowder sacks, measuring jugs and fillers, the tower with its whispering gallery acoustics, and, of course, the comfortable domestic arrangements of the lucky Robinson Crusoes who caretaker this historic mini-island.

Staying on the low path which leads to Mrs Macquarie's chair, we turn south again and stroll along the edge of Woolloomooloo Bay, which in the past was often full of grimy grey ships. The eastern shore of the bay is dominated by the Captain Cook Dock, and the sweet-potato-shaped peninsula of the Garden Island Naval Dockyard.

Once Garden Island really was an island, a little double-hump separated from Potts Point by a channel some 300 metres wide. In 1940 reclamation of this seabed commenced and here the Captain Cook Graving Dock, 'capable of accommodating the largest capital ships of the British Navy for repairs or refit' was constructed. In spite of round-the-clock shifts, and the employment of thousands of workmen, the dock was not ready for use until March 1945. At 347 metres long and nearly 46 metres wide, it was the largest in the southern hemisphere. The vast crane, looking like a vertical hammerhead shark, was installed in 1951. It was then one of the world's biggest. Garden Island is again under long-term reconstruction.

The first ground on the island was cleared by a party of marines from HMS *Sirius*. Governor Phillip had ordered that a small garden be planted there, for the use of the First Fleet's officers. Under glass near this historic spot are three sets of initials carved in the rock in February 1788 by these amateur gardeners. The initials are regarded as the first inscribed in Sydney. However, there is evidence that Garden Island's cabbages appeared before Farm Cove's cabbages – a matter of a week or so, but Farm Cove's boast of having the first garden has Governor Phillip's signature on it, so let it stand.

Much of what we know of Garden Island's early history comes from the logbooks of *Sirius* and other later ships. It has had an almost continuous association with the navy, though for many years from 1911 it was government and not navy property. The island has many historic buildings including the tall, three-storey barracks erected in 1887 after the old Georgian style and now used as clerical offices, also the sail-loft on the northern end, now used as a non-denominational dockyard chapel.

In 1830 the Aboriginal rover Bungaree died in the naval sick bay on Garden Island, and, so tradition says, was buried nearby. (Rose Bay also claims to be the burial place of Bungaree and one of his wives.) Bungaree, an honorary Navy man, was the first native Australian to circumnavigate the continent twice, once with Matthew Flinders and again with Captain Phillip Parker King. A tall strong Aborigine of manly countenance, Bungaree was an important personage in the Central Coast tribe. He took easily to white men's ways, was a competent interpreter and reliable seaman. When Governor Macquarie left the colony, he presented Bungaree with a general's uniform, possibly one of his own, and a fully-equipped fishing boat. In this, 'with a load of dusky retainers', Bungaree liked to meet incoming vessels. Peter Cunningham describes this ritual in his book *Two Years in New South Wales*. Stripped of its sneering tone the passage gives a vivid picture of the Aborigine's courtly and self-confident manner. '[He] lifts up his beaver with the right hand a full foot from his head, with all the grace and ease of a court exquisite and … lowers it in a gentle and most dignified manner down to the very deck, following up this motion by an inflection of the body almost equally profound.' Bungaree is one of the two natives mentioned in the 1788–1850 *Dictionary of Biography*.

Ghostly clangs sound across the glassy water. This man-built peninsula, sprouting with all the fantastic disorder that any form of engineering seems inevitably to create, is majestically ugly. It is not alone in its disorder. Let us face it bravely: the graceful amphitheatre of

Woolloomooloo is a calamitously jampacked squodge of unit blocks, many painted in Federation colours, ochre predominating. Yes, yes, these neat tidy buildings are undoubtedly drier, lighter and airier than the tumbledown, crumbling stone and brick cottages and workmen's terraces they replaced in the early 1970s. And certainly the State Housing Department was faced with a crisis in those years, immigration being steady and robust.

But why so many buildings in this small enclave of narrow, difficult streets and selfwilled lanes? Does the sunshine enter many of these windows?

Woolloomooloo was Sydney's first suburb. But it might have been much more. Captain Phillip was a sharp man. He must have cast an eye over this impressive inlet, far longer and deeper than today, its high eastern cliff a shelter against the prevailing wind. Why then did he rather choose Sydney Cove as a site for the settlement? Perhaps he did not see the copious stream that splashed downhill through the mahogany and cedar forest that grew thickly on the heights of a Darlinghurst that was to be? It seems it was the Tank Stream that made him decide on Sydney Cove.

Before the 'Loo became a suburb it was mostly called Jacky Palmer's Farm. The low land was not well thought of; it became swampy where the stream dispersed, and there were mangrove mudflats that were believed to breed low fevers and malaria. The abrupt eastern ridge, then called Woolloomooloo Hill, was described as 'barren, rocky and desert land, suitable only for windmills'.

Still, we have some angelic watercolours from Lycett and others, and we know what an enchanting landscape was enjoyed by the resident Womerah, kinsfolk of the Cadigal, well fed and friendly, shown picking oysters from the rocks, the children chasing pelicans and cranes. The Womerah were not wanderers; their territory provided for all their needs. These happy people lived in amity with the white settlers until late into the nineteenth century, when there remained insufficient natural habitat to support them any longer. They vanished together with the emu and wallaby.

We expect the water of the bay to be scummy and polluted but it is clear as glass. We can see little fish, jelly blubbers and rocks covered with de-oystered shells. Eating oysters in the bay was once a constant joy, and it was many years before the shores were eaten out. Mrs Governor King, that pleasant dumpling, writes in 1791: 'Here we have feasted upon oysters just taken out of the sea; the attention of our sailors, and their care in opening and placing them around their hats in lieu of plates, by no means diminished the satisfaction we had in eating them.'

Lacking sailors, hats and oysters, the 'Loo Bay still must have fish, for here and there on the low stone embankment sit meditative fishermen. The sparse scrub above the rocks on our right is full of birds, and pigeons and seagulls shuffle peaceably away along the path.

We are walking towards John Palmer's old estate. Here he built an exceptionally fine house and called it Woolloomooloo after the cove's supposed native name, which was unusual for those early landowners, who usually christened everything in sight after the villages where they were born, or even their papa's favourite horse at Home. The name is richly comical, and has been described as the sound uttered by a man wobbling a red hot potato around his mouth. Sydneysiders have from time immemorial tended to call the locality the 'Loo.

John Palmer bounds into colonial history – 'prancing, dancing little atomy', as one of his jealous enemies recorded. He was certainly a tiny elfin person, so light on his feet that he could dance a hornpipe on the dining table without spilling a drop of wine. He had come to New South Wales rather older than other officers of the First Fleet. His career had been eventful, beginning at the amazing age of eight. He had survived several naval battles and twice been a prisoner of war. The French made fun of his stature, but the Americans treated him extremely well, even more so when he married an American girl to the applause of all her well-connected friends.

Remarkably for a man who had only the extremely specific education required for life in the navy, Jacky Palmer was a brilliant business man. He saw opportunity everywhere. Aside from his work as Commissary, which brought him only ten shillings a day and woefully heavy responsibilities, he very soon built a windmill and a bakehouse, became a magistrate and as soon as he acquired capital, joined the sealing and whaling industry, owning his own ships. His star shone even brighter when a young sister of his wife Susan, visiting Sydney, married Merchant Campbell, the colony's wealthiest settler.

Woolloomooloo House was the centre of fashionable society. The bay probably reached its apogee of ordered beauty and prosperity at that time, for paintings show fields of grain, orchards and sweeping pastures.

It is plain that the mudflats at the head of the bay had not yet been reclaimed, for Palmer's grand house is situated somewhere near modern Cathedral Street, though it is shown at the waterside.

Both Campbell and Palmer suffered grim economic losses because of their perfectly correct loyalty to deposed Governor Bligh. Although Governor Macquarie upon arrival re-established Palmer in a position of responsibility, it was too late. Palmer's splendid estate was sold at a loss. The house was demolished in the 1850s after an uncertain history as residence for various religious dignitaries.

Commissary Palmer's choice of Woolloomooloo as his estate meant that other rich ambitious men followed him, building magnificent mansions, some of which still stand today. Even the small dwellings of artisans and mechanics, closer to the water and the growing shipping industry, were 'clean and commodious and fitting the requirements of their tenants'.

At the western end of the bay we ask one of the fishermen if he has any clues about the crumbling old stairways that clamber up the stone scarp to nowhere. He thinks they were for coming down rather than going up, coming down to the bathhouses, like. There's a splendid swimming pool quite close, full of kids yelling and churning, and others lashing up and down roped lanes, while a young coach holds a stopwatch.

'That swimming pool, you mean?'

'Nah, that's the new one, named for Boy Charlton. I mean the bathhouses.'

What can he be talking about?

'The old Dom Baths, of course. That's where the big Aussie swimming tradition began.'

He is right of course. Better still, his dad used to swim here, and in the manner of old chaps, the son has adopted his father's stories as well as his own. We learn that locally the baths were called the Fig Tree Baths, because of the huge tree hanging over the water. The kids dived off its branches. Kids were free, but grown people had to pay sixpence for a towel and a cozzie. The cozzies came in two sizes, too big and too small. The baths were all netted in with wood grating because of sharks. No, his dad hadn't ever seen a shark, but sharks had come into the Harbour with the whaling and never went away.

'There was a religious crank kind of. He used to baptise people in the Baths. He'd say they'd go down cursing and come up blessing, but in the wintertime it was the other way around.'

The things you pick up! But the fisherman is correct. In 1880 the Port Jackson Swimming Club, probably the first such in Australia, began to hold regular races at the Domain Baths. We are told all the contestants used the peculiar limping stroke called sidestroke. The sport became such a craze that someone thought of an indoor swimming pool, and at some unspecified date, possibly 1882, 'the Old Nat.' was constructed in Pitt Street. The Natatorium claimed to be the first indoor saltwater swimming pool in the world. Even so, it still had Woolloomooloo connections, for its water was pumped up by steam engine from the 'Loo Bay. The water was changed only once a month, yet one does not read of epidemics of ear and eye viral infection, typhoid or other diseases.

Sports history proceeded. In 1892 the New South Wales Swimming Association was formed and held most of its carnivals at the Old Nat. But by then Australian water sports had broken away from the old European idea of indoor baths. The Old Nat closed down in 1905 and the Salvation Army converted the building into the People's Palace.

While the Domain Baths as described by the fisherman sound casual and homemade, swimming as a sport was already taken seriously. In 1908 the City Council provided £10,000, a truly large sum for those days, to update the baths, which then became 'the finest of their kind in Australia'. Fred Lane, the first Australian Olympic swimmer trained there, and Barney Keirnan, one of the 'destitute boys' of the hulk *Vernon* and then the *Sobraon*, smashed all world records from 100 yards to a mile right here. Other names, now faded and ghostly, were associated with this spot, Fanny Durack, and Frank Beaurepaire, Duke Kahanamoku who is credited with bringing the crawl from his native Hawaii to Sydney, Arne Borg the Swedish world champion and Andrew 'Boy' Charlton who beat him in 1924.

While the old man hauls in three leatherjackets, well under the statutory length, we recall the earliest Domain Baths of which we have heard. They were not used for swimming but for bathing. Strange! But seawater was considered therapeutic in its own right. In fact right here they used to heat it. Hot seawater was thought curative for rheumatic complaints, bunions, swollen glands, eczema. Possibly it was.

One of these medicinal baths, Robinson's Hot and Cold Sea Water Baths, was opened in 1833, and the legend is that the first woman to bob around at the end of the rope was Mrs Biggs, the wife of Macquarie's ex-coachman. The baths, for both men and women, were conducted with the most genteel propriety, an old hulk being moored between men's and women's sections. Her decks were fitted up as a teahouse.

The old man smartly chops the head off an infant leatherjacket and stows it in a Glad Bag. 'Got a cat waiting,' he explains. 'G'day to you.'

Thus dismissed, we wander past the swimming baths. Beyond it are old jetty steps half-hidden in lantana and blue periwinkle. But there's no jetty. We climb up towards George Lambert's statue of writer Henry Lawson, high up under a gum tree in a waste of droughty golden grass. Lambert has caught very well the faintly haunted expression of a deaf man. Lawson gazes abstractedly over the Captain Cook Dock, Garden Island, and the cement wastelands. Henry Lawson isn't so popular now that everyone's protesting, but once his was the loudest of the few lone voices squawking against the establishment, colonialism, sweatshops, cultural snobbery and the hard lot of the working man. His facile verses are easy to remember; for a long time he was the most quoted writer in the land, and quoted by the people he liked and understood best, the underdogs.

Henry and Bertha, who was to become his wife, used to walk to Mrs Macquarie's Chair in 1895 when they were sweethearting. I remember Bertha Lawson, dainty and pretty-voiced, and all of eighty, murmuring abstractedly: 'He had the most beautiful eyes I ever saw in a human face. Mother, of course, said he had no prospects, and George Robertson said 'My dear girl, you must be crazy.' We used to sit under the fig trees and feed the birds, blue wrens and wagtails. We loved each other so much. He used to chant his poems softly in a singsong voice and I'd write them down.'

The marriage was disastrous, George Robertson (of Angus and Robertson, Lawson's publisher) being right as usual. Henry, who had been a hopeless alcoholic for a long time, died in 1922. Poor Henry. 'Sorrow and poverty taught me to sing,' he said.

God knows what sense of the ironic caused the Establishment to place Lawson's statue where it is. This is the part of the Domain called Dossers' Alley, where the homeless unemployed used to sleep, huddled around rocks and trees like a lot of newspaper-wrapped grubs. It is said that the fussier ones would go down in the morning to wash in the horse-troughs still remaining near the docks. As Henry said, there's not much to look forward to when your pants begin to go.

The road now becomes Art Gallery Road, running along what must have been a very high ridge. Woolloomooloo looks as though it is in a ravine, and the Art Gallery itself perched on an artificial sandstone precipice. We cross the bridge over a huge cutting, with traffic shrieking along the Cahill Expressway below.

No one with an eye in his head could praise the painful overcrowding of apartment blocks in today's 'Loo. The planned renaissance of the bayside village in the 1970s fell flat somehow, possibly because of failure of funds. But, as we stroll along Art Gallery Road, we recall what the locality was like in the previous century and a half – old Woolloomooloo, gone in the teeth and gone in the knees, decrepit, neglected, despised. It was unlucky from the beginning. As soon as John Palmer and other enterprising farmers vanished, it was the prey of greedy land grabbers who would have slapped up hovels of bark and reeds if Authority had permitted them. Instead they built tiny slab timber cottages and the ubiquitous terrace where only the end dwellings had one wall of their own, and all other walls, floors, roofs, drainage if any, were shared.

'Where slum developers go, slum landlords follow. Slum landlords mend and replace nothing, dwellings become ratholes, and soon only the poorest and most hopeless, and after them the petty criminals, are the possible tenants' said the writer, Frank Clune, who lived there in childhood. 'They used to send missionaries into the 'Loo as if it were darkest Africa. It was a dangerous place.'

'The grubby little brick pigsties were penned in by strong iron railing fences as a precaution against the hovels developing feet and walking out of their unsavoury environment' wrote George Finey, the artist, who knew the place well.

Most of these terrace houses, as squalid as any in Cardiff or Nottingham in Industrial Revolution times, had frontages of 2.5 metres, attics made of rusty corrugated iron, stairs with no safety rails, open fires for wives to cook on. And of course there were no bathrooms and only a 'dunny' in the box-sized yard. The three dreaded Ds – dysentery, debility and death – were rampant. Drainage from the fine mansions of Darlinghurst and Potts Point ran into Woolloomooloo Bay, with poor results for the lowland residents. But the rich people on the highlands got lead poisoning; they had lead water pipes.

By the 1930s much of the old 'Loo had gone, except for romping tales of razor gangs and 'pushes, rampaging drunken seamen, fearful fights with chains and crowbars; the smallpox outbreak, and the houses boarded up as though in the plague; famous pubs, The Little House Under the Hill, with a narrow door you had to go in sideways, and the Cottage of Content in Bourke Street, used as a poste restante by sailors from all over the world. Woolloomooloo had the first Police Boys' Club, started in an old lock-up in 1937 by Police Commissioner McKay, to get the boys off the streets. It was a terrific success, gathering one thousand members in two weeks.

One thing that remains is the bronze drinking fountain set into the cliff on Cowper's Wharf Roadway. Its simple inscription is this: 'To commemorate the place of farewell to the soldiers who passed through the gates opposite for the Great War, 1914–1918.'

The cliff shines rusty red with seepage from the gardens of houses above in Potts Point, perched on the lip of the rock like castles. Trucks come and go with cargo loadings, taxis sweep around the sharp bend into Wylde Street, which will take them quickly into King's Cross. The famous piecart, Harry's Café de Wheels, is parked nearby. But it's Café de Bricks now, permanently at rest beside the busy road. Open all hours, pies and sausage rolls, strong coffee, chat and good cheer as of old.

There's really nothing but the fountain to remind one of the laughter and tears of those bygone days when the troops embarked. They have left a quaint awkward song, those soldiers, a parody, of course:

> *It's a long way to Woolloomooloo-oo*
> *It's a long way to go.*
> *It's a long way to Woolloomooloo,*
> *And lots of good old girls we know.*
> *Goodbye bully beefo.*
> *Hooray cobbers square,*
> *It's a long, long way to Woolloomooloo,*
> *But we're going back there.*

Up the stairs, a more modern café overlooks the gentle downland dip of the Domain. The arch of the Bridge is visible, and above the trees slowly moves a huge crane like the neck of a browsing dinosaur. The Art Gallery can be a hard place to get to. The shortcut across the Domain via Art Gallery Road is the most pleasant route from the city; a cab is a still better thought.

When reconstruction began on the Gallery in the early 1970s, the Government Architect intimated that the aim was to double the space, but to be polite to the old section. The old section, weightily Roman and constructed in peculiarly dead brown Pyrmont sandstone, is what confronts us. It scarcely deserves respect, being one of the Victorian architect Horbury Hunt's more derivative designs. How could he have produced this khaki railway station, a man so eccentric and original, who designed his bicycle to double as both steed and fully-fitted architect's studio?

The newer gallery provides five storeys behind this façade; it begins directly behind the massive arches of the lobby, in a curiously tacked-on style. It is air-conditioned, fitted with highly sophisticated security systems, provided with ample workshops, a linear 1.25 kilometres of racking space, restaurant, exhibition rooms, a sculpture courtyard, administrative offices and so on. Most of these were exasperatingly lacking in the old gallery. The architecture of the new block has been described as New Brutalism; flea-bitten concrete, lofty roofs and ceilings with no ornamentation, pebble colours, grey, white, beige. Yet there's wonderful space, airiness, and superb lighting. At the corners lofty glass panels let in a troll's cityscape, the highrise buildings of King's Cross and Darlinghurst, leaned-upon by rainclouds; rusty ships, dull sleeping water of Woolloomooloo Bay.

The Gallery will disappoint those accustomed to the opulent collections of Old Masters found in the famous European galleries. Its aim is different: it is primarily a showcase for Australian art. You will find representative works of all periods from Martens through Roberts, Streeton, Drysdale, Nolan, to today's favoured genius. Quail-like flocks of school children scuttle everywhere, often in uniform, Sydney-style. Little green girls cluster about a modern exhibit with their trendy teacher:

'What are all those red hoses, Miss? Why are they supposed to be marigolds?'

Larger clerical-grey boys scuffle in front of a painting. Somebody bearded and two months their elder, says: 'That is a purely selfish work, it doesn't give out. It's not only unilateral, it's paranoic.'

There is a judicious selection of Dobells, many of the old London drawings, as well as Mary Gilmore in her Mickey Mouse gloves, cloudy Margaret Olley, and the strange *Night of the Pigs*. The attendants are exceptionally friendly and pleasant. Asked where the Victorian paintings are, one says: 'Oh, the wrinklies are down below.'

There is a fine collection of Victorian and Edwardian genre paintings. Personally I view these with real gusto. They are suitably situated in the old wing – slippery parquet floor, arched glass roofs, jumbo pictures in rococo gilt and rubbed frames on succulently mulberry walls. Though most of these represent the work of the renowned Australian artists of the Golden Age, some are from overseas. There's a Ford Madox Brown which was for a long time regarded as the Gallery's most valuable acquisition. 'A piece of monstrous bravura,' says the youthful, bearded teacher who, with his grey flock, has caught up with us.

There are some pleasing landscapes in the wrinklies' wing; Conrad Martens, Gruner, Heysen. They all seem spookily derivative, the artist's eye is looking backward at some fatherland which his heart will not farewell.

A grand new wing added to the Gallery in 1988 provides further space for travelling exhibitions, special displays, and a delightful small theatre, for films of art interest.

Finest experience of all for the visitor is a dreamlike wander among the Aboriginal paintings, unlike any other art, mysterious and beautiful. One has a disturbing perception that here is something coded, a message, a communication from an ancient past. But, alas, we cannot understand and go away deprived.

The Gallery has a good bookshop, a restaurant and coffee shop, and there are often great exhibitions from overseas and interstate.

We return to the city across the Domain, which still looks touchingly like the town common. Even the northwest path we follow meanders along serpentinely, and it is easy to discern where the ferny creek came tumbling down the vale in other times. Intensely green, with paternal trees grouped here and there about the edge, and an extremely scant population of statues, the Domain is simply and admirably an open stretch of grassland. It is the Sydney people's jealously-protected place for playing games, flying kites, state ceremonials, mass meetings and public speaking.

There's been a good deal of boring under the Domain for the railway, the Cahill Expressway and the extensive Domain parking station, but in latter years the only encroachments upon this treasured open space have been the Art Gallery, and the much later (1939–1943) Public and Mitchell Libraries.

Though history says that the Domain was opened to the public in 1888, it seems to have been free to them, perhaps on certain days, for long before that. B.C. Peck in his *Recollections of Sydney*, written about 1848, mentions Monday afternoons, between four and five, when the band of the 99th Regiment played lively polkas for the fashionables and the unfashionables. He describes charmingly dressed ladies, in their splendid carriages, 'with favoured gentlemen leaning on the doors to chat with these admired ones'. The unfashionable are 'settlers from the interior whose immense beards and moustaches, monkey jackets and cabbage-tree hats give them a Robinson Crusoe-like appearance'.

Some curious things have happened in the Domain. In 1820 there was a procession round and round, and then west to St Phillip's behind a band playing the Dead March from Saul. 'All, wearing crepe and suitably composed expressions, from the highest to the lowest, marched lamenting.' This was to mark the death of George III.

Here, too, occurred the first fatality connected with flight in Australia, The Great Balloon Catastrophe. This extraordinary event occurred in December 1856. For six weeks before the fatal date, the name on every tongue was that of Pierre Maigre, heroic French balloonist and shrewd PR man. His extensive advertising campaign whipped public interest to such intensity that when the day of his proposed ascent came, more than ten thousand people, including Governor Denison and his entourage, assembled in the Domain. It was the first recorded balloon flight in Australia, and the balloon itself, when inflated, almost reduced the crowd to hysteria. Sketches of it indicate that it was somewhat larger and more ornamental than the Taj Mahal, painted red and green, and intricately laced with golden ropes.

The balloon, thirty metres high and almost fifty metres in circumference, was inflated by the 'effluvium from a large iron furnace which burned stable straw saturated with spirits'. Naturally enough it refused to ascend, but dragged both basket and intrepid aeronaut painfully along the ground. The hysterical crowd, believing the whole thing a hoax, tore Pierre's hat from his head and shoved it in the furnace. Then they chased him across the Domain and into a cottage in Macquarie Street, where he took refuge in a locked scullery while the foremost members of a crowd of three thousand kicked in the windows and tried to set the roof shingles alight.

Meanwhile, those left at the Domain had found greater sport in burning the great balloon as well as the grandstand and chairs arranged for the show. 'It was a scene of unparalleled disorder and riot. No bigger *feu de joie* was ever seen in the colony.' During this riot young Thomas Downes was crushed when the crowd dragged down the balloon's 50 foot anchor poles. He is buried in historic Camperdown Cemetery, and a balloon is carved on his headstone.

There were colossal gatherings to protest against conscription in 1917, and even greater ones (judged in excess of 100,000) to protest against the Governor's dismissal of Premier J. Lang in 1931. 'From north, south, east and west they came, until it seemed that the whole of the city and suburbs had taken to the roads that led to the Domain . . . "Are the people of New South Wales going to say they will give a nominee governor powers which the British people took away from a hereditary king 300 years ago?" asked Mr Lang. With a response that could be heard through the wide expanse of the Domain, the citizens shouted their most pronounced "No!".'

On Sunday the Domain is the battleground of the public speakers, still noisily debating the same old issues of religion and politics, daylight-saving and gay rights. Occasionally some inspired daylight-saving lunatic, a Flat-Earther or a Sex-Abolitionist, will draw from the crowd a brisk cross-fire of good heckling. Things have never been different. In a *Sydney Morning Herald* editorial in 1888, we find the acid comment: 'All visitors to Sydney should spend a Sunday afternoon in the Outer Domain, if they would witness the fierce blaze of light a person can throw upon a subject of which he may know little.' Reaching the far side of the Domain, we walk along Hospital Road behind Parliament House and the Sydney Hospital. This used to be Richmond Terrace, one of the best parts of town.

So we come into Prince Albert Road, which curves around the Law Courts. On our left is the mighty bulk of St Mary's, the Roman Catholic Cathedral. Standing between the Domain and Hyde Park, St Mary's position can scarcely be bettered. Church authorities must be grateful

To think that this masterpiece came from the materialistic sixties!
And the worse seventies! You go away with your faith restored
in humankind.

On the other side of the great passage in the sandstone known as the
Argyle Cut.

Macquarie Street was commandeered by authority to be the grand street of the infant colony, a high place from which the posh could look down upon the rabble. Governor Macquarie designed it.

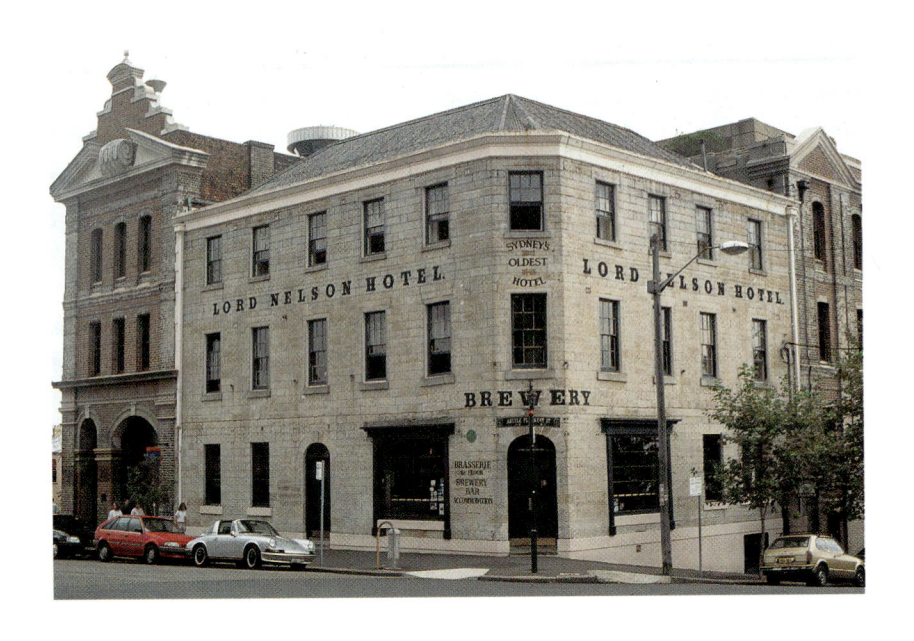

The austere Georgian Lord Nelson Hotel, licensed in 1838, was built by emancipee Billy Wells, who probably fought at Trafalgar.

Victoria Barracks are one of the finest examples of British imperial barracks. They were designed by George Barney, who also built Fort Denison and reconstructed Circular Quay.

The pampered, expensive terraces of Paddington are pretty to the point of romanticism. Several of the curly leafy streets will make you smile, they are so charming.

The Gap, where traditionally the sick and sorry jump to their deaths.

Bondi Beach is the most famous 1,000 metres of sand in Australia.

that Governor Macquarie did not heed the plaintive cries with which the original land grant was received by Father Joseph Therry, the builder of the first St Mary's. He had his heart set on a more fashionable site, on the Rocks ridge, but found himself cheek by jowl with convict barracks, hospital and racecourse, not to mention the ramshackle slum of shanties and bothies already clustering around the brickfields and potteries to the south.

Macquarie (a Mason and Protestant) laid the foundation stone, and slowly, over a period of thirty years, the huge Gothic church arose. It was paid for by the city's Catholics, mostly ex-convicts and poor Irish migrants, and completed in 1837. Twenty-eight years later, in 1865, St Mary's burned to the ground, in a roaring blaze which was seen thirty-two kilometres out to sea 'like God's own pillar of fire before the Israelites'. The temporary wooden cathedral which replaced it also was destroyed by fire. A third brick building was demolished when the present cathedral was opened in 1882.

It is an astonishing church for what was then a tiny remote city; built in thirteenth-century style and much larger than many of the European cathedrals. Its length is 107 metres, its width 39 metres and its height more than 46 metres. Its nave is over 30 metres high. It is said that when the cathedral was built, nothing of its style and magnitude had been attempted for two centuries. Certainly nothing resembling it is likely to be built again.

St Mary's possesses one of Sydney's ten belltowers. The last time its peal of eight bells crashed out over the city in the famous and complex Grandsire Triples was during a Papal visit.

While St Mary's tradition and beauty makes it worth visiting, I find the crypt the more unusual and fascinating feature. It is open to the public during office hours, and there is usually a guided tour the first Sunday of each month. In the floor of the crypt Australia's largest mosaic makes a dazzling pathway to the sanctuary. It is contrived in the angelically pure blues, greens and scarlets of antique Celtic enamelwork. One is dumbfounded that such a treasure should be in a crypt though the latter is, in truth, as vast and impressive as many a church. Upon closer scrutiny we can distinguish in the jewelled stone a chain of motifs depicting the six days of Creation.

This masterpiece was the work of Peter Melocco, who came to Australia as a migrant in 1908. The mosaic was completed in 1961, the year of this quiet, slight genius's death. We have already noted the Tasman Map on the floor of the Mitchell wing of the State Library, but the crypt was Peter Melocco's greatest gift to Sydney.

We leave St Mary's, and cross the road to Hyde Park. We rest near the Archibald Fountain where the spray can waft over a heated face. All is green and heavily foliaged. The birds are somnolent – into the fountain, a desultory shake of the wings and back to a snooze on Apollo's head.

Before us, a bright point in the sky, is the golden crow's-nest of Sydney Tower, the elegant addition to Sydney's classic symbols, the Bridge and the Opera House. It is misnamed, being not a tower but an attenuated spire, rising out of Centrepoint, a vast shopping centre with almost 200 specialty shops and a complex of subterranean tunnels that lead to other fashionable emporia.

At a little over 300 metres, Sydney Tower is the highest city observation point in Australia and (although it must surely be overtaken any minute) the tallest in the Southern Hemisphere. For an unsurpassable view, on a cloudless day extending from the Blue Mountains to Palm Beach and beyond, you may take a two-level lift, travelling at an unspeakable 70-odd metres per second. Of course there are stairways as well. At the top you will find the observation deck, two restaurants and a conference chamber. One of the restaurants is revolving, somewhat unnnerving, I always think, as you have no sooner sussed out the whereabouts of the Ladies than it vanishes on its endless round.

'You wouldn't get me up that thing,' observes a nearby woman, placidly injuring a pigeon's digestion with fragments of pizza.

'Why not?'

'Bet it sways.'

A momentary vision of that fragile stem juddering before a brisk southerly makes one judder oneself. But of course that never happens.

The public relations department of Centrepoint know why, and we can scarcely improve on their explanation. The golden pod and the almost invisible telecommunications antennas weighing close to 2,000 tonnes are locked to the top of the spire. The latter is not one immensely high, thin structure, but is composed of forty-six separate units, anchored to the roof of Centrepoint with a spiderweb of steel cables. But tall structures, natural or manmade, are of their nature flexible, so how does Sydney Tower differ? Most ingeniously. A vast water tank containing 162,000 litres, we are told, hangs in suspension in the turret. It moves to the same frequency as the tower, but out of phase.

'Could you say the slosh of the water minimises any sway?'

'Well, we might put it another way ...'

The aerial delicacy of Sydney Tower, its bold display of imaginative engineering makes one feel that here is the forerunner of a different architecture, a futuristic architecture springing from the inconceivable technology of the third millennium, as different from our largely rectangular Sydney as that Sydney is different from Greenway's dignified, Quakerish Georgian.

THE EASTERN SUBURBS

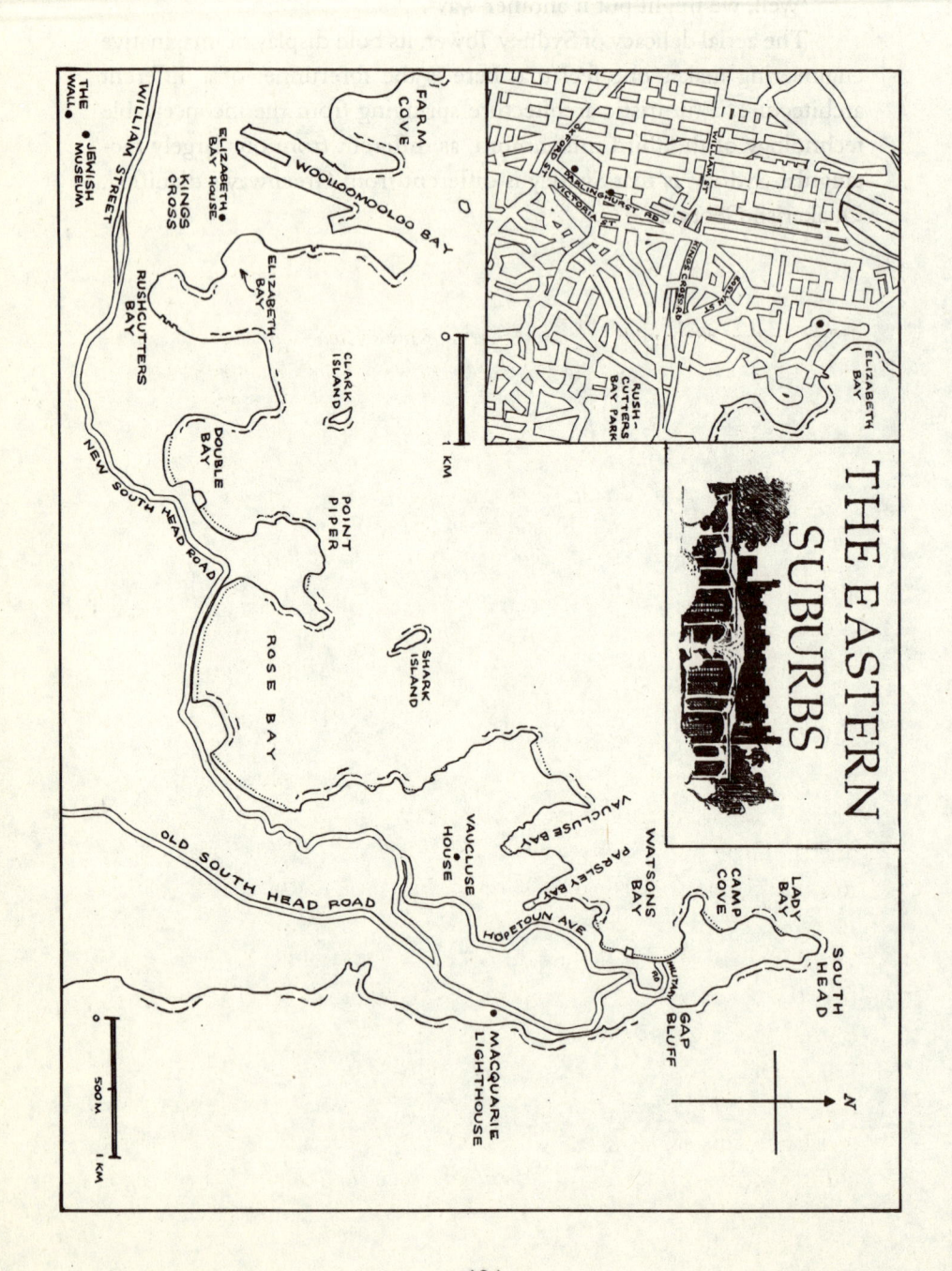

CHAPTER 5

WILLIAM STREET TO SOUTH HEAD

What are they doing with William Street? – King's Cross, wicked or wonderful? – the aristocratic opportunists – battle of Victoria Street – a mysterious disappearance – Elizabeth Bay House – the great wall of Darlinghurst – death of a gentleman murderer – the Jewish Museum – birds of yesteryear – manorial houses – Ensign Piper, prince of the Point – a man who walked on water – Did the Spanish discover Australia? – Vaucluse House – father of the constitution – Macquarie Light.

EARLY in Sydney's story, as we have seen, the Tank Stream, as by a stroke of Divine propriety, separated the sheep from the goats. On the east side Phillip and his officers erected their tents and little dwellings. Convicts and troops were disposed to the west.

As the city grew, things remained thus. The rich, noble or privileged built their sumptuous mansions ever more and more to the east. Not for them the thrombotic lanes smelling of gaspipes and capricious drains. Their lanes were leafy, bordered with stone walls and rambler roses. And, just as the very old slums of Sydney, the Rocks, for example, show a certain prenatal influence from St Giles and other fearful London rookeries that sheltered their builders in youth, so do the status suburbs between King's Cross and South Head display the well-bred Englishry of an earlier time.

Some of these incongruously English houses, marooned by the floodtide of highrise development, but saved by the enchanted word 'heritage', still stand beneath their mossy slate roofs and barleysugar chimneypots with an air of aristocratic inconsequence. Others, even nobler in style, went down like ninepins before armies of backpackers or survive shamefaced under false ceilings and chipboard partitions as last-stand residentials for the indigent or done-for.

The great Crown grants were made, the splendid houses built, in the early nineteenth century. While the residents of western Sydney, fierce as a nest of bull ants, fought and sued and badmouthed each other in the public prints, 'ran away to the woods', drowned themselves, promised their assigned servants 'short shrift and a bloody shroud', life in the wealthy east went on as though Mayfair were but a short drive from Darling Point. Ladies wearing sashes under their armpits sat beside bow windows reading *The Mysteries of Udolpho*, or *Orphan of the Rhine*, both prodigiously horrid. They sang Moore's Irish melodies, gossiped about that cosseted barbarian, Lord Byron, and deplored the vile London crowds that pelted horse-dung at the unpopular Prince Regent. Wearing costly bonnets, they attended refined entertainments, escorted by young gentlemen of the military persuasion.

Under the surface of the good life, of course, there was a subfusc band of unprincipled rapacity and gross materialism. It was a time of unparalleled opportunity for the audacious. The portraits of that time tell the story. We ponder the braggadocio of the side-whiskers, the truculently-lifted chins above tall stocks, the foxy, self-seeking something that peers out of those supercilious Regency eyes. They are successful opportunists all, these men, from John Macarthur with his uniformed train of convicts, to blondish barmy Captain Piper, who nevertheless parlayed a post worth £400 into a taxfree £4,000 a year. Of all these colonial gentlemen, only poor Governor Macquarie, grown old, with few teeth and scant brindled hair looks exactly what he was, a worn-out, good old Jock, with no friends at Court. In a word, a failure.

In the old days, it was as though a briar hedge grew up around the eastern marine suburbs, as in the story of the *Sleeping Beauty*. They were insulated from the vigorous, squalid Sydney without. Enclaves of this genteel, drowsy world still exist. All the more astonishing, then, that the very gateway of the envied eastern suburbs is King's Cross, frightful, wonderful, infamous, beloved, a place so small that on the map it takes up very little space. In fact, it is difficult to say just where King's Cross is. Teetering on a cliff above Woolloomooloo? A little to the left of ladylike Elizabeth Bay? Somewhere near the Fleet Base, anyway, Garden Island and all that Navy whatnot.

The approach to King's Cross, the unlikely gateway, is ambiguous.

For there's no doubt that William Street has something upsetting about it. What was it meant to be? It is a street of majestic width, preposterous for Sydney, a city mostly at home with roads both narrow-gutted and cantankerous. The fact that they named it for the King of the time must mean something. It is sadly true that William IV was called Silly Billy by his loved ones and had a head shaped remarkably like a tea caddy. Still, he was the monarch. William Street was therefore significant, designed to be an imposing boulevard with a vista at the end – an obelisk, a war memorial, even a sweep of summer sky. Instead it is traffic jammed, lined with a hodge podge of buildings that somehow contrive always to look uncomfortable and terminates in a perpendicular Coca-Cola sign as big as a cow paddock.

Town planners have been nagging away at William Street since convicts hacked it out in 1831 and they are at it again. Now there's a traffic tunnel to be put underneath it, to link up with Park Street and Darling Harbour. This is not a new idea. During the large upheavals of the 1970s, such a tunnel was a part of the City Council's Strategic Plan. Ten years later the familiar words were heard: 'Planning guidelines must be reviewed. The scale of vision has been reduced by the economic climate.'

The old William Street, horse or steam tram William Street, was not respectable. It was coarse and colourful, intimately connected with dockside Woolloomooloo, and the first 'bit o' town' for seamen who put up in lousy lodging-houses in Bourke, Riley and Forbes Streets. The poet Kenneth Slessor, who for years lived in King's Cross, 'eating, sleeping, loving, arguing, sausage-frying and head-scratching in a small room of stucco ... seven storeys higher than the top of William Street' speaks of such a seaman.

> ... walking down William Street,
> with a tin trunk and a five pound note
> Looking for a place to eat,
> And a peajacket the colour of a shark's behind
> That a Jew might buy in the morning.

That old William Street had a smell of its own, frying hamburgers, frangipani, sun on dust and the faintest flavour of mudflats from the 'Loo Bay. Now if the wind is easterly, you get a blast of cardamom, coriander and marihuana from the Cross.

Here is Darlinghurst Ridge, surprisingly and abruptly high. An abrasive wind whips along Darlinghurst Road, full of grit and crust-brown leaves, and one is reminded that it was the wind that first brought settlement to this osseous ridge. Here, some 40 metres above sea level, were the important windmills.

During Sydney's first seven years, the sparse grain harvests were ground to flour by convicts 'marching like mules about a capstan, their eyes gummed up by the bran'. The millstones, which had come with the First Fleet, were said to have ended as tombstones in the Town Hall graveyard; they may still be in existence, in some lost cemetery. The first windmill arrived with Captain John Hunter in 1785, when he returned to the colony as its second Governor.

That windmill took ten minutes to grind a bushel of corn. Even when a more efficient mill was erected, people still had to queue all night to have their corn ground, and we have a resentful note from Alexander Sawdrey, aged twelve at the time, who was left in the queue while his papa, a small George Street grocer, righteously went to see if the taverns in the Rocks were as disreputable as people said. 'Papa arrived home to sermons and soda water, I stiff with cold, during eleven hours of waiting outside the mill, was indisposed four days with affliction in gizzard. Mama very sullen.'

From the mid-1820s, high Darlinghurst Ridge bore five or six windmills. Later there were others at Paddington and Waverley. Sketches show these Darlinghurst windmills gaily spinning, a frivolous ornamentation to the almost bare hogback. Some seem very substantial, perhaps built of stone. Others are rickety wooden structures perched on posts like dovecots, supported by splayed legs and reached by crazy stairways. Their oak shingle roofs were, we are told, painted bright blue.

The Cross seems mostly to have had the shouting vitality of the social outsider. Razor gangsters, conmen, beggars, female driftwood, writers, actors, great painters like William Dobell, revered icons like Mary Gilmore, saints such as the people who run the Wayside Chapel, weirdos like the lady who set up house in a stormwater drain – all have lived, and live there, mostly contemporaneously.

'But is it dangerous?' a visitor asks a tourist courier. Well, taxi drivers readily go there, although there are several streets in Sydney where they won't drive at night. Any place where drugs are used and traded has its dangerous spots, dark lanes and deep doorways particularly. There's no denying King's Cross has its cardboard castles and dumpstervilles, but on the other hand there are wonderful old streets like Victoria Street and Macleay Street, which have survived all their battles.

But you may well feel a faint frisson in the evenings when all the night folk are awake, the air is full of barbaric yawping and the ghoulish light of neons halates the trees and the bald bumpy heads and thumb-tacked noses of the fashionable.

Though no longer 'Sydney's entertainment centre' – during the R&R boom from 1967 it was 'south-east Asia's entertainment centre' – it is a weird, electric place by night, exorbitant, often as bent as a bicycle wheel, offering venal and dubious pleasures as well as four-cornered ones. It swims out of the dusk like a blob of spilled oil, all rainbows and reflections, and gamesome groups of middle-aged tourists noosed with cameras, excitedly speculating whether the epicene person in an exoskeleton of painted leather is a drag queen of the new cosmic variety.

Upon these aliens, the austerely-clad old voluptuary spidering in the coffee bar smiles his abstracted scholar's smile; the adolescent prostitute heaves up her furry eyelashes and looks right through them. The zonked boy sitting on his kidneys beside the El Alamein Fountain, soaked with the spray, does not even glance their way as they boldly take his picture for a souvenir.

Well, some love it, some hate it. It is true that hardcore 'official' King's Cross is a formula for grossness. But somehow the place is never self-deceiving. It knows what it is and pretends to nothing. Its unmistakable message is: 'If you don't like it, rack off.'

King's Cross in the daytime is something entirely different. One sees how minikin the place really is. The charm of Darlinghurst Road, heart of the Cross, is that it is always sunny; it has a fortunate northeastern lie. The sunshine lends an innocence to the gaiety and brightness always present. There's a great smell of roasting coffee, the patisseries are full of fresh cakes, tiny shop windows gape with the moist maculated mouths of orchids. A Hare Krishna monk floats past, suspended in a dozen metres of apricot cotton, shaven head rimmed in metal down.

In the daytime, one sees that King's Cross is truly a village, one of the several sewn indistinguishably edge to edge in the municipal ward of Fitzroy. This particular village, already well-established when the intersection of five streets was officially named Queen's Cross in 1897, picked up its present name when the Cross was renamed to honour King Edward VII in 1905. The villagers have always been there, housewives buying food, children marching off to school, pensioners of various kinds dawdling in the sun. In this characteristic lies much of the charm of the Cross, an ordinariness and continuity which the residents themselves have fiercely championed during the many attempts at developing, facelifting, and cleaning up.

The most notorious battle was that of Victoria Street in the 1970s, so to Victoria Street we must go to view it in its triumph. When the writer first saw it, it seemed the saddest street in the city, fine townhouses frowsy, their front steps heaped with dried leaves, fast food cartons, dead newspapers; trees neglected or chainsawed; the houses interspersed with curry establishments; laundromats; dark doorways plastered with nudie photographs left over from R&R days; demolition hoardings everywhere. Even so, the dignity of Victoria Street was plain to see. It was a carriage road, if ever we saw one, handsomely proportioned, sweeping from Oxford Street in the south to dwindle into doglegged lanes above the Potts Point escarpment.

Most of the old houses had long left behind their time of glory; they had travelled down that *via crucis* of the grand mansion, through the humiliating days when the two old remaining family members rented out the front bedrooms to paying guests, to the ultimate mould and rot of the cheap boarding house.

'They're going to knock us down and build skyscrapers,' said a passing woman. 'But some have been glad to sell, get out, buy a bungalow. You can get through that French window there if you want a squiz,' she added obligingly. Behind the smashed French window was a cavernous drawing room cold as death, a ceiling six metres high seemingly painted with flower clusters, which turned out to be fragments of hamburger or chiko roll hurled presumably by the same tenants who had lit small fires on the priceless kauri floor. An armchair spewed kapok beside the gap where the marble fireplace had been ripped out. Something in the armchair awoke with a snort.

'You get out. This is MY squat. Go find your own!'

Many of the squatters were destitute or on the run. Others more responsible were placed in the doomed houses by the Builders Labourers Federation, under the Napoleonic leadership of Jack Mundey, whom we first met saving the Rocks. But in spite of the

Federation's Green Ban on Victoria Street, the developers were resolute. Early one morning in 1974 they sent in a team of toughs armed with sledgehammers and iron bars to clear out the squatters, defenders, protestors, tear down the barricades, block the street to police vehicles. Many squatters took fright at this time.

King's Cross lovingly recalls this and several other highly publicised Victoria Street battles. It must have seemed a great lark until the middle of 1975 when the outspoken newspaperwoman Juanita Nielsen, one of the last two residents of Victoria Street, disappeared. Perhaps it was a mismanaged abduction for she was heiress to one of Sydney's great mercantile fortunes. More likely it was plain murder, to shut her up. Her body has never been found, nor the mystery solved.

At the Cross, Mrs Neilsen is regarded as a martyr, for her sad fate abruptly halted all the melodramatic nonsense. The plans for the updating of Victoria Street quietly vanished. The State Government bought the site and all but ten of the condemned houses were marked for immediate restoration. They stand today, many, of course, reincarnated as restaurants, clubs or bijou hotels, but in all ways as charming as ever. Flights of ancient stone stairs still descend unexpectedly into the crowded glens of Woolloomooloo; the flame trees bloom at the northern end on the doorstep of Potts Point.

If colonial architecture of the wealthy kind is your interest, there are still many wonderful houses to be seen in the vicinity of the Cross. In Darling Point, for instance, Lindesay, Carthona, St Vincent's College (not Hospital) where five Irish Sisters of Charity began to care for the sick in 1838. It is said they brought with them a crucifix with a black Christ because they believed all Australians were black. Don't believe it. The Irish Church was sending out priests to New South Wales forty years before that date and was well-informed. Besides, it is obvious that the Sisters were bright as buttons; look at the superb site they chose for their foundation. Still, a nice story and one of many to be read with pleasure in the several books published about Sydney's historic houses.

If time is short settle for Elizabeth Bay House. In fact, if you have only a day or two in Sydney, pick up the Sydney Explorer Bus almost anywhere and be driven straight to this perfect treat of a William IV home. Its magnificent gardens have long gone, but in itself it is a livable, graceful house that escaped death by neglect by the skin of its teeth. Because of its name you'd think it would be in Elizabeth Bay Road, but it isn't. You could approach from Macleay Street, but the lovely old house is really in a kind of cul-de-sac named Onslow Place. All of this apparent disorder indicates the immensity of the old Macleay Estate.

Alexander Macleay was a Highland gentleman of flashing eye and ornate nostril; like John Macarthur he modelled himself on the republican Romans. Though he had served Britain in various governmental posts, his heart was in science. He was a member of the Linnean Society from the sixth year of its existence, his special interest being entomology, closely followed by ornithology. He came to the colony in 1826 at a somewhat advanced age for a colonist. He served as Colonial Secretary, and then Speaker in the first representative Legislative Council until his retirement.

He said himself that his grant of 23 hectares was the finest on Darlinghurst Ridge, and it was characteristic of him that he spent nine years designing and planting his garden before building the house. Though not a rich man he imported rare plants and trees from China, Brazil and Africa. From the exquisite paintings by his friend Conrad Martens we can see that the garden was justly described as a botanist's paradise.

Macleay borrowed heavily to build Elizabeth Bay House, designed by John Verge and described as 'quite the finest house in the Colony'. Newspapers described its style as Grecian Revival, though actually the projected row of Palladian pillars across the front façade was never installed. There were, naturally, no bathrooms, but the first two flushing toilets in the Australian colonies astonished all observers. No expense was spared, although Macleay's originally highly productive investments in sheep properties quickly diminished in value. His daughter Fanny worried 'Where are the revenues to come from?' and worried even more as her father marched ever closer to bankruptcy and the huge staff required to keep the mansion in order were one by one dismissed. The unmarried daughters found themselves doing the housework. Fanny wrote to her brother, himself a nabob in Cuba, 'Very often I wish myself in a bark hut. At least I should not be striving to keep up an appearance of respectability.'

Alexander Macleay held on to his gardens as long as possible, though he had to auction part of his demesne to pay his debts. Yet the gardens were still wondrous enough in the reign of Alexander's son, William Sharp Macleay, to be visited by every important person who came to Sydney. There, for instance, the naturalist Thomas Huxley proposed to his future wife Henrietta Heythorn. William Sharp was the rich brother to whom poor Fanny complained. He was a friend of Cuvier and Darwin, and eventually a trustee of the Australian Museum of which his father was first president. Together with another William, Sir William John Macleay, nephew of Alexander, and an explorer, ichthyologist and MP, William Sharp added greatly to Alexander's natural history collection. In 1890 Sir William John left this priceless collection to Sydney University, where it can be inspected by the public.

Alexander Macleay had seventeen children, and it would be gratifying to know that Elizabeth Bay was named for his wife, the enduring Eliza. But it was not. Young Lachlan Macquarie named the charming bay after his mother during a picnic held there on his birthday.

When in lieu of his father's debts, William Sharp Macleay took over the house in 1845, he sold its furnishings to the interior decorators of the new Government House for £300. Thus from the inventory, and remaining pieces of furniture, the 1970s restorers of Elizabeth Bay House were able to replicate the style of its heyday with remarkable exactitude. From 1911 when the house passed out of the hands of the Macleays and their kin by marriage, the Macarthurs, its history was unstable and usually deplorable. It was squashed by dire unit blocks, partly demolished, vandalised, tarted up for weddings and social gatherings, and finally divided into no fewer than fifteen studio flats. One of these was occupied briefly by the present writer. The miniscule room with its immensely high ceiling gave one the feeling of living in a chimney; the entire house was a twilit semi-boarded-up warren that smelt of decay, drains and tomcats.

But today the noble portico, its domed drawing room; the alcoves for priceless bijouterie, cedar joinery, the lantern-lit oval staircase down which the Macleay daughters must have swept in their youth and beauty for the frequent balls and banquets, but above all the house's abiding air of wealth, good taste and leisure – all these features never fail to please thousands and thousands of visitors. Don't miss it.

Now you could wander down the hill to Rushcutters Bay and its complex of parks and sportsgrounds, not to mention the first place where convicts and Aborigines met in conflict. Otherwise, let us walk on to what is probably Sydney's most menacing stone wall. There are, of course, walls and walls and not every one makes a statement. But this one does. It looms, threatens, looks daggers. It defies you to even try to get inside. Which is perverse, as it was erected expressly to keep people from getting outside.

This formidable wall is a prison façade. It was built mostly because of Governor Macquarie's inability to please the cranky commissioner sent by the British Government in 1819 to report on conditions in New South Wales. Commissioner Bigge, who so effectively pulled the plug on Macquarie's city-building ambitions, severely criticised the elderly Scot's 'unfortunate propensity to ornament and architectural effect'. He announced that what Sydney needed was not a model school, or a cathedral, but a new gaol. It should be near the South Head Road, he said – that is to say, on the fringe of civilisation. We call it Old South Head Road now, but then it was the only one.

This 'new gaol' is Darlinghurst Gaol, now largely a training centre for TAFE (Technical and Further Education). As our favourite busybody and journal writer Louisa Anne Meredith said of Sydney in the 1840s, 'no single building of durability stands that has not something to do with convicts'. Thus convicts not only occupied this dread fortress, but built it. It has the unmistakeable look of stone quarried, worked, carried, put in place by hungry wretches, many in irons, under the tyranny of savage overseers. It also has the air of a building determined to last five hundred years.

However, the wall is the oldest part, dating from 1822, and is so ponderous it might well have satisfied poor Macquarie's yearning for grandeur. Most of the buildings within were constructed from 1822 to 1885 under a number of architects beginning with Francis Greenway. The redoubtable entrance, with its coat of arms and medieval towers and portcullis was built by free men.

The interior is pragmatic and scarcely worth seeing, so unimaginative and dull has the intermittent renovation been – though one does get a faint feeling of atmosphere in the old morgue, now the switchroom, and the gallows yard where you find the toilets. Hanging in semi-privacy actually came quite late in the prison's long history. As we already know, Victorian and pre-Victorian opinion about public executions differed from our own. They were believed by authority (and the churches) to be decidedly edifying.

Just outside the gaol gates is a dusty plot of grass where Sydney folklore says the gibbet used to stand. Some celebrated felons were disjointed here, including Frank Gardiner, John Dunn and other bushrangers, but the most interesting must surely have been Captain John Knatchbull, RN, a gentleman of good family and a remote connection of Jane Austen's, who brought a versatile black sheep's career to a smashing climax when he walloped a widowed shopkeeping lady with a tomahawk. 'The devil made me do it,' he maintained. But he was really after her rumoured savings, which he intended should pay for his wedding and set him up in business.

The murder was characteristic not only of his psychopathic concentration on his own immediate needs but of his careless and finally fatal arrogance. There are well-documented accounts of this man's career and trial. The latter is of peculiar interest to a modern reader. Although the McNaghten Rules had not yet 'penetrated the fastnesses of the legal processes' of remote Sydney in 1844. Knatchbull's defender, the dazzling albino barrister Robert Lowe, quoted the McNaghten case of 1843, and did indeed make a plea of moral insanity, the first time it had happened in a British court.

Lowe's defence was unsuccessful, and Knatchbull's execution beside the Darlinghurst Gaol gates attracted the largest mob of thrilled sightseers ever known in a city already famous for the ghoulish curiosity of its populace. The weeks before the hanging had been marked by public processions of 'the lower-class, carrying black flags marked with death's heads, who feared that because of the accused's higher station, he would be reprieved. Equal punishment for high and low was their cry.'

The Sydney newspapers covered the hanging to 'the last light quivering of the body', albeit adopting a righteous and hectoring tone towards the 110,000 spectators who stood for hours in the February heat of that early morning, pressing against the chain which held them at a distance from the gallows, and chiacking the mounted police who patrolled the barrier.

Knatchbull wore a new suit of fine black broadcloth, reputedly a gift from Lady Gipps, the wife of the Governor, so that he could die like a gentleman and not let the side down. He didn't. He had been converted to religion some time prior to his execution, and conducted himself with dignity, being 'launched into another world with a noble and fervent prayer trembling on his lips'. The crowd was shocked into a dismayed silence, and dispersed quickly and quietly.

Robert Lowe, after a brilliant legal and political career in New

South Wales, returned to England in 1850 to take up a position as leader-writer on *The Times*. He had a notable career in the House of Commons, held several ministerial posts, and was Chancellor of the Exchequer under Gladstone. He was created Viscount Sherbrooke and took his seat in the House of Lords, dying in 1892 at the age of eighty-one.

Darlinghurst Courthouse, plainly part of the same complex, was built about the same time as the gaol. The central Court is dated 1836, but the lateral Courts are 1884–88. The High Court at the west is circa 1922.

Almost opposite the Gaol, in Darlinghurst Road, stands the Jewish Museum, covering the history of adherents of the faith from the First Fleet, when a Jewish clerk arrived on the ship *Scarborough*. There are many mementoes of the Holocaust and occasionally a survivor of that fearful period to show you around. But don't think a visit will leave you only with sadness; there are many richly evocative things to see and hear as well.

Returning to King's Cross we decide to be spendthrifts and take a taxi. Most taxi drivers are fairly knowledgeable unless you're unfortunate enough (as happens occasionally in this multicultural city) to come across the man who arrived from Afghanistan only last week.

First to Rushcutters Bay, a sheltered, shallow bay, devoted to the navy, prestigious yacht clubs and marinas, its shores so lavishly endowed with green spaces it is difficult to see where one ends and the next begins. Sharp-eyed as we are, we note that where demolition or rebuilding is proceeding, perfect avalanches of sand cascade or fountain before the mighty machines, and recall how Darlinghurst Ridge was once an almost impassable wall of dunes.

The existence of the complex of parks, which run past Darling Point and Edgecliff, down a precipitous gully and deep into Paddington, is due to the fact that almost all the land below the dunes was estuarine swamp. The swamps were fringed with mangroves and overgrown with rushes, which from the earliest days provided cottage thatch. The entire locality was regarded as wasteland and development eastwards was very slow indeed until Chinese market gardeners contrived to drain the marsh, elevate little islands here and there and plant vegetables. In the earlies the only access was by boat and it was by boat that several convict rushcutters were sent, in May 1786.

Two of these were speared by Aborigines. William Okey and Sam

Davis were the first recorded white men to be killed thus. Captain Phillip, who had been much struck by the apparently gentle nature of the black fays, who were one moment visible in the bush about his settlement then gone like shadows, investigated the killings and said: 'The first injury had been offered by the unfortunate men. They had been seen with a canoe, which they had taken from one of the fishing places.'

In recent years this first tragedy has been sensationalised – the convicts seizing and raping the women, black warriors rushing out of the bush in fury, etc. In fact nothing of the sort happened. One simply must believe Captain Phillip, so pragmatic, dour and exact in his record of events that one could kick him.

At Rushcutters, too, occurred that touching incident, when the Aborigines, observing a convict being flogged for stealing some of their fishing-gear, burst into tears of compassion and the woman whose tackle had been stolen physically attacked the flogger.

The Aborigines were so little feared by the Europeans that free settlers, enchanted by an astonishing new countryside, wandered at will along these shores. Like most educated people in those days they drew and painted, and we have watercolours of mangrove bitterns, egrets perched in treehouses of sticks, countless ducks, darters, and in their season migratory whimbrels and godwits. Alas, nothing to be seen now but gulls and the occasional meditating pelican. But wait, as we alight at Darling Point in order to see the fine houses, what should whizz overhead but a large group of ibis. This causes slight consternation, as they are not native ibis but unmistakeably Egyptian, straight off a tomb. How? What? Truly? The truth is that these Egyptian ibis belong to Taronga Park Zoo but spend their days freeflying, going home only for supper and a trouble-free night.

Darling Point is the snubbed-off promontory between Rushcutters Bay and Double Bay. There are few places in Sydney where you may see so many well-preserved old mansions. Take any road on your left. They all meet and meander around the point. Darling Point began as a heavily wooded peninsula called Yarradabbi. In the 1830s when the foresters began to strip the bush, erosion was so great that the Surveyor-General, Major Thomas Mitchell, suggested that the best way to preserve this pretty point would be to subdivide it. Mitchell was one of the first residents of Darling Point, and his splendid house, Carthona, where he reared his family of twelve children, is still in fine condition. Major

Mitchell modelled his home on a famous house near Lake Windermere and carved much of the ornamental stonework himself. He was also a literary man and translated Portuguese poetry for relaxation.

His was a versatile and idiosyncratic personality. He is described as being of 'dire aspect', but I trust that is a misprint for 'dour'. He surveyed the battlefields of the Peninsular War and is credited with working out Wellington's lines of defence. In Australia he was a distinguished explorer, and, as we have seen, Surveyor-General. He was pretty peppery, and fought a duel with Sir Stuart Donaldson, who was destined to become, briefly, the first Premier of NSW under constitutional government. The duel was fought in what is now Centennial Park. Donaldson had accused Mitchell of wasting public money, and Mitchell very properly put a bullet through his enemy's silk hat.

Thomas Mitchell, worthy gentleman, has been memorialised in many ways, but my favourite is the exquisitely pretty cockatoo, which comes in delicate shades of pink and is called the Major Mitchell. Not far away from Carthona is Lindesay, built in 1834, battlemented and parapeted, with octagonal chimneys. The Mitchell family lived here whilst Carthona was being built, and it is usually considered the first house on the point. Fortunately it was presented to the National Trust in 1963 and has been lovingly restored. The Trust follows its admirable custom of allowing certain exhibitions and displays to be held in this historic house.

Other elegant and historic old buildings you may care to see from the road are: Bishopscourt, Greenoaks Avenue, the residence of the Archbishop of Sydney, which was built in 1847 for Thomas Sutcliffe Mort; The Octagon, Octagon Road, said to have been built as a guardhouse and later occupied by Henry Gilbert Smith, the Father of Manly; St Mark's Church, as well as the rectory and cottage close by. The church was the work of a very young Edmund Blacket, possibly his first design in Australia. Though the tower was not added until 1875 (the gold rushes having robbed the builders of suitable labourers), the church always was a landmark, standing upon its high ridge like a sentinel. It was described in the 1870s as 'a perfect toy of a church, [which] sits as plumply on its stone mound as a castle, done in white sugar, on a twelfth night cake'.

To the east of Darling Point is Double Bay, famous for fabulous shopping. Some people call it Double Pay, but you don't have to believe everything you hear. By car one seems to approach it through lagoons of jacaranda bloom and the occasional bauhinia like a coral cloud. It appears always to have been a pretty place. In 1868 the governor of the time tried to find some Aborigines to show to the horrid young Duke of Edinburgh, who was visiting, and the only place where he could find enough tribesmen to give an exhibition of boomerang throwing was at Double Bay. The last Cadigal camp is supposed to have been here, though for many years pockets of the detribalised continued to live around the fertile shores.

Double Bay is peculiarly associated with the jacaranda. One of its earliest professional gardeners successfully acclimatised the exquisite Brazilian, the blooms of which make so frequent a chalky lavender smudge upon the Sydney landscape that many Australians think the tree a native. Michael Guilfoyle came to Australia as gardener for Thomas Mort, but in 1851 he established his own large nursery at the corner of Ocean Avenue. For over twenty years Guilfoyle imported and grew exotic plants. Tradition says we are also indebted to him for the ubiquitous frangipani. One of Guilfoyle's sons became director of the Melbourne Botanic Gardens in 1878. Michael Guilfoyle himself has an avenue in Double Bay named for him, but every jacaranda that blesses out streets and gardens is his memorial.

On its eastern side, Double Bay is bounded by the peninsula of Point Piper. From the Harbour, the point is regrettably overbuilt; it resembles a settlement of the wild bees that build their combs in crannies of the rock. And yet, as one walks the long twisting roads, one is conscious of its nostalgic air. It has not grown mummified with age; there is a gentle rosy lustre still. By some magic a little of the original bush still remains in pockets here and there. Walk along Wolseley Road from New South Head Road, and descend the stairs into Duff Reserve. Here are red gums and stringybarks that were growing when Captain John Piper, 'the great buck, prince of hosts, leader of the world of fashion' built here his grand, double-domed house in 1820.

Lovable Piper looks a shade goofy in his portraits, but he is undeniably fashionable, for his head sits in an extremely high stock as an egg sits in an eggcup. Arriving in 1791 as a poor, eighteen-year-old ensign, John Piper commenced one of those spectacular colonial careers so frequent in the early history of New South Wales. Already, though so youthful, he had a curious distinction. He was the first Englishman to go beyond the Great Wall of China. (He was actually a Scotsman.) In 1814, he became Naval Officer of the port; in effect he was controller of shipping and collector of customs and harbour dues. On the government revenues he collected, he was allowed a commission of five per cent. Very shortly he was immensely rich, and having the temperament of a doge, proceeded to live like one.

His house on Point Piper, Henrietta Villa, must have been magnificent. In so many early watercolours it floats, insubstantial as a dragonfly's wing, against the hanging woods. Before it is the dark-foliaged orangery, and behind it 'a most excellent garden which supplies an abundance of the choicest fruits, peaches, apricots and nectarines and every other species'.

It is amusing to see that this splendid garden was enclosed with clipped hedges in the form of a St Andrew's cross. The banqueting room, which lay under one of the impressive domes, was also in the form of this cross, representative of Captain Piper's distant homeland.

Henrietta Villa was the scene of imperial entertainments, balls, picnics, dazzling fetes of all kinds. The estate carried a hundred servants, a stable of racehorses and a perfect army of spongers. It must have been a dreary day for social Sydney when in 1825 Governor Darling, the martinet, had Piper's official accounts examined, to find that the gay cavalier had been not dishonest, but negligent and imprudent.

He was dismissed from his post and shortly left the primrose fields for ever. In grave financial difficulties, Piper lost his wonderful home and subsequently his estate. A glance at the map of modern Sydney shows the extent of his property, the value of which today would be incalculable. It was bounded by William Street, Double Bay, Ocean Street, Jersey Road to Oxford Street, Old South Head Road as far as Rose Bay. The world being thus so cruel to 'the Prince of Australia', he determined to leave it in a fitting manner. He had his boatmen row him out to the middle of the Harbour, and having commanded his piper to play a lament, he jumped overboard. What a shame that this characteristically theatrical scene was ruined by humble human affection! His boatmen, like everyone else except Governor Darling, loved him dearly. They fished him out, tipped the seawater out of him, and to the strains of a rousing strathspey, rowed him back to safety and ruin.

Piper retired to a little pastoral property near Bathurst, but through extravagance lost this as well. He died in poverty in 1851. His magnificent villa survived him only a few years. It was demolished in the 1850s to be replaced by an even grander home, Woollahra House. This mansion was demolished in 1929.

In spite of a sad jungle of apartment buildings, Point Piper has a dry sweetness. Very clearly one hears the voice of the past – a William IV and Victorian past. The gardens are still beautiful, with a nostalgic sigh for the wilful English exiles, who wanted and got gardens with a haha, parks with coverts and a brushed-and-combed wilderness, Florentine urns, follies and summerhouses with geckoes instead of earwigs. One cannot help but be glad that they achieved them.

Point Piper has a long roll of distinguished residents, political, legal and academic. One of the most interesting was the aeronautical pioneer, Lawrence Hargrave, who lived on Woollahra Point from 1902 to 1915. He was an agreeable, rather absentminded man, 'the crank with a kite'. This English immigrant was fascinated by the flight of both birds and kites. He either had no business sense, or was one of those noble souls who believe that science, like music, hath no boundaries, for when Wilbur Wright contacted him in 1900 about the use of his aircraft models, he told the American inventor that he had no patents, and his aeronautical discoveries were 'at the disposal of all'.

Point Piperians were occasionally treated to the delightful spectacle of Mr Hargrave strolling on the water across Double Bay. He wore on his feet 'something like blown-up tennis racquets'. The major Hargrave legend still drifting about Point Piper is his strongly-held theory of the Spanish rock carvings. In brief, he believed that one ship from Mendana's expedition from Callao to the Solomons in 1595 was blown south and sought shelter in Port Jackson. There are many rock carvings and letters on the rockfaces of Point Piper, and Hargrave wove these into a fantastic but credible story. His papers and sketches about this romantic curiosity can he seen at the Mitchell Library. Odd clues to early Spanish discovery of Australia do turn up in coastal waters now and then, chunks of metal, nubbins of china, cannonballs. They are as baffling as the sixteenth-century Spanish helmet dredged out of Wellington Harbour in New Zealand in the 1920s.

Rose Bay, as bays go, is a beauty, with a fine beach two kilometres long. The huge ballooning bursting growth of Sydney seems to have missed this middleclass suburb, which doesn't care a bit. Boaties love the bay, in spite of always having to keep one eye peeled for seaplanes, which buzz in and out of the old Lyne Park base at the head of the bay. Locals sometimes call it the Water Airport, for this was the terminus for the mail and passenger flying-boat service between Britain and Australia. In those days flying-boats were considered safe, as in a crisis they could land on the water. Anyone, however, who has spent an hour in a ditched flying-boat will know that death from seasickness is a certain hazard. Rose Bay was tremendously busy from 1942 to 1945, the flying-boats being in constant service ferrying Australian and American troops back and forth from New Guinea.

The New South Head Road, which we are travelling, passes behind the seaplane base and to our right we see a vast cupola-shaped green swathe cutting towards Bondi. It comprises playing fields and sportsgrounds, including the Royal Sydney Golf Course which takes up most of the green space. It occupies the lowlands where, in prehistoric times, the sea swept across the peninsula, islanding South Head. When the first settlers took up their land in Rose Bay, the area was still a peat bog covered with teatree, with a little river dribbling out close to the present seaplane base. In the 1860s it was still marshy, the only occupant being an irascible old crippled Aborigine called Rickety Dick, who lived in a gunyah beside the road and scatted any child who wandered nearby. He was a kind of pensioner of W. C. Wentworth, the lordling of nearby Vaucluse.

Most of the first drainage and clearance of what is now the most exclusive private golf course in Sydney was done by ever-industrious Chinese market gardeners, and was resumed, we hear, on somewhat peremptory terms.

Rose Bay and its neighbouring suburbs, boast many fine colleges. The Gothic pile which mounts the hill above Rose Bay, in one of the most fabulous positions around Sydney, is the Sacred Heart Girls' College. The original house, Claremont, was built about 1852, and a portion of it is still in existence. It was leased in 1882 by the newly arrived Sisters of the Sacred Heart, who later bought the property. A new edifice, designed by the popular Horbury Hunt, was built of sandstone quarried on the estate. This dates from about 1884. There are also many newer buildings but the entire complex retains a formidably dignified character.

Horbury Hunt was a marvellously funny fellow, a Canadian who arrived in Sydney in 1862. A tiny man in granny glasses and bright, self-designed clothes, he was a walking (or rather pedalling, for he always rode a bicycle) architectural office. His clothes were full of pockets, and the pockets full of scales, tapes, pencils, compasses and so on. His hat held sheets of paper, and his bike had an attached drawing board. He began his Sydney career by working for Edmund Blacket, but in 1869 started his own business. His work is fresh, simple and original. He preferred brick to stone, and is credited with inventing the sawtooth roof which is so much a feature even of modern industrial design. Very absentminded, he occasionally turned up in his pyjamas for work on the Rose Bay convent.

Vaucluse takes its name from the property owned by Sir Henry Browne Hayes, the unlikely convict, who abducted the unwilling and spirited Corkonian heiress Mary Pike, in 1797. In spite of his being but little pockmarked and having remarkable whiskers the lady did not take to him, and after an exciting interlude of screechings, ring-throwings, unmasking of a bogus priest and similar fantods, Sir Henry gave the game away and rushed out into the night and into hiding. One applauds the heiress's good sense, for Sir Henry seems to have had a head like a ham. He was also a tactless troublemaker, and although transported to New South Wales on a life sentence for the disastrous abduction, behaved to all as though he were visiting royalty. Constant putdowns seemed not to penetrate his conceit, although some were of the blistering order of this one from Governor King, delivered after Sir Henry demanded permission to form a Masonic Lodge. He, naturally, would be president. Said Governor King, a mild and kindly man for those times: 'If H. B. Hayes is not sensible of the indulgence already allowed him, instead of being president of a Freemasons' Lodge at Sydney, he will be put under a "president" of another kind at hard labour.'

Vaucluse is rocky, irregular terrain and therein lies so much of its idiosyncratic charm. Walkways descend between ferny clifflets, flights of steps show us gemmy glimpses of seascape one moment and pink bosses of pigface in some secluded rock garden the next. We descend stairs into the sheltered valley, 'the closed vale', where stands Vaucluse House. In January and February the place rings, vibrates, with the deafening stridulation of the giant cicadas, so that those with sensitive hearing flee between the avenues of huge trees, longing for the silence of the house that hides half its vanilla-coloured Gothic façade behind dense green foliage. Once the very wide verandah was wreathed in wistaria, and people went on 'wisteria picnics' to view the sumptuous spring display. The vine has been cut back to allow architectural details to be seen more easily.

These details, indeed the entire exterior of the house, are unusual for Sydney. Vaucluse House looks rather like a cross between an Indian bungalow and a fortified Scottish manorhouse. It has never quite worked for the present writer, though the interior is lovely. Henry Browne Hayes bought the estate for £100 in 1803, and probably his small stone house was built shortly afterwards. No one really knows if this original building was entirely demolished when William Charles Wentworth, really the only begetter of Vaucluse House as we know it, bought the estate in 1827. It is possible, I expect, that portions of 'the genteel dwelling house of eight rooms, with outhouses', are incorporated in the present mansion. The famous moat filled with Irish soil is under the present polygonal stone-paved verandah and has been seen several times during repairs.

The story of the Irish soil, so characteristic of the slightly cracked nature of Sir Henry, began with his hysterical visit to a military friend.

'My dear Major,' he cried, in the measured periods of a man educated in the eighteenth century, 'for the last eleven days I have suffered agonies of mind, and have been praying from early dawn to dusky night . . . to my favourite saint, St Patrick. But he seems to take no more notice of me than if I were some wretched thief in a road gang with manacles on my legs and a stone-breaking hammer in my hand.'

He went on to describe in equally stately terms the snakes which invaded his sylvan domain . . . black snakes, brown snakes, grey snakes, yellow snakes, diamond snakes, including 'a gentleman six feet long and as black as a coal, coiled up on my white counterpane, and another of the same dimensions under the bed'.

He proposed to import 150 tonnes of genuine Irish bog, a sure remedy against a serpentine invasion. An amused Governor gave permission, and about 1808 the soil arrived in biscuit barrels. It was taken to Vaucluse by water, and interred in a two metre wide trench, which ran all around the house. Sir Henry gave a party for his friends while the sacred soil was dug in, behaving meanwhile in his usual crackbrained fashion, lauding St Patrick, telling funny stories and singing Irish songs. The superintendent of convicts, himself an Irishman, and the many Irish convicts in the gang of seventy-five wept over the chocolate soil, and begged Sir Henry for handfuls of it. 'Take it and welcome,' he said. Afterwards the guests were entertained 'in a tent made of old sails'. Altogether, it was a memorable St Patrick's Day.

Later tenants of Vaucluse, including Wentworth, reported that no snakes were ever seen within the enchanted circle, but alas, of later years one or two snakes have been caught on that shady verandah. Perhaps the sacred earth requires to be refreshed.

Sir Henry's later career was one of constant misadventure. Born into a lowlier class, he would undoubtedly have ended on the scaffold. As it was, he returned to Ireland in 1812. There he died at the age of seventy, and now rests in the crypt of Christ Church in his native Cork under this marvellously unsuitable inscription: 'Most sincerely and universally regretted . . . a kind and indulgent parent and a truly adherent friend . . . endeared to every person who had the honour of his acquaintance.'

Bidding farewell to Sir Henry and his remarkable whiskers, we step into the gracious shadows of his successor Wentworth's 'palace on the green bay shore'. William Charles Wentworth, editor, liberalist, explorer, lawyer, elder statesman, Father of the Constitution, was born to a young surgeon, D'Arcy Wentworth and a convict girl in a little stone house which still faces the peacock lagoon of Norfolk Island. The year was probably 1793.

Both D'Arcy Wentworth and Catherine Crowley survived the disastrous Second Fleet, which lost 400 out of one thousand convicts through disease, cruelty and most lamentable conditions.

The rich fields of exploitation opened before Surgeon Wentworth. He acquired enormous tracts of land, and was one of the beneficiaries of the so-called Rum Hospital. During the time D'Arcy Wentworth was chief surgeon of the Rum Hospital, conditions were scandalous. However, he died a wealthy and respected man, and we are indebted to his good sense in sending his son William Charles off to England at the age of eight for an excellent education.

A brief biography of Wentworth can be bought at Vaucluse House but here are a few details of the life of this formidable man who called himself the first Australian. Unlike most first-generation native-born, he never looked back at his fatherland. The fluffy-whiskered toby jug of later years was autocratic and attracted enemies like flies. As a rich young radical, he was a different person, passionately involved in everything he undertook. In 1813 at the age of twenty, he, with Blaxland and Lawson, found a way over the colony's Great Wall of China, the Blue Mountains, which barred all enterprise to the west. While at Cambridge he published a notable book on New South Wales, and also wrote his famous frightful poem on Australia: 'May this, thy last-born infant, then arise to glad thy heart . . .' etc.

In 1824 he and his friend Dr Wardell started their newspaper *The Australian* (not connected with the present one), which was a bitter opponent of the Establishment as represented by the detested Governor Darling. His lifelong interest was the creation of a constitutional and representative government in a colony hitherto ruled arbitrarily by a governor responsible only to the English Government, grossly ignorant of the needs and desires of its distant colony. Within the walls of Vaucluse House, on a leather-topped oak table still to be seen, was drafted the Constitution Bill, giving responsible government to the State of NSW. This took effect in 1856.

The house is a tribute to the devoted housewifely care given by the Vaucluse House Historic Site Trust. Not very much of Wentworth's original furniture, which he loved to collect on his voyages abroad, still remains, but the rooms have been furnished with period pieces from other old homes around Sydney. Many of these have histories of their own. The worn Pompeian tiles on the floors are truly from Pompeii, and the legend is that they were given to Wentworth by Garibaldi in gratitude for the large financial support the Australian legislator gave to the Risorgimento.

In spite of the many charms of the Henry VIII-type kitchen, the drawing room is my favourite. Instead of wallpaper, painted panels adorn the walls. These were done by a convict, Bryant Payne, who ran away several times during the process. These panels feature formal entwinements of roses, convolvulus and passionflowers, probably painted from specimens from Wentworth's garden. They have been restored with china-painting delicacy by a small band of Sydney art teachers.

When Governor Darling retired from Sydney in 1831 Wentworth celebrated by inviting four thousand people to the greatest party the city had ever witnessed. The lawn was dotted with gay marquees 'filled with four thousand loaves and casks of beer and Cooper's gin'. Here and there a spit, presided over by a brawny blacksmith, revolved with a whole bullock, one of twelve sheep or many small fowl. Here the joyous assemblage, with loud acclamations, proclaimed their relief at the departure of a governor so unpopular that when his health was drunk at the annual dinner party of the Turf Club of which he was patron, the band played 'Over the Hills and Far Away'. Even the grim martinet Darling must have winced when he heard that the hills beyond Vaucluse House sparkled through the night with two immense bonfires, and that an illuminated frame, surmounted by a fizzing crown and two detonating stars, bore the words: DOWN WITH THE TYRANT.

Though Wentworth was at the peak of his liberal era (later he favoured political power being in the hands of the propertied rather than the grubby paws of the proles), one may be sure that his guests were of both le ton and the genteel bourgeoisie. He died in England in 1872. His body was returned to Sydney, given a State funeral and interred in the family vault, which is just a little stroll away in Chapel Road. The estate has long been subdivided, and the vault, with its citrus-striped roof, sits rather forlornly between two houses. But trees and grass cluster close about, and it's not undignified.

If you have time and inclination, you can stroll back to New South Head Road, which is not far at all and gives you a chance of seeing the old houses oozing good care and no penny-pinching. Catch a Watson's Bay bus on New South Head Road, which now mysteriously changes into a serpentine minor road, and wiggles across the middle of the peninsula to join Old South Head Road, close to Christison Park, a sandy, exposed green patch which is part of the Macquarie Lighthouse reserve. The lighthouse is white, harmoniously designed. It looks faintly oriental except for the Australian background of enormous sea, sky, and sunburned grass. It is open to visitors but you must first obtain a permit from the Marine Branch of the Department of Shipping and Transport. If you wish to photograph the exterior of the lighthouse, wait till you have seen South Head, and then walk back along the historic coastal road from the Gap.

The Macquarie Light was designed by Greenway, the convict architect, but it is the second of its family, being built to the same plan in 1883, when Greenway's first building, then sixty-five years old and crumbling, was demolished.

The work on the first tower was commenced in 1816, and concluded in seventeen months. The governor, Mrs Macquarie, their friends and the architect drove out to South Head in a December dawn to view the 'noble, magnificent edifice' against the Pacific sunrise. The kindly governor presented Greenway with his pardon, and they all sat down to breakfast.

The light first shone in 1818. It is an eerie thought that before this almost 20,000 kilometres of Australian coast had been completely dark; when night fell the continent vanished to become once more the ghostland of the early navigators. It is true that since 1794, a fire had been lit at night in an iron basket on South Head as a beacon and warning to ships nearing the land. But this dim spark was not to be compared with the first flash of the Macquarie Light. An American whaler, forty-eight kilometres to the south was so amazed to see it, he described it in his log as an astronomical phenomenon.

Robert Watson of Watson's Bay, who had come to the colony as quartermaster in the *Sirius*, was the first lightkeeper.

The present tower, which is very close to the original site, is twenty-six metres high; the light is 106 metres above sea level. The old light continued to operate until the new one was opened, so there has been no dark night on South Head since 1818. It has a range of forty kilometres. In the intervening sixty-five years between the two lighthouses, total trade in Port Jackson had increased from 34,000 tonnes to 3,000,000 tonnes a year.

The present light was first popularly called the Electric Lighthouse. However, the primitive generator was not reliable, and the light was later powered by oil and then kerosene. But during that first electric period it must have been remarkably bright. An immigrant who approached the Heads by night in 1886 wrote: 'Two hours before the Heads are reached it has grown to be a flash of intense brilliancy, and its long rays ... divide the darkness with lines of living fire. Between it and the red light on the end of the Peninsula [the Hornby Light] is a dip in the cliff, over which the lights of Sydney were seen.'

The dip is the Gap, where traditionally the sick and sorry jump to their deaths.

The revolving beam, though its brightness is very much reduced as it wheels over the Harbour, is an old friend to passengers on homegoing ferries. It is switched on fifteen minutes before sunset, and a familiar game is to watch the flaming westerly windows of Vaucluse and Watson's Bay, and try to pick from among them the hardly observable twinkle of the Macquarie Light. Then, as the sunset fades, the double flash of the light becomes slowly visible, a reassuring wink.

Only a little further on, almost opposite Cambridge Avenue, is the Signal Station. The present building, also rather resembling a lighthouse, dates from the 1840s, but the Signal Station itself has been manned without a break from January 1790.

The Signal Station at first consisted of a flagstaff and a few huts to house the lookout. It was agreeable for the men, who planted a vegetable garden, had a boat for fishing, and occasionally, when off duty, walked to the settlement via a track which is now fairly closely followed by Old South Head Road.

The homesick longing for news of home is well expressed in an entry in Watkin Tench's journal: 'Here on the summit of the hill, every morning from daylight till the sun sunk, did we sweep the horizon in hope of seeing a sail. At every fleeting speck which arose from the bosom of the sea the heart bounded.' At last on June 3, 1790, the shout of 'The flag's up!' resounded through the settlement. Tench scrambled up to the heights above Dawes Point and saw the flag. 'A brother officer was with me. We could not speak; we wrung each other by the hand, with eyes and hearts overflowing.'

As we know, the incoming ships were the Second Fleet, laden with death, disease, disaster and few stores. But at least they brought mail from home.

'"Letters, letters!" was the cry. They were produced and torn open in trembling agitation. News burst upon us like meridian splendours upon a blind man. We were overwhelmed with it, public, private, general and particular. Not...until some days had elapsed were we able to methodise it or reduce it into form.'

Poor Tench, one would think him in the first colony on the moon. In 1791 he speaks of rowing six miles out to sea to greet a ship, only to find that they had brought no mail, no newspapers, and were as ignorant of world events as the Sydney settlers themselves.

'Are Russia and Turkey at peace?' he cried.

'I have heard talk about it, but don't remember what passed.'

The Signal Station is very impressive. It has the complacent look of a building which has been of immense utility for countless years.

The suburb of Watson's Bay runs down to a flat, picturesque little foreshore, trim and well kept. It has an archaic look, as though it were once a fishing village. The streets are little more than lanes, and there are some nice old stone cottages. The blue sky, the coral trees, the jetty where housewives are buying fish from a boatman, all add to the relaxed atmosphere of this countrified, serene suburb.

Surgeon John White, who came through these Heads with the First Fleet in 1788, said 'the Harbour is safe from all the winds that blow' but fortunately it isn't, and the most indolent viewer feels profound pleasure at the sight of hundreds of little Sydney yachts scooting before a hard nor'-easter, their spinnakers lit with reflected radiance from an ever-shining sea.

To Watson's Bay come hundreds to view the start of the internationally-contested Sydney to Hobart race, one of the world's great long-distance sailing races, over 1,000 kilometres from the Heads to Hobart estuary.

There are numbers of things to look at in Watson's Bay: the Moreton Bay fig tree on the waterfront under which Governor Macquarie and his party picnicked in 1811; the obelisk which marks the completion of the thirteen kilometre South Head Road by the soldiers of the 73rd Regiment. St Peter's Church is a simple little village church by Edmund Blacket. It was built in 1864, 'to be the first building to greet the eyes of newcomers to Sydney'. It has a funny little gallery, and its organ used to be owned by the Emperor Napoleon. Dunbar House, in Robertson Park, is a comely old colonial. Built before 1840 for the Colonial Treasurer, it is named for the tragic immigrant ship which smashed into the Gap cliffs on a wintry night in 1857.

If you have time, walk the few hundred metres along the waterfront to Camp Cove, which is a lovely little crescent tucked down behind the giant's breakwater of South Head. Close to the end of Pacific Street is the Victorian house of that interesting Russian explorer-biologist, Nicolaus Miklouho-Maclay. Here in the late 1880s he established the first biological research station in Australia. From the footpath on the northern side you may spot his monogram engraved on one of the house's pillars. It looks rather like the Masonic emblem but is really two entwined Ms under a crown.

On the shore is the obelisk which records Captain Phillip's landing here on January 21, 1788, when he sailed up from his unsatisfactory Botany Bay camp to explore unknown Port Jackson. So this is, as far as we know, white men's first landing place within Sydney Harbour. This little cove has always been associated with the pilots, who used to row out in open boats. Next-door Watson's Bay was the inspection point for ships' documents, and customs and medical examination. There are several navigational marks still remaining from these days of sail.

About 800 metres offshore, the ebbing tide creams over the rocky shoal called the Sow and Pigs. This divides the fairway to the main harbour into two channels. Always a menace to shipping, the Sow and Pigs were marked by lightships for many years; the most noticeable of their present warning complex is the tall striped tripod. The rocks are a natural rounding point for yacht races, and are mentioned in the description of the first recorded race in Sydney Harbour, when the boats' crews of two British warships competed for a purse of Spanish dollars. This 1827 event foreshadowed the famous Anniversary Day Regatta, which began the following year, and is still the most magnificent spectacle on Sydney Harbour.

Camp Cove is a great place for swimming, sunbathing and rock-fishing. However, let us retrace our steps and visit the Gap. It's strange that this cliff should be Sydney's traditional place for saying 'Goodbye, cruel world'. North Head is much higher, and a satisfyingly majestic place for a dramatic exit. Perhaps the Gap has always been a favourite because first the trams, and now the buses, carried the would-be suicide conveniently close. For there's no getting away from it, Sydney people hate to walk.

For one even slightly timid of heights, it is a dizzying experience to look over the rail to the sandstone platforms below, half revealed in the waves' wash, black, glistening, cracked with strange regularity into long vertical gutters. A toothpick-sized fisherman is away down there, perched like a cormorant amidst the sloshing sheets of shallow foam.

Only two or three people have survived the jump from the Gap.

The grief and despair of so many has not lingered in the fine keen air. This is a noble place, with a thousand kilometres of sea before you. The ocean is navy blue, patched with aquamarine and bottle green, prowled by the shadows of the thunderheads marching across from the east. In air that tingles with suspended vapour, one watches the endless rollers smashing upon the sandstone ledges far below, spilling away in effervescing sheets. What is the fetch of these long waves that chug in the grottoes and shake the mighty bluff? One imagines them rising near the western shore of South America, momentarily dividing and joining around the three thousand kilometre reef of the islands of New

Zealand, surging irresistibly across the Tasman to this ruinous defeat.

The sandstone of these cliffs is particularly richly coloured; here and there on ledges are lonely patches of scrub. The twenty-nine metre cliff is strongly fenced, but you could easily slip under or over, if you really wished to do so. A half-submerged submarine butts out between the Heads.

The anchor of the *Dunbar*, cemented to the rock, is enormous, cumbrous. Its striated iron looks fossilised. Shortly before midnight in 1857 the doomed ship struck the cliff broadside on. At dawn, in a gale that blew spray over the top of the cliff, the sea was dense with broken timbers, floating cargo, 121 mutilated corpses, and mobs of sharks. One young seaman, thrown ashore, clung to a ledge halfway up the cliff throughout that nightmare night. He was there for thirty-six hours, kept company by an Icelandic boy, who climbed down the fissure in the cliffs called Jacob's Ladder. Extraordinarily, this sole survivor of the *Dunbar*, James Anderson, ended his life some years later by drowning in shallow water.

Those bodies found are buried in a common grave in Camperdown Cemetery. The anchor was recovered in 1907 and since then skindivers often fossick in the rotten remains of Sydney's most tragic wreck.

Turn now towards the Harbour. There are seats among the sandstone terraces and boulders that take their familiar form of half-buried dragons. It is inexplicably sheltered, warm; the sea-sounds but a sustained shush. Chirps and creaks of insects are all that can be heard in this gentle wilderness of scrub, banksias and wildflowers. In the swimming western light, Sydney is grey as cobwebs. All shapes are there, turrets, ghauts, domes, parallelograms, silos, everything except the pyramid. The Bridge's arch seems to float suspended above the hanging forest of Bradley's Head. One can see the highrise buildings of distant northern suburbs. As the church spires disappear, these great spaghetti packets take their place as the eminences of the cityscape. A super jetcat skids across to Manly, where the dying pines look thin and gauzy, like the tails of elderly possums. North Head has the profile of a sperm whale. One is reminded of Mundy's fancy that one day the two enormous sandstone jaws of the Heads would snap together, and turn Port Jackson into a land-locked lake. Lieutenant-Colonel G. C. Mundy, a wonderful gossip, wrote entertainingly about the Sydney of the late 1840s. This was his favourite ride as it was for many. 'On Sundays there is a general rush of horsemen and chaise men and women towards the Heads.' He records that in D'Urville's *Voyage d'Astrolabe* of 1830 there is a stylish picture of this Sunday rush – the Macquarie Lighthouse against a tempestuous sky, foliage blowing, horsemen galloping past in tall hats and tightwaisted coats, spanking equipage with windblown ladies. All is animation and flurry, which seems to indicate that Sydney Sundays were once decidedly more mettlesome than they are now.

Lieutenant-Colonel Mundy goes on to describe a 'brickfielder', a duststorm swallowing up the town in clouds of red and white, flying into his eyes and grating in his teeth. Then came torrential rain and hail, drenching his patent, self-ventilating gossamer hat and his filmy paletot, and after that a bright stripe of western sky, upon which the town lay in silhouette, as it does now. Most of the buildings he mentions are still standing; they are all in the vicinity of Macquarie Street. But now we cannot see them 'for the houses in between'.

It is time for us to catch the bus back to the city. But first, turning to the north we observe the high green tip of the South Head peninsula now given over entirely to naval and defence purposes. When Louisa Anne Meredith drove out here in 1828, she mentioned the 'mat-like plats of the fig-marigold, adorning the hot sandy banks with its bright purple flower'. And blow me down if the occasional gardens of South Head's military installations are not still splashed with cascades and avalanches of blowsy pink from this native mesembryanthemum, which the convicts christened pigface because of some fancied pigginess about its five-sided fruit.

South Head, which as a defence post is under the control of the Commonwealth Government, was originally fortified in 1859 for a curious non-military reason. The authorities feared, and on good grounds, that armed Yankee privateers might raid the town and lift the many tonnes of gold held in bank vaults during this period of the great gold rushes. Pictures of South Head fortifications show the soldiers wearing topees as though they were on the North-west Frontier.

The Hornby Light, a red and white striped tower, was erected on Inner South Head in 1858 as a response to the wreck of the *Dunbar*. It is an entrance guiding light. Near it is the shore establishment of the Royal Australian Navy, HMAS *Watson*. Its chapel of St George the Martyr is very fine and well worth a visit. It is a non-denominational memorial to all those of the Royal Australian Navy who died on active service. It stands alone near the cliff's edge, and the glass wall behind the altar frames a seascape in which North Head stands like a colossal abstract monument to the durable spirit of man. The whole restless sea seems to fill this tiny building, and one finds it fitting that the chapel is marked as a landmark on Admiralty charts.

Riding home in his soggy paletot, his collapsed self-ventilating hat, Lieutenant-Colonel Mundy in 1842 observed that the Antipodes had little twilight, that while the ravines were in darkness, the sunbeams still gilded hilltops and gum trees. It is no different now. The sunset still flashes signals from top windows of houses, dazzles passengers on the righthand side of the bus. Shop windows are lit in the dusky valley of Rose Bay. As we lurch around a high corner, we look backwards to see the first blink of the Macquarie Light. In fifteen minutes the sun will be gone.

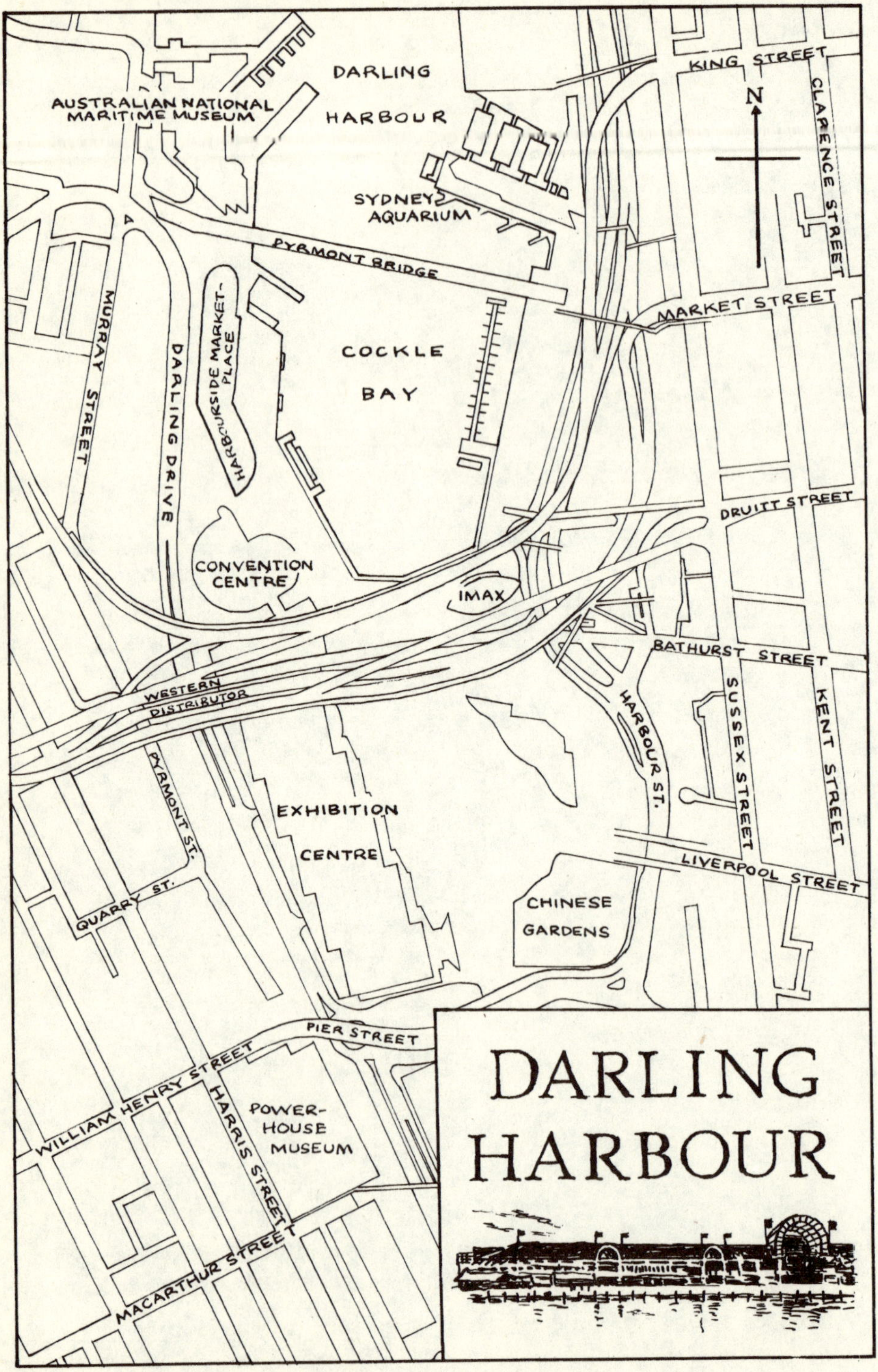
DARLING
HARBOUR
AUSTRALIAN NATIONAL MARITIME MUSEUM
DARLING HARBOUR
SYDNEY AQUARIUM
KING STREET
CLARENCE STREET
N
PYRMONT BRIDGE
MARKET STREET
MURRAY STREET
DARLING DRIVE
HARBOURSIDE MARKET-PLACE
COCKLE BAY
DRUITT STREET
CONVENTION CENTRE
IMAX
BATHURST STREET
WESTERN DISTRIBUTOR
HARBOUR ST.
SUSSEX STREET
KENT STREET
PYRMONT ST.
EXHIBITION CENTRE
LIVERPOOL STREET
QUARRY ST.
CHINESE GARDENS
PIER STREET
WILLIAM HENRY STREET
HARRIS STREET
POWER-HOUSE MUSEUM
MACARTHUR STREET

CHAPTER 6

HOW DARLING HARBOUR BECAME THE ENT CENT

Harbour of King Herod of the Antipodes – coming of the container ships – the railway goods yards of yesteryear – a brilliant impresario – a gift from Guangdong – the amazing Powerhouse Museum – the sorcerer's eye of IMAX – The Aquarium, who stares at whom? – the highly important Maritime Museum – soldiers coming and going – the rebirth of Pyrmont – eating at the Fish Markets.

NOW for a change of pace – a visit to a place of fun and entertainment – Darling Harbour.

Darling Harbour, like so many places about Sydney, was called after that governor who was, in the hearty manner of his day, described as 'the archfiend', 'Beelzebub', and 'King Herod of the Antipodes'. However, Governor Ralph Darling seems to have been competent, if unlovable. It was his predecessor, Lachlan Macquarie, who discerned that there are few things a glorious city-to-be needs more than a tradesman's entrance, a rear end, a backyard that can be as noisy and dirty as it has to be. Currently, Sydney's back door is Port Botany and its environs, but in Macquarie's time the bay was too far away. He thanked Providence for the long, narrow, though often shallow inlet on the west side of Sydney Cove. It terminated in enormous tidal flats, dense with mangroves, veined with fresh or brackish runoffs from the higher ground to the southwest. Here settlers and Aborigines amicably gathered shellfish, speared flatfish and trapped black swans and swamphen. It was referred to as Cockle Bay.

The breakneck shore of Cockle Bay was impassable for horses and vehicles; the west border the precipitous edge of an uninhabitable tick-infested peninsula later to be named Pyrmont. Cockle Bay, therefore, was scarcely thought of as a viable extension to the colony. However Macquarie, like most governors with an unlimited supply of free labour, understood that landscapes were created to be pushed around. He reclaimed enough land along the east side of Cockle Bay for vehicular access roads to be constructed. We have already looked at them – the streets of the Wicked Uncles. He banged down cliffs, built jetties, moved the city markets south so that industry and commerce would follow, and approved and opened the first steam mill in 1815. The Industrial Revolution had come to New South Wales.

From the 1840s, the dredges were at work in Darling Harbour and its immediate neighbours, Blackwattle, White and Rozelle Bays. From that time anyone could predict that Darling Harbour would become the growling gut of Sydney. The city map tells the tale. Every northern side street from Parramatta Road, the first highway in the South Pacific, is laid like the spoke of a fan, angling down to the foreshores of Blackwattle Bay and Darling Harbour.

There was obviously only one site for the railway goods yards. Twenty-four hectares of the old tidal flats were drained; the yards were upgraded and enlarged once more in 1922. The fill used was sandstone from the city underground rail tunnels. Sidings reached like long black fingers along the wharves and within the yards' own compound were more than forty-eight kilometres of track. Before the 1970s the goods yards handled over four million tonnes of freight annually.

Darling Harbour, Pyrmont, White Bay, Walsh Bay, for more than a century were the most intensely industrialised areas in Sydney, dirty, noisy, immensely wealthy, everything blackened or rusty or inhumanly bright – cranes, hoppers, ships' masts, titanic Meccano sets, graveyards of corroded metal waste, and sophisticated loading complexes. Ever and anon, sounded the colossal groan of a gantry crane swinging like a mantis amidst the smoke.

Can this be so? The genial bluewater cove of today, thronged with visitors, prosperous, with five-star hotels, monorail humming overhead, an aquarium, a casino – was it once as we have described it? What changed it?

Time changed it, other needs. And of course the City of Sydney

Strategic Plan which, by a circuitous route and a million difficulties, dug-in toes, fund lapses, anguished letters to newspapers and government ministers, transformed Darling Harbour and its environs into what it is today. But first the vast complex had to lose its reason for existence. 'It was the container ships that began it,' says one of the now elderly waterfront unemployed. The growing use of containers totally changed dockside activities, and the increasing reliance on road transport provided Port authorities with new problems. The eccentric network of narrow Sydney roads could not cope with the huge rigs and semi-trailers. Port Botany responded by rapid expansion of its facilities and by the installation of then novel giant travelling cranes to service the new methods of cargo handling. Railway freight transport slowed to idleness and the goods yards at the head of Darling Harbour became obsolete.

A curious side effect was that the massive woolstores, built long before by Thomas Sutcliffe Mort and other early industrialists, were abandoned. Shipping wool in containers meant that the auction and general handling of the clip could be transferred to more accessible locations far from the wharves. What was to be done with the historic woolstores, fortresses built to last centuries, with priceless pitsawn hardwood floors, beamed ceilings, immense arched windows barred with iron? They were architectural dinosaurs in some of the best positions in the inner city.

An imaginative property developer, Tom Hayson, bought several of these cumbersome structures, which stood around forlornly for years, getting in everyone's way and having their windows smashed by vandals. Each eventually became a select coven of trendy loft apartments worth a fortune.

Hayson was also the moving spirit behind the reconversion of the dismantled goods yards, by then a terrible wasteland and dumping ground behind a rusty fence, into something Sydney might cherish. He brought together the culturally minded Premier Neville Wran, and the American urban developer James Rouse. Rouse had invented the suburban shopping mall in the 1950s. He also had a remarkable flair for revitalising decayed old dockside areas. Government sat on its tail and dithered in the customary style, until James Rouse himself came to Sydney and delivered an inspiring speech. But it was the mid-1980s before a consortium of government and private enterprise transformed what was a useless eyesore into a futuristic place of information and entertainment.

Darling Harbour was opened for the Bicentennial celebrations, 1988, and we are now going to visit it.

You can travel by monorail, of course. Or if you enter Sydney via Central Railway Station, then it's the light rail for you. This is a kind of supertram, nothing at all like the malevolent old 'toastracks' which Sydney dumped in 1961. Indeed no, the light rail, which began operations in 1997, is whispery smooth. It can drop you at Paddy's Market, the Casino, the Harbourside shopping centre, or take you on to the Fish Market and Wentworth Park at the head of Blackwattle Bay. Extensions are constantly being planned so by the time you read this who knows where this admirable tram might carry you?

You can drive, or you can walk, the latter venture taking you over the old Pyrmont Bridge, now used only for pedestrians. Sometimes kids are allowed up into the tower that houses the mechanism that swings the middle of the bridge around to allow the ships to pass through like sheep through a sliprail. This is a good place from which to survey the entire sweep of Darling Harbour's buildings and facilities. Sydneysiders are increasingly and inaccurately calling the whole box and dice 'the Entertainment Centre' or, more familiarly, the 'Ent Cent'. And the more Darling Harbour as an entity extends itself via Cockle Bay until it reaches Broadway, not to mention up and down the Pyrmont Peninsula and north to Walsh Bay, the more we're going to talk about the Ent Cent.

However, there's a real Entertainment Centre, on the city side, next to Chinatown. Immense and opulent, it is a multifunctional venue, catering for sports, ice ballets, great international performers like Pavarotti, pop concerts, basketball – any type of performance in fact that may attract very large crowds.

And the Star Casino, over there in Pyrmont, not only has its own hotel, but its own entertainment centre as well, separate from that luxurious palace where you hope to win a fortune.

The Ent Cent is just what Sydney longed for – a lively, even elegant city within a city, certainly with something for everyone. The situation, looking into the sparkling northern waters, sheltered from the sometimes sharpish south winds, is perfect.

Problems, problems, what to see first? I can offer you a look at the underside of a crocodile's belly at the aquarium, which is downright horrible, or a refreshing wander in the Chinese Garden, which was given to the Australian people as a Bicentennial gift by the folk of Guandong Province. This part of China provided colonial Australia with thousands of goldminers and traders. The garden is lovely, grass, windbells and waterfalls.

However, the first thing that happens to most people is that they lose a child in the Powerhouse Museum. What a splendid place this is! It really was a powerhouse, a longish time ago, providing the electricity for Sydney's trams and other things.

The exterior is one of ponderous solemnity. The interior is large enough to hold the Opera House, and an attendant gaily remarks that when the Opera House is obsolete it'll go on exhibition too.

The Museum does rather specialise in monstrous intimidating metal objects that the kids fearlessly clamber over, going vroom, vroom.

We must take it seriously, however. The Powerhouse is the largest museum in Australia and the most significant part of the Museum of Applied Arts and Science, a collection which grew from the exhibits at the International Exhibition held in the Sydney Garden Palace in 1879. We recall that the Garden Palace was the one that so spectacularly burned down. The original infant collection was called the Technological Industrial and Sanitary Museum, a characteristic Victorian boast that cleanliness was next to godliness and Sydney possessed them both. Which at that time it certainly did not.

The great blessing of the Powerhouse is that you can touch, push and wiggle some of the exhibits, which gives a delightful sense of freedom. You can make things happen with interactive exhibits and be amazed at your own manual dexterity. Or you can indulge that secret longing to play around with mechanical and electronic toys. Some of these toys are very large, such as Locomotive Number One which pulled the first trains in New South Wales in 1855.

Of course there are many other displays. You could spend an entire day seeing and touching. Sometimes special exhibitions too – the world of the circus the day we were there. And yes, you can get a meal right on the spot.

Now for other things to do and see. You can't do the lot on one visit, so the choice is yours. The Harbourside Festival Marketplace, with its two hundred odd stores, is for those essential souvenirs as well as for serious shoppers. At Harbourside you are offered many things, one of them being elegant artwork. Local artists and craftspeople have contributed banners, suspended mobile sculptures, painted murals, decorated pots and patterned terrazzo floors featuring native animals and wildflowers.

The Ent Cent rather preens itself on ultramodern roof shapes. The roof of the Aquarium is a breaking wave; the Exhibition Centre shows a mast and rigging. Probably you won't want to inspect the latter unless something that interests you is being shown, but it is a fascinating building. It is said that the architect was instructed 'No pillars!', very difficult when dealing with a space of 25,000 square metres. He achieved this by stepping back the five halls to provide independent areas. The Convention Centre is next door, the venue for many Olympic events, judo, tennis, weightlifting and so on.

The IMAX Theatre gives some people the shrieks. But if you remain stable during other virtual reality operations, you will survive this. The awesome screen – the largest in the world, it is said – is ten times bigger than the everyday movie theatre screen. It shows images so stunningly clear that when you put on the magic liquid crystal glasses and find yourself in three dimensions it is almost, as one dazed patron said, 'an out of body experience'.

Our 'best place', as children say, will always be the Maritime Museum. Even more than the Aquarium.

Not that the Aquarium isn't an eye-opener. The unusual building is designed so that two-thirds of it are under water. This means you can take a fantasy walk with beautiful or deadly sea creatures flying and flirting beside you and above you, and not drown. No one can convince us they're swimming; the water is totally invisible. Can they see us? I don't think so. When you are eyeball to eyeball with an octopus, it's not his tentacles that break out in goosebumps. And as for the sharks, seen from below, what power, what real majesty, what a great argument for one to remain a land person. Here there's a special tank where children can touch things, sea grapes, starfish, hermit crabs, certain little creatures that don't seem to mind at all.

But, for the writer, the Maritime Museum is the most significant cultural establishment at Darling Harbour. How plainly its exhibits speak of the often forgotten fact that we live on an island, no matter how immense. The ocean is our wall; the nation's founders were seafarers. Along the museum's jetty are moored a string of ancient sailing vessels of all kinds, including a floating lighthouse. You can inspect these survivors, possibly resolving that you will take a half-day voyage on one of the five real live sailing ships gracing Sydney Harbour, if only to find out how they make the thing go where it's supposed to go.

The museum is a repository of maps, charts, and logs, including a copy of the record of Captain Bligh's astounding feat of navigation after the mutiny on the *Bounty*. Aboriginal and Islander rafts, canoes and paddles, some remarkably ingenious, are among the multitude of water craft displayed. The evolution of the surfboard, and the development of the winged keel that helped *Australia II* win the Americas Cup in 1983 always attract keen kids.

This eastern Pyrmont shore used to be as seductive as a boilermaker's yard, a wilderness of stacked cargoes, factories, mountains of coal, cumbrous transport vehicles, and the awfulness of heavy industry dumping grounds. The railway goods yards did not cover only the old Darling Harbour swamp – they stretched almost to the present venue of Star City Casino and its lavish attendant complex.

Huge freight berths occupied the shoreline as far as the Colonial Sugar Refining Company's monstrous compound on the northwest. In front of the Maritime Museum were three cargo wharves used for the embarkation of Australian soldiers during World War II. Somewhere about here is an inadequate plaque commemorating those who did not return. The American soldiers have a grander memorial of their arrival on these shores, but that is on Glebe Island at the far end of the Anzac Bridge.

'Through those gates passed some of the most beautiful GIs in the world', was the saying in those days. The Americans, more than eight thousand of them, arrived on the *Queen Mary* which anchored in Athol Bight on the north side of the Harbour. Ferries took the men to Glebe Island, whence they were dispersed by troop trains to various camps on the city fringes. Nowadays Glebe Island may look the very heartland of industry, particularly servicing grain exports, but during the war it was an outpost of the US – off limits to civilians. It was also the handling and storage depot of all US Army supplies.

Pyrmont has always seemed to us a queer old place, a stubby oblong peninsula, so close to Sydney on the east and on the west hemmed in by a three-pronged family of bays that defend it from the silt and flood debris of two big rivers. For many years no one seemed to want it; it was part of a John Macarthur grant. What wasn't, one might ask of that great landgrabber. He used to take people there for picnics. There were many creeks, 'an abundance of rock lilies, and parrots of the brightest hues', an exquisite aspect on every quarter and contiguity to the new settlement. Yet while smart people were staking out land and building themselves mansions at Darling Point and Double Bay, no rich official settled at Pyrmont. Perhaps it was the ticks. Or maybe that curious social division into east and west we noted in earlier chapters.

Even when part of the old Macarthur land was eventually cleared, the new proprietor chose to build his impressive new home, Lyndhurst, high up on the southern slope behind the Blackwattle tidal flats, halfway to Parramatta Road. This was Dr James Bowman, the capable English doctor who cleaned up wretched Sydney Hospital after its riotous years in the charge of D'Arcy Wentworth. Dr Bowman came into possession of the magnificent estate because of his marriage to the heiress Mary Macarthur.

Lyndhurst was designed in the Regency style by John Verge, who also built Elizabeth House in Elizabeth Bay. It was to Lyndhurst that Mrs John Macarthur fled, when the persecution of her deranged husband drove her from Elizabeth Farm in Parramatta.

Dr Bowman did not enjoy his fine house for long; the great crash of the 1840s came, and gradually Mary's dowry was sold off, right down to Blackwattle Bay. All the wide meadow-like parkland of Wentworth Park, including its greyhound track was once Lyndhurst Estate. Of all the splendid colonial mansions that were mutilated, burned or knocked down whenever the passion for progress seized Sydney, Lyndhurst had one of the narrowest escapes. It became in turn college, convent, boarding house, but stood up long enough to be photographed, tottering on the verge of collapse amid a reef of rubbish. It was acquired by the Department of Main Roads as part of the then current plan for the northwestern freeway, with consequent fierce quarrels with the National Trust and other pro-Lyndhurst groups. In 1976 a new Premier, Neville Wran, ensured that Lyndhurst should be restored. Now one of Sydney's most charming old villas, standing in its own garden, Lyndhurst is the headquarters of the Historic Houses Trust.

At the Ent Cent there are a thousand places to eat – well, maybe a hundred or more – but we are going to suggest hopping on the light rail and quickly and comfortably sailing along the northern Pyrmont loop.

This passes through Star City Casino complex and terminates at the Fish Market where you can enjoy a marvellous seafood meal of any ethnic variety. Of course, if you wish, you can leave the tram at the Casino and watch other folk losing their money, but it is fresh and interesting to see the elegant modern 'outer inner' suburb that has sprung up where the senile cottages and sagging, reeling shops and desolate, empty factories stood as late as the 1970s. The tram will let you off beside the Fish Market carpark, almost under the Western Distributor.

Before you is Blackwattle Bay, a sheet of silk, with the trawlers lined up in a marina like horses in stalls. Rozelle and Blackwattle Bays are overlooked but not dominated by the futuristic Anzac Bridge. Its massivity is made airy and almost insubstantial by the changing light flitting up and down its maypoles of steel braces. Compare it with the poor old 1902 workhorse, the Pyrmont Bridge, all ponderous piers and crisscrosses and pillars with stone mushrooms on top, and be thankful that the 1990s architect of the Anzac Bridge realised that it was possible to make it an outstanding work of art.

We are too late for the wholesale fish auction, open daily and early to the public. The open market area, as big as two football fields, is already being hosed down. But the retail markets, arranged as a spacious arcade, are a revelation. Who would dream that fish are as beautiful and varied as birds? These creatures, presented in shop after shop in shoals of their own variety, cannot be related to the damp nameless substance that so dismays us when we defrost fish. No indeed, at the Fish Market we see *fish* – shining steel barramundi, parrot fish, freckled and rosy red, the monstrous bullheaded cod, his cold eye still bright. What could be more gorgeous than a blue swimmer crab, so neat and satiny, a cornflower and mauve body so admirably topping those violet legs? And sardines! The seas outside Sydney are seething with them, but only now after years of misplaced obduracy, will old-style Australians eat them. Here they are, filleted, close together, headless, with curled tails, bright as polished aluminium. Cheap, too!

Other shops sell other edibles, but in a modest, polite way, as though the proprietors feel they really are out of place. An Italian deli, bread shops, fruit shop – but we see no butcher. Tables are everywhere, inside and out, so we sit outside, beside the gently lifting brown water, marooned patches of drifting rubbish slowly circulating. To our left the enormous black disused coal loader indicates Blackwattle's industrial past, though the extensive tidal swamps at the head of the bay always discouraged commercial investment. From the mid-nineteenth century, after the Bowmans had dispersed their Lyndhurst estate, these flats were a nauseatingly befouled place. They took the drainage from the Glebe abattoirs, designed by Edmund Blacket, the nearby sugar refinery and a brewery, and were also a sewerage outfall.

After a while it became the place, along with the head of Rozelle Bay, where old boats went to die. People towed them there and marooned them, and there are some sad photographs of the old cockle beds, where a dinghy lies like a dead cockroach, or a rusteaten scow, bottom glistening with black barnacles, is tipped over in the mud. Later this ruined and filthy locality was cleared, filled with the sludge raised by the ever active main harbour dredges and turned into Pyrmont and Glebe's main recreation area, Wentworth Park.

The High Victorian suburb of Glebe looks very fine from across Blackwattle Bay, unit blocks showing among the elderly and often decrepit houses. Glebe was originally Anglican Church property, the Glebe, in fact, granted by Governor Phillip to that mistreated First Fleet parson Richard Johnson. It was covered with the densest possible bush, and poor Mr Johnson was given only eight convicts to clear it. Even the eight wouldn't work, but skived off into the bush and smoked figleaves and gave him cheek when he went after them. Poor Mr Johnson seemed destined to suffer in this world, and he did.

Despite small sales and leasings, some clearing for farmland and orchard, the Glebe was still heavily forested countryside when Edmund Blacket and his family decided to move from Darlinghurst and build a new home there. His daughter's sketches indicate that even in the late 1860s, the Glebe looked like Sherwood Forest, and we are told that Blacket travelled from his city office by ferry to Glebe Point, where he hired an escort of four men to take him home along a bridle-track 'infested by footpads and bushrangers'. It sounds desperately rash for one so frail in health as Edmund Blacket – swelled feet, putrid throat, toothache, bilious attack, low fever, inexplicable pain in the side are a few of his recorded ailments – and one can imagine him riding through the twilit bush with his rustic bravos and starting at every cheep. But he remained at Glebe for thirteen years, doing much of his finest work in that period.

Blackwattle, Rozelle and their upland settlements have changed their mode of life so many times. But their residents made the most of it even in the hard times. Here is one orchardist who supplied the early fishermen of Blackwattle Bay – almost all Portuguese, it is said – with sly grog. Devoid of plant though not of ingenuity, he writes in a letter: 'The flying foxes having nipped my piches, I distild 400 gals strong cyder from damaged fruit by hollowing the butt of native oke and employing wooden padle to crush fruit. After frumentation one glas put parson in the whelebarrow.'

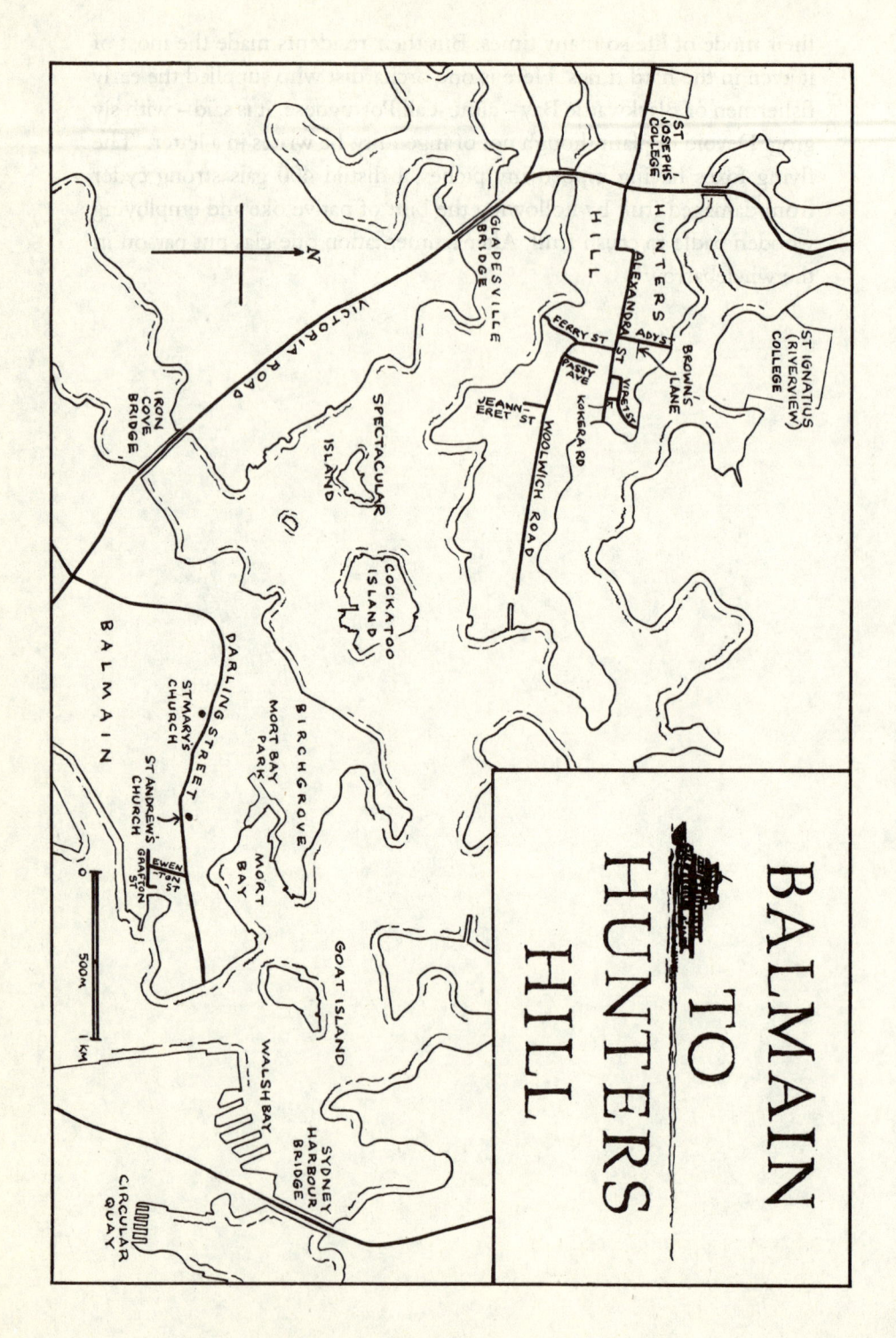

BALMAIN TO HUNTERS HILL

CHAPTER 7

BALMAIN TO THE RIVERLANDS

Ships at the bottom of the garden – dolls' houses of Balmain – palms but no olives – the remarkable Thomas Mort and his achievements – the cheapest real estate deal in history – the renaissance of Goat Island – the man chained to a rock – how Captain Maconochie turned a beast into a man – dreaded Cockatoo – Mary Reiby settles at Hunter's Hill – the admirable Freres Joubert and their legacy – two fine bridges – Homebush bound for glory.

THERE'S a place in Sydney where but a few decades ago, people lived in symbiosis with ships, the only suburb where I've seen the bow of a large overseas vessel nuzzling someone's garden fence. Often there were no fences. Senile cottages, half lost in overgrown grapevines and mossy cherry trees, crouched a few feet above slipways, boatsheds, repair yards, and all the rusty disarray of engineering works.

Of course the years have brought progress, the tottering old homes have been restored handsomely and are now worth millions of dollars. A block of home units on the site of Birchgrove House isn't too upsetting, though the locals, who mounted a tremendous protest when the historic Didier Joubert house was doomed to demolition in 1967, still mourn. The cherry trees bloom, the gardens are a dream, the trees thick as moss. But you still see masts and flitting sails through the foliage, and, though the residents do their best not to look that way, also the huge Caltex installation to the southeast, on Ballast Point.

Generations ago the shores of Balmain were grabbed by maritime industry as it moved out of Sydney Cove. And in more recent times, from the 1830s, came steam sawmills, chemical works, soap factories,

Mort's Dock, oil tankers, tug and lighterage companies, all of which needed more of the precipitous green peninsula so near to and yet so separate from Sydney. So Balmain is not beautiful. But to my mind it is a rare, felicitous place. Long ago industrial man set its horizons close. They press against kitchen windows and turn nice bandy little seagoing streets into blind alleys. But everywhere, unexpectedly, this horizon is broken by enchanting fragments of green and blue and glimpses of the silvery city set about like a circular wall.

It is a place where you may walk for hours in a perfect daze of curiosity and pleasure. Such a walker is a time-traveller, for Balmain is a miniature replica of Sydney itself as it was in that expansive era when steam took over industry. Its ethos springs from an older colonial world; its people have strong roots in a free, native society.

Its history, too, is different from that of other suburbs. It was settled neither by worthy ticket-of-leave farmers, nor by the bashaws of the South Head suburbs or the North Shore. Shipmasters, stevedores, marine engineers and dockworkers built Balmain.

It has many migrant residents, yet you never notice them. It is still the most Australian of villages, perhaps like Surry Hills and Redfern before World War II. Balmain absorbs all comers, the foreign seamen of a century ago, as well as the Greeks and Italians of today. Its close-knit community admits to only one alma mater, Balmain.

'Yeah,' says a drinker in one of its numerous hotels, 'One of these days Balmain may join the Commonwealth. But I dunno. We're still chewing over whether we'll join New South.'

For those with only two or three hours to spare, I recommend a ferry trip from Circular Quay, for Balmain, even more than Manly, is associated with ferries. Balmain's watermen preceded the ferries. They excelled in the boat races which were the principal spectator sport of the 1840s onwards. In fact, though the Sydney Harbour Regatta began in 1828 and continues to this day, Balmain had a famous regatta of its own from 1849 to 1914.

Early residents rowed themselves or engaged a waterman, but in 1841 the first homemade ferryboat ventured forth. It was accurately called *The Experiment* and kept the passengers in a fury of nervousness because of all the pumping that had to be done.

Our ferry fusses under the Bridge like a little waterbug, heedless of the howling steel above. The view of Sydney from its deck is unusual.

Opposite Walsh Bay, we get an impression that the western horn, Miller's Point, was once very long and thin, like Long Nose Point perhaps, and that much of its north and west is reclaimed land. Notable lines of terraces arch up precipitous streets from Miller's Point towards the glimpsed grid of Hickson Road, Kent and other streets named for Queen Victoria's uncles. And we recall that these streets, for us workaday and historically diminished, were for a century or more the picturesque haunt of people connected with coastal and intercolonial shipping.

Governor Macquarie laid out the two lower roads, Kent and Sussex. They were directly behind the huge George Street Barracks, and indeed present-day Erskine Street marks the old track the soldiers made down to their bathhouse which was the first swimming enclosure in Sydney Harbour. This was almost exactly where the Western Distributor now meets Day Street. The streets became so industrially important that municipal authorities were constantly improving them, filling potholes, knocking down hovels, improving their gradients, so that houses and shops were sometimes left perched seven metres or more above the roadway, to be reached by ramshackle wooden stairs.

These can be seen in most early photographs, and indeed the careful observer today, now that so much current reconstruction is going on, can often spot ghosts of old stairways on temporarily exposed stone cuttings and back walls. (We have already seen the old house in Kent Street, Noah's Ark, which was marooned in this manner.)

The tumbledown cottages were occupied by longshoremen, sailmakers and ships' carpenters; many were lodging houses for seamen. There were also chandlers, pubs and produce stores that stocked Hunter River lucerne, New Zealand potatoes, kegs of salt butter, North Coast maize, eggs, live hens and bacon. This area from Walsh Bay to Pyrmont Bridge once bore the sardonic name of The Hungry Mile. Here, in Depression days, the unemployed waited hopefully at wharf gates, sometimes camping there all night in the hope of an early morning pickup. Sometimes a thousand men waited for a stevedoring job which would require only a hundred, and it was bitter knowledge that the latter were often selected because they would 'give a sling' to the foreman when they were paid.

When Macquarie built Kent and Sussex Streets Darling Harbour was still Cockle Bay. Pyrmont Bridge hides from our sight the easily-discernible tidal flats where the first settlers gathered cockles and speared flatfish. The salt marshes, which had been encroached upon over the years, vanished entirely when final reclamation took place in the 1920s.

As the ferry rocks across the deep green water, we are actually crossing north of Darling Harbour, which formally ends at Peacock Point, Balmain, south of the Darling Street wharf where we will land. Peacock's Point was for many years an appalling eyesore of the kind peculiar to an engineering and maritime locality. That is to say, it was a dreadful jumble of garbage, discarded power poles, bashed-in tin sheds, rusty corrugated iron fences, and weeds high enough to hide a horse.

From 1835 until the 1960s ships were repaired and refitted here and several small shipyards operated. Eventually work fell off and closure followed. Peacock's Point was a hideous wasteland until it was transformed into what is probably the greenest, quietest waterside park in Sydney. It is now called Illoura Reserve. Its ancient maritime associations have been retained, with old wharf piles and seagoing timber being used both structurally and ornamentally.

With a swish the ferry bustles close to the small Darling Street wharf. A deckhand throws across half a gangplank, lends a brawny arm, and we arrive on the dripping steps, before us stony hills with roads carved into them, following the easiest slopes. Not Darling Street, though. It plunges straight up from the jetty, a very steep road just here. Yet down it a tram used to run, hooked to a monster restraining weight called the dummy.

'Tonnes it weighed, tonnes. Boys would ride it ... some got killed, others had legs squashed, terrible dangerous, but they wouldn't listen.'

People speak to you in Balmain. The nullities of casual City conversation are absent; people have things to say. This young boy, eight or nine, idling on the steaming wharf, readily answers questions:

'My granddad worked in the mine. He was a mine engineer. Did you know Balmain had a coalmine? He said Sydney's sitting on the biggest and richest black coalfield in the world. One end of it's up Newcastle way, and the other end's in Wollongong. And the other side's maybe halfway to New Zealand.'

'We did hear that they found coal at Cremorne Point, at a great depth. But it was never mined.'

'Balmain mine was deep too, nearly 900 metres, I've heard. And there were long drives right out under the harbour. As far as Vaucluse, my granddad said. And he said that the men working down there used to hear the anchors thumping on the floor of the harbour.'

The existence of the huge coalfield was postulated and accurately assessed in 1847 by that remarkable geologist parson, William Branwhite Clarke, rector of St Thomas's in North Sydney. The Balmain Colliery was worked steadily for only fourteen years. Competition from the top end of the Sydney Basin coalfield, the Hunter River mines, made it unprofitable. It seemed, as well, to be plagued by inefficient management. Several old Balmain miners have left memoirs, and they are hair-raising. The mine was so deep the heat was unbearable, and the men worked almost naked.

'It was as dark as a dungeon, the air full of coaldust and dried horse manure. Lung trouble was rife. In the cage that lowered us some of the sideplates were eaten with rust. Thirty-six of us at a time were lowered in this bucket. We never could tell if the day might be our last.'

This cage did fall once. Fortunately only five workmen were in it at the time; all died after crashing forty metres through the dark.

The horse manure mentioned above reminds us that wretched blind pit ponies lived almost permanently in the depths of this mine until it was closed in 1932. The shafts were concreted over in 1957.

Darling Street is an archaic street with an air of importance. After the steep ascent from the ferry wharf it tends to follow the contours of the land, and this makes Balmain an idiosyncratic place. The foundations of the village are much as they used to be. People just live here; they haven't pushed the earth out of shape. One side of Darling Street is often higher than the other, and to cross over we have to go down three or four steps. Gutters are mostly of the old tipped stone slab type. Footpaths of side streets often descend in broad ramps, and there are little flights of stairs between lanes, and houses, as there are in the Rocks.

Where would you see such marvellous domestic architecture as you do in Balmain? The houses are squeezed among pubs, corner shops, disused factories – 'all the moss on my slate roof died because of soap fallout from the detergent factory' – shipyards and metal works. The sea shows in bright blue slivers through lattices and around chimneypots; it lives at the end of every canted street, not openly so, as in Mosman, but seen through the interstices of masts, winches and chimneys. The whole suburb lives with ships and the sea. This uniquely natural, joyful atmosphere is Balmain's own.

The houses are mostly small, some regular dolls' houses stubbornly individual in shape and ornament. We see gables with broderie anglaise bargeboards, windows with Art Nouveau picture panels, sandstock bricks, iron lace, stone urns, stucco scallop shells and grapevine garlands, octagonal bow windows, Welsh slate roofs with inset red and yellow mosaic bands, Scriptural Dutch tiles on verandahs and stair-risers.

'Well, you see,' says a resident, 'the old shipowners often built terrace cottages for their steady men, and according to where the shipowner come from, Bristol or the Clyde or Aberdeen, that could be the kind of cottage he built, people always thinking that what they know at home is the best.'

Here are a few of the many to look out for. Fortunately some of these have been restored beautifully by modern owners. The Waterman's Cottage is naturally enough near the water, No. 12 Darling Street. Stern and reserved, with a stuck-on upper balcony that ought to come off, it has walker-unfriendly front steps that protrude across your path, so be careful. Built about 1840, it was first occupied by Henry McKenzie, who rowed people to and from Miller's Point. In 1907 he was still living in this house, aged ninety-five.

Not far away is a grand two-storey, Ewenton, in Ewenton Street, a stylish stone house of the 1850s, with a magnificent view over Johnston Bay. It was built by the notable businessman Ewen Wallace Cameron, partner of Thomas Mort, and a Balmain pioneer. When the writer first saw it, it was derelict and cockroachy, with shattered windows and dry, dead garden. It was marked for demolition. Children were playing inside, walking the rotted beams and jumping gaps in the magnificent cedar staircase. Warning them against rusty nails and rats, we moved on, continuing up Darling Street to find St Mary's, a thirteenth-century decorated Gothic Anglican Church, one of Edmund Blacket's first Sydney works. It was consecrated in 1848.

This endearing, squat little church has a worn, homely look; splintery and uneven floors; cluster timber pillars with touches of faded cherry and gold at their capitals, and a rather fine chancel window, the gift of Ewen Wallace Cameron. Edmund Blacket lived at Balmain in his later years; his house Glendinning is still standing at No. 393 Darling Street and is the Methodist Church's Social Centre.

The Watch House, No. 179 Darling Street, is a foursquare little structure designed by Blacket in 1854. It had a narrow squeak in the 1950s. Disgracefully neglected, long used as a dosshouse for homeless drunks, it was due for demolition. However, it passed into the hands of the National Trust, and the remarkable restoration does credit to the very active Balmain Association. The Watch House served as police headquarters until the building of the present rather resplendent police station and courthouse in 1887. It had a dwindling history after that, at one time being occupied by a private family with twelve children, who used the cells as bedrooms. It now serves as an information centre.

Turning right, one wanders into Grafton Street, which has some picturesque better-class residences. Here Sir Henry Parkes, the Father of Federation, lived at the height of his political career. These Victorian houses should look across at the city skyline, but they all face a vast baleful object, which turns out to be the Container Terminal on Johnston's Bay. The Great Container Terminal Battle commenced in 1965, and in spite of ardent resident action, was lost. The $15 million terminal was opened in 1968. Residents are still lamenting the noise, the obstruction of views, the general awfulness of industrial advancement. However, these titanic installations, underpinnings of a great city, have to be somewhere, and they are here.

Still and all, industry has almost left Balmain. Mort's Dock, practically the heartbeat of Balmain from 1855, employing many hundreds of men in its shipyards and engineering works, quietly closed down in 1959. Mort Bay retains hardly a trace to indicate that a fabulous enterprise operated there for over a century.

Colgate-Palmolive – traditionally associated with Balmain, where there's even a Colgate Street – and Lever Brothers, around the corner in White Bay, went away to the western suburbs. Thus vanished a three-generation tradition for girls to 'work down at the Olive' among the soap, talc and other toiletries.

'Both those firms brought in mountains of copra. All Balmain's cockroaches came with the copra. We got South Sea Island cockroaches' laughs an old lady living near the disused old grey Palmolive building. It is not really disused; all elderly buildings in Balmain seem to be converted into something – offices, restaurants, craft centres, cafés. Only the churches have held out.

St Andrew's Congregational Church, circa 1854, pretty spire sticking up out of a mass of dark trees like a hollyhock, is famous for its Saturday market day which Sydneysiders attend in force. A bystander says that it's here at St Andrew's that young Japanese couples come to be wed. A stall lady hung with forty-four strings of hand-moulded beads says no, it's St John's Anglican, over in Birchgrove, Andrew's is romantic but John's has class. This stimulates a discussion on why young Japanese couples should want an Aussie wedding at all, during which we cross the road and visit a splendid pub, The London, which displays a dauntingly large stock of Australian beers of many brands.

Here we learn some more about copra, a coconut palm product. That's the palm in Palmolive soap. We note the historic fact that Lever Brothers began operating about 1895.

'The first boil up of Sunlight Soap south of the equator was done right here in Balmain,' says a patron and is topped by another more serious customer: 'That's not important. The Labor Party began earlier than that, in 1891 down there in Mort Bay, mind you. We've got real history, if that's what you want.'

This name Mort, now. An unusual name surely. Yet it is everywhere in Sydney, Mortlake, Mortdale, nine Mort streets and roads. A quick look in the phone directory shows us a small clutch of live and prospering Morts. It is time to think about this remarkable pioneer and businessman who created or developed so many of Sydney's early industries. The best place to do this is while walking around the tranquil Mort Bay Park, which, for many years now, has occupied the site of Mort's Dock, for so long the most important industrial installation not only in new South Wales but in Australia.

Strolling amid the green spaces, we recall a statue of Thomas Mort, somewhere near Macquarie Street, a frockcoated person of imposing stance and mad affronted eyes. Can that be our Mort? One thing we do know, Thomas Sutcliffe Mort did not resemble his statue – probably Sydney's only statue erected to honour an industrialist. It was cast in 1883, the 'likeness' obtained from photographs modified by the artist's High Victorian passion for pomp, arrogance and the heroic mode.

No, Thomas Sutcliffe Mort was a handsome man with dark curly hair, fine features even in old age, an upright figure and an outgoing personality. In addition to these blessings he had a character which fell very little short of nobility. In brief, he was exactly the right young man to arrive in Sydney when its first towering figures of shipping, land development, trading, whaling, stock breeding and banking were either withering on the vine of life, returning to England to play nabob, or retiring into obscurity.

He was born in 1816, the son of an affluent Lancashire family sadly brought to ruin. As he was well educated, certainly a gentleman, he was sent forth to recoup the family's fortunes. Naturally he travelled as a gentleman in a modest cabin with a washing basin, shaving mirror, a wardrobe and a special tall box for top hats. He had no contact with the emigrants 'tween decks, packed like sardines, sleeping, eating, socialising and fighting in the same space.

The twenty-year-old Thomas, like all youthful empire builders, was desperately homesick, but wrote in his diary 'I whistled off my regrets and replaced them with happy hopes'. He arrived in Sydney in February 1838. It was a boisterous time, when the colony was snapping its braces and blowing its own trumpet. Darling Harbour jostled with ships loading colonial wool, hopeful immigrants poured in through Sydney Cove; the North Shore and the 'upcountry' offered wealth in the form of cedar, mahogany and lesser timbers. There was even talk of a harbour bridge, and if not a bridge, a string of linked steam punts to carry the bountiful produce from the two big rivers and the distant peninsula of Barrenjoey.

Because he was a gentleman Thomas was at once welcomed into all the best houses, and soon had a group of powerful friends. Nevertheless he apprenticed himself to an established importing and auctioneering firm, quickly becoming familiar with the exciting mercantile opportunities of the colony. At twenty-four he had enough capital to marry and open his own auctioneering business.

Thomas brought to auctioneering something unheard-of, the concept that wool sales could be a lark. He used patter, local jokes and a witty delivery. Soon the sales became a popular entertainment. The Mort fortunes in the Old Country were restored, the younger brothers brought out to Sydney, mother and sister comfortably set up, and faithful elder brother William who always remained in England to look after the womenfolk, staked to a business enterprise.

Meanwhile what of Balmain? One cannot imagine that sharpeyed Thomas, rushing around buying land, building cottages and investing in ships, did not visit Balmain.

What of the Balmain peninsula's beginnings? It must have been swept by bushfire in prehistoric times, for it was treeless when the First Fleet arrived, scrubby, rocky, well-watered, its soil unsuitable for farming, its beaches rich in oysters. During the first rush for land grants, no one wanted Balmain. Despite its nearness to Sydney it was 'fit to grow only geebungs and native currants'. Almost the entire peninsula was granted in 1800 to Dr William Balmain, who had come in the First Fleet as surgeon of the transport *Alexander*. The Scot Balmain looks a right sobersides, trap firmly closed, eyes riveted on the portrait painter with a 'Do your worst, damn ye!' expression. No gay or vicious tales of his Sydney life have descended to us. He had a convict mistress, but then almost every officer did.

He was in favour with Governor Phillip because on that disagreeable occasion at Manly when an Aboriginal warrior hurled a spear at the gift-bearing Phillip, piercing his shoulder, Balmain was at hand to minister. It is rather a disturbing picture, for the Governor refused to have the spear removed before he had written a dispatch to his superiors in England, and insisted on tottering to the boat, with Balmain supporting the four metre weapon on his head. Balmain later extracted the spear safely, though painfully.

Aside from Surgeon-General John White (of White's Bay), Balmain is the only one of the First Fleet's eight sawbones who is commemorated on our map. The only local memorial to William Balmain is near the Darling Street wharf, a small rose garden with a plaque. It is a curiously soft and tender memorial for this tough and somewhat mysterious eighteenth-century doctor.

Balmain had little to do with the village that bears his name. He sold the peninsula for five shillings within fourteen months, some say in settlement of a gambling debt. Balmain held responsible positions in the new colony. He was medical superintendent for four years at Norfolk Island, and served six years as chief medical officer in Sydney. He died in London, aged forty-one, leaving his other estates at Windsor and Ryde to his two illegitimate children in Sydney. Balmain's curious sale of his now priceless grant is immortalised in the once-common Sydney saying: 'It's all Balmain to five bob.'

The purchaser, John Gilchrist, was a merchant and shipowner. He held Balmain for thirty years, during which time it was visited only by fishermen and kangaroo hunters. Yet the bush must have regrown, for travellers of the time called it 'one of the most charming valleys of the harbour and a paradise of tropical trees and scenery'. Gilchrist, who had been paymaster to Macquarie's 73rd Regiment, put a cart track from the Parramatta Road down to 'the point opposite Miller's Point' and named it after Governor Darling. He subdivided and sold his property, reputedly for £50,000. People must have moved in almost at once, for a pleasing pencil sketch by John Hardwick, dated 1853, shows what was to be Mort Bay (then Waterview) with land cleared to the ridge, many meadows and farmhouses, and, overlooking all, the spire of 'romantic' St Andrew's, though bare of its present enfolding ruff of trees.

About this time, 1853, Thomas Mort startled the community. Although already immensely wealthy, a speculator in gold, copper, railways, wool, shipping and public buildings, he planned a fully extended dry dock where overseas ships could be refitted before the Home voyage.

The squared shape of the sparkling bay before us is all that remains of astonishing Mort's Dock. In February 1854, when the mangrove marsh was driest, work on this grand engineering project commenced. It necessitated arduous digging. The hole was 195 metres long, 21 metres wide, and 5.5 metres deep, all excavated with picks and shovels. The dock was planned to be large enough to take the biggest vessel then afloat. The work was finished in a year, the first ship entering for repairs in March 1855.

With the dock in operation, the P&O Line decided to mount a regular monthly mail service to Australia. What joy this decision must have brought to the isolated colonies in the South Pacific! Mort proceeded to build a wharf, slipways, an iron foundry and an engineering shop. He employed fifty blacksmiths, wheelwrights, and fettlers as part of a permanent workforce which eventually expanded to 1,100 men. His ironworks produced railway locomotives and carriages, rails, girders, bridgework.

Remarkable as Mort's industrial achievements were, we marvel even more at the radical changes he brought to the historical concept of labour. He was not an egalitarian, any more than Thomas Jefferson or Robert Owen, but he believed in justice, no matter who gave it or received it. For instance, he offered his entire workforce shares in the great enterprise. This proposition was so revolutionary, so shattering to the minds of men mostly trained in Britain where master and man were different species, that many refused to accept it. To tradesmen who satisfactorily fulfilled their work contracts, he presented a freehold allotment in Balmain, and financial assistance in the building of a family cottage.

He believed in good health, and looked to the ventilation of his workshops; kept doctors and medical inspectors on hand; was the inventor of the Australian custom of the smoke-o mid-morning and afternoon, and encouraged a community spirit among his employees. He could also be bossy, advising them all to be in bed by 10.30 pm.

Thomas died in 1878, but his company continued to expand. The Dry Dock's importance began to decline during World War II, when government contracts were increasingly awarded to the official docks and shipworks on Cockatoo Island. Mort's Dock closed in 1959.

Mort Bay Park is a beautiful green space from which one can watch the tall city catch the sunlight and turn it from east to west. There is no sound except that of birds and the occasional plunk as one of the nearby kids catches a soccer ball on his toe. One tries idly to imagine the cacophony that shattered the surrounding air for over a century, but fails. Still, the great dock and Thomas Mort himself surely shaped Balmain by providing constant work, apprenticeships, housing, a way of life that was based on Thomas's own – resolute, individual, humorous, interested in many things. A great idiosyncratic place to visit, Balmain.

One of the pleasures of Sydney is the number of points and peninsulas that remain wooded. Directly before us is one that appears to have floated away from its moorings. But in fact it is an island, and keen eyes can soon discern roofs of buildings, a crane like a damaged spider, and shores extended by jetties and slipways. Like almost all the islands in Sydney Harbour, this one was long ago seized by the navy – Governor Phillip was not a Royal Navy man for nothing – and put to work.

It is curiously named Goat Island, though no one knows why. The original proprietors, who used it as a fishing base and general weekend lollabout place, called it Mel Mel, for the flocks of sulphur crested cockatoos that nested there. Goat Island is probably, aside from Cockatoo in the Parramatta River on the northwest side of Birchgrove, the most interesting of all the Harbour islands that remain to us. There were once thirteen of these exceptionally hard nubbins of sandstone that resisted disintegration during the drowning of the Harbour river valleys. Phillip hardly had his tent raised before island bashing commenced. Some were quarried down to the water's edge thus neatly providing platforms dangerous to shipping but useful for erecting bell buoys and signal towers to warn that shipping. Some were gradually destroyed by gunfire and explosives. The larger became prisons, quarantine stations, laboratories for sinister chemicals, ammunition dumps. One thing common to all was that the noble red gum bush was cut down and European trees, along with the ubiquitous Norfolk Island pine and the Port Jackson fig, planted instead.

Goat Island, which is one kilometre from the city, is 5.5 hectares in area, all of which has been utilised from the early 1830s. At that time 'hardcase' convicts, those who had been convicted of further crimes after transportation, were more or less homeless, being crowded like animals in the old hulk *Phoenix*, moored in Lavender Bay.

Surveyor-General Thomas Mitchell, obsessed like most of the Establishment with defence, pressed for development of Goat Island, which could, he maintained, be converted into a fort to protect the top end of Port Jackson. The *Phoenix* convicts were moved to the island and set to work, many in leg irons, to quarry stone and erect some of the finest and best preserved colonial buildings in Sydney. The men were worked mercilessly, tradition says, probably under vile ticket-of-leave overseers, always the greatest tyrants.

The island is, in fact, an original convict village, even more complete and unchanged than Port Arthur. The official buildings are graced with mahogany floors, cedar staircases, and various small refinements in the masonry. The prisoners' barracks are full of stony chill and a barefaced determination on the part of their gaolers to make life as wretched as possible. Toolshops, storehouses, messhalls, the triangles, solitary confinement cells have been preserved mostly because of the insularity of their environment. When the shipyards closed, Goat Island was simply left alone with a caretaker to chase off bold picnickers and souvenir hunters.

In 1998 a government department saw at last that the deserted island was a treasurehouse, not just for archaeologists but for visitors who wished to step into a living past. The ten million dollar fund provided for restoration and protection of Goat Island will continue to be called upon into the new millennium. In the meantime guided visits can be arranged. Inevitably they sadden; there are too many reminders of the shameful years of slave labour that built this strange place. One recoils from the exposed rock with its slight overhang where a man was chained for two years, the rusted bolt, the hollow where he slept. This man is scarcely known in Australian history, yet his story is the summation of convictism, its cruelty and remedy.

He was Charles 'Bony' Anderson, born in a workhouse in 1816, apprenticed in a coal ship at nine, and transported for seven years in 1834 for a drunken fight in which some shop windows were smashed. Anderson was illiterate, spoke 'thick as a beast, should a beast speak', and bore a depressed scar from a head wound received in battle during his navy years. It is possible he had some brain damage from this wound. As he had an unbreakable spirit, he presented a sporting challenge to his gaolers. His term at Goat Island is a monotonous record of floggings (for such things as staring at a passing steamer), escape, apprehension, floggings, escape, apprehension, and finally his inhuman sentence as an intractable felon to be chained to a rock in the open for two years. His chain was eight metres long, so he had limited movement. To make things uneasier, he wore trumpet irons on his legs. Such a savage beast was dangerous to approach, so the gangrenous morsels with which he was fed were conveyed to him on the end of a long pole. Under a penalty of one hundred lashes, his fellow convicts were forbidden to speak or look at him. His former working mate risked and received this penalty by throwing him a quid of tobacco.

Free people who passed in boats and often tossed him bits of food, reported that his back, covered with infected lacerations, was infested with maggots. When rain fell he rolled in the puddles to assuage the torture. The representations of these free settlers to the governor finally had the man's sentence shortened. After this he was sent to the Port Macquarie limeworks where he carried sacks of lime on his back, which was burned grotesquely. He absconded, being given shelter by the Aborigines. Recaptured and flogged, and 'seeking mercy by the gallows' he killed an overseer with a spade. But he was denied death, being sent instead on a life sentence in irons to dreaded Norfolk Island.

There Anderson remained turbulent and intractable, teased by the other prisoners as though he were a wild animal, often flogged, frequently in solitary confinement, until Captain Maconochie took charge of Norfolk Island. Most of us know little of this intelligent, brave humanitarian who, in an age that regarded the sadistic abuse of such as Anderson not only as acceptable but as eminently moral, could say: 'Vice is a disease and penal science is just moral surgery. The means it employs must often be painful but its object should always be benevolent –

always the speedy discharge of the patient.'

In 1840 then, these two unusual men were brought together by fate, the highly literate and compassionate naval officer, and the brutalised Anderson, 'twenty-four years old and looking like an old broken man'. The Superintendent 'cast about therefore for any means of reclaiming the unhappy creature'. He did exactly the right thing; he put the man who spoke thick as a beast with the beasts, the island's team of half-tamed bullocks. Bony lived alone with these animals, all men being strictly enjoined not to interfere with him. To paraphrase Maconochie's words, he became less wild, felt himself of some value, he and the bullocks grew tractable together. It is touching to learn that he would not use the whip on his animals.

As Anderson became a human again, Maconochie gave him further responsibilities. Three years later Governor Gipps, visiting the island, noticed 'a prisoner, trimly dressed in sailor's garb, going about his duties'. Anderson was then in charge of the Mount Pitt signal station, and had surrounded the high, isolated spot with a flourishing garden.

In later years Anderson became deranged. Fortunately he died before he could be passed over to the brutal hands of Major Joseph Childs, who supplanted Maconochie as Superintendent of Norfolk Island and inaugurated a reign of such disorderliness and capricious cruelty that it culminated in the famous insurrection of 1846.

Alexander Maconochie himself, who had such success with his humane theories of prison reform, was recalled in disgrace. He died in obscurity, though he left behind several books enlarging on his revolutionary ideas.

There are three other islands visible from various parts of Balmain. Snapper, a training depot for sea cadets, is whimsically laid out like a ship, its ends shaped as bow and stern. Spectacle is a storage site for munitions; its buildings include a naval storehouse and museum certainly worth seeing.

Cockatoo Island is more interesting still. Sydneysiders probably recall this island as a comprehensive and inaccessible complex of dry docks, slipways, jetties, machine shops, engineering works and ships in various stages of construction or repair. At eighteen hectares – some land gained by reclamation – Cockatoo is the largest Harbour island, situated midstream in the mouth of the Parramatta River. (Glebe Island was once the largest but it has been united with the mainland.) Cockatoo is regarded as the birthplace of professional, large scale shipbuilding in Australia.

Responding to the desperate need for a reliable docking and refit facility, Governor FitzRoy ordered the construction of a dry dock by convict labour. His order was ratified by the Legislative Council in 1847, excavation commenced in 1850 and the Fitzroy Dry Dock completed in 1857. Radical newspapers pointed out that the work might have speeded up if the penal authorities had taken the leg irons off the wretched convicts. A visiting Royal Navy brig HMS *Herald* was the first ship to make ceremonious entry.

The Cockatoo Dockyards' long and varied history continued through depressed or prosperous decades until the later years of the twentieth century. At the time of writing the island is silent and uninhabited, poised between the furious industrial past and its future as a historically treasured reserve. For like Goat Island, Cockatoo Island is an archaeological goldmine, not because of its century and a half of continuous service to shipping, but because of the poor devils who made it possible. In 1833 Governor Bourke, a humane man, fretted over the fearful conditions of the George Street Gaol, overcrowded, infested with rats and riddled with disease. He decided to put a small, subsidiary prison on unoccupied Cockatoo Island, sufficient to accommodate 250 of the most intransigent charges. The island was a suitable place for a quarry, heavy labour in which would keep them out of mischief.

Fragments of the cell block, the guardroom and kitchen built by these men still exist amidst the wealth of convict era relics on Cockatoo. Governor Bourke in due course went his way, the prisoners who had constructed the fine buildings on Goat Island were transferred to Cockatoo to do it again. They were joined by sixty 'lifers' from Norfolk Island penal settlement, which was due to be closed. There were now far more than 250 convicts on Cockatoo, and Governor Gipps ordered extensive enlargement of the prison buildings. These are being restored today.

Cockatoo Island was a desperately unhappy place, quickly famous for the severity of its regime, the shortlived but ferocious mutinies, and the many attempts at escape. The writer Louis Becke, who as a boy lived at Woolwich, which we can see just beyond Cockatoo, described how he and his brother would listen on foggy days (when most attempts were

The gates to the Botanic Gardens, part of old Government House's original demesne and farm. It is fairly firm tradition that the Gardens were laid out mostly by Mrs Macquarie.

Observatory Park is one of my favourite places.

Mosman: you will never see so many and so diverse cupolas in another suburb.

Mosman Bay: the many small boats flitting along its shores, the ferry wharves and boatsheds, the ferries themselves ceaselessly trundling back and forth like domesticated waterbugs.

Clyde Bank

The Macquarie Light was designed by Greenway, the convict architect, but it is the second of its family, being built to the same plan in 1883, when Greenway's first building, then sixty-five years old and crumbling, was demolished.

Durham Hall, Albion Street

Sydney Harbour, beautiful as a dream, laid upon the map like a branch of blue coral.

made) for 'the muffled clamour of that dreadful bell and the sound of someone panting hard in his swim for liberty. One winter's day, a wretched creature was found clinging with bleeding hands to the oyster-covered rocks beneath our house, too weak to drag himself further from his pursuers.'

In 1863, Frederick Ward succeeded in swimming from Cockatoo Island, and survived for six years as the bushranger Thunderbolt.

Among the many massive stone structures erected by these convicts are some of great historical interest, such as the twenty bottle-shaped wheat silos excavated in the living rock at the command of Governor Gipps. The silos speak of almost unimaginable labour. They are nine metres deep and six metres wide at the base. Each could hold over 100 tonnes of grain, safely sealed away from weather and the armies of weevils. They might well have conserved New South Wales's plentiful production of wheat, but they were never used. Similar silos had been constructed at the Norfolk Island settlement many years before. These are still in existence, curiously called 'the Mummies' or 'Momies' by the residents. The silos were unsuccessful; the wheat turned mouldy, a tragedy for the always underfed prison settlement.

At the time of writing Cockatoo is out of bounds, but there are sometimes special tours. This is good news for island-lovers for God knows we are an obsessive tribe; there is even better to come. A scatter of small maritime companies will arrange Island Events – a scoot around the Harbour visiting the remaining nubbins, with inspections where possible, and maybe a picnic on Rodd Island, in Iron Cove, a traditional place for hijinks. Information from tourist offices.

Iron Cove Bridge carries the important artery Victoria Road from the small, crowded suburb, Rozelle to the spatulate Drummoyne peninsula. Drummoyne looks tremendously over-built; it is a favourite home unit area, with many of those twinkling windows getting great views of the Parramatta River or oil tank installations as the case may be. The peninsula was not settled until the 1880s, when the poor farmland and peach, fig, and China orange orchards were subdivided. From this era remain a few grandmotherly family homes, tottering at the water's edge above mossy seawalls and crumbling boat steps. Though Drummoyne has considerable light industry, most of the residents work in the city, only 6.5 kilometres away.

The introduction of the River Cats in 1993 brought new life to all the riverside suburbs, which languished somewhat after World War II. The Cats, trailing their long tails of foam, make the trip Sydney to Parramatta in fifty-five minutes, a delightful voyage.

The first settler of consequence up this way was nasty Surgeon Harris, who was a great beauty and went on like one. He was a tremendously rich person who spent most of his post Second Fleet life in Ultimo, which he named. His grant of 290 hectares covered almost all the land between Iron Cove and Hen and Chicken Bay; he called his farm Five Dock. For a century or more it has been a solidly respectable working class suburb.

Through the lower end of the peninsula runs the cryptically-named Great North Road, which plunges decisively away from the Parramatta Road and ends at the Parramatta River at Abbotsford. Once it was met by the Bedlam Point punt, operated by winch and cable. It was then truly the Great North Road, connecting the important farmlands of Ryde and beyond with the mother settlement.

We are able to read many personal accounts of the exciting journey to Town from the northern farms, mostly by people who recalled childhood experiences of that damnable punt. 'Mother and me sat with the two oxen and five pigs bound for market and murder ... the ferryman was drunk as a prince, Father did the hauling on the rope, with fiery language ... A gentleman who did not assist told us of a stormy night when the chain broke and he and Honble. Blaxland whirled down stream, coming to grief on a sandbar, and were saved for posterity by a farmer with a long pole. That night we camped halfway to the high road [Parramatta Road] and mother and me shook all night for fear of dingoes in the bush.'

Hen and Chicken Bay catches the eye; its shores are marked with unexpected names. It has three deep baylets of its own; Canada Bay, Exile Bay and King's Bay. In 1837, French settler rebellions against British rule in Canada were brutally quashed by a figure familiar to us, Sir George Arthur, ex-Lieutenant-Governor of Van Diemen's Land. Transportation was still an alternative to the death sentence, so fifty-nine most unusual convicts were sent off to Sydney. They had been convicted of 'aggravated treason'. Ninety-one of their colleagues, who were of British extraction, including some sympathetic Americans, were sent to Van Diemen's Land.

They were received with acclaim by certain free spirits among

Sydneysiders, who themselves would dearly have loved to rebel against British rule. Sensible Governor Gipps treated his French Canadians more or less as prisoners of war. The Canadian exiles were all educated men; several were doctors who generously treated the settlers round about. They lived in a stockade between Burwood Park and Parramatta Road, and are still kindly, though vaguely, remembered in Concord folklore. By 1844 most of them had been pardoned and repatriated to Canada. The three deeply indented, reedy bays named for them are their memorial. Some say the name of Concord itself commemorates these visitors.

All the peninsulas in this river country are eccentrically shaped. Onions Point looks like an angry chook. It is the eastern end of probably the most handsome peninsula, ornamented by the lovely suburb of Hunters Hill, and the interesting Woolwich. Here at Onions Point is the official confluence of the Lane Cove and Parramatta Rivers, but no one has told the rivers. They are very different, flowing at their individual pace, the Parramatta carrying, alas, some pollution, the Lane Cove countrified and serenely slow.

The Parramatta was always significant, as it was the waterway – indeed the only way if you did not fancy a huge cross-country hike – between the intended capital and the port of Sydney. Produce and wool came down the river in sailing vessels; passengers travelled via cart, soldiers still marched overland. In 1790 a fearful contraption, the first 'ship' built in Australia, took to the Parramatta. It was named the *Rose Hill Packet*, was propelled by both oar and wind and the voyage took a week.

The Woolwich/Hunters Hill peninsula enjoys both the Parramatta and the Lane Cove Rivers, but somehow it seems to belong to the latter. The district has many of the finest houses in New South Wales. As usual Hunters Hill seems to float in a private light. From this golden gauze arise like djinns the spires of little churches, for Hunters Hill, like Balmain, has a low profile.

What kind of place is it?

'There are stone walls with doors in them,' says a child's poem. 'And what is on the other side isn't today.'

For nearly half a century, no one wanted what we know today as Hunters Hill. The District of Hunters Hill, something quite different, was early settled by farmers, orchardists and timber-getters. It was a vast area, broken down under Governor Bourke into parishes; the parish of

Hunters Hill embracing practically all the country west of the Lane Cove River, with the old settlement of Ryde, or Kissing Point as it was then known, as its market town. The peninsula had poor soil, was tick infested, and benighted wallaby and koala hunters were worried by fairy voices wailing about their camps in the dark. Undoubtedly these fairies were of the same race as those others that unnerved lonely sentries during Sydney's first months – 'they whispered "Warra warra!" and it was not until much time had gone by that we understood this meant: "Go away! Go away !" '

So it was not until 1834 that serious settlement was made on the peninsula, the first purchaser being a Sydney merchant called Billy the Bull. The same year Mary Reiby settled near the south end of present-day Fig Tree Bridge. Being a prudent woman, she took heed of the local tales of bushrangers and had the shutters of her riverside house lined with sheet iron, so that she could withstand a siege if need be. This house was bought in 1847 by the Joubert brothers who added a wooden tower and balconies and used it not only as a family home but as the ferry terminus for their Lane Cove River service. Fig Tree House (No. 1 Reiby Street) still stands, looking extraordinarily country-French in spite of its mixed ancestry.

Hunters Hill's early nickname, 'the French village', is due solely to Joubert frères, whom we imagine as a jolly pair of Cheerybles from Bordeaux, intent on dabbing the colonial woodlands wild with a little chic. But Jules Joubert, his brother Didier and their partner the Comte de Milhau were accomplished and comfortably wealthy men. They were the first large scale speculative builders in Sydney. They built for the plump in pocket, and we are thankful that the latter were content to be guided by the elegant good taste of their architects. The Jouberts began to build about 1848 and it is said that two hundred of their houses are still standing in Hunters Hill. The partners used local materials wherever possible, but they imported French and Italian masons, as well as shiploads of European tiles, glass, marble, and decorative fittings.

Hunters Hill, therefore, though not historic in the usual sense, is a curious and delightful place to explore. The houses are not all grand by any means. Many are the handsomest bijou cottages, some built at a later date in the Joubert manner by Italian stoneworkers who put up at the Garibaldi Inn. The 1861 inn, once used as a corner grocery shop, is on the corner of Ferry and Alexander Streets.

Though we mention a few favourite houses, you'll spot many others by just mooching around. If you decide to make a day of it, best to take the ferry from Circular Quay, and then the bus straight up the middle of the peninsula to Gladstone Avenue. After that, drift. The streets are uncommonly narrow, some of them as steep as stairways, which seem to dive straight into the water, especially on the north side. The leafy pedestrian lanes are fetching, occasionally less than a metre wide, with willows overhanging them, and perhaps on the other side a fortress wall of sandstone brick. Above these walls show quartettes of scrimshawed chimneys, roofs overgrown with virginia creeper, and overgrown trees. If these gardens are haunted, it must be by contented ghosts.

A purring contentment, in fact, is the resident spirit of Hunters Hill. The adorable old houses in Brown's Lane, Viret Street and Kokera Street radiate the same serenity as do the dozens of mousy, one-storey cottages with verandah, two front windows, centre door, like a child's drawing. Nearly every street has a blue glimmer at the bottom; some have romantically misty vistas of headlands and bays across the way. New and restored houses seem perfectly to mingle with the old ones. We owe this partly to the revived craft of handmade bricks. These lively bricks can be every colour from pale rose to coffee brown, each brick individually brindled or freckled with white, sepia or auburn.

Here are some houses to look out for. Passy, in Passy Avenue – Jules Joubert built this classic late-Colonial in 1854 for the French Consul of his day. It was later occupied by Sir George Dibbs, the Premier of New South Wales. If you stroll down Passy Walk, you may see its unusual twin staircases.

Wybalena, probably Hunters Hill's most-photographed house. It is No. 3 Jeanneret Street, a somewhat awkwardly-shaped house with very good wrought iron.

Innisfree, No. 11a Ady Street, built in 1858 by Jules Joubert. It is notable for a gatehouse and a magnificent arched gateway leading to a stone courtyard. In its drawing room in 1861 Hunters Hill was proclaimed a municipality.

Gladstone Hotel, on the corner of Alexandra Street. This 1881 structure was built as a private house, and became an inn about eight years later, while preserving to some degree the architectural integrity of the original building.

You will also want to see the old shoe shop in Ferry Road, an aged stone building so small it is without doubt occupied by brownies; Fig Tree House where both Mary Reiby and Numa Joubert, son of Didier, lived; the Town Hall, where a historical Museum is open Monday to Friday, business hours.

The tiny municipality is also associated with the French Marist missionaries who settled in the peninsula in 1847, and in 1857 constructed, mostly with their own hands, the dignified Villa Maria Church. In 1881 they opened St Joseph's College, Hunters Hill, which claims to be the largest boarding school for boys in Australia.

Hunters Hill people surely must be ferry people; the small waterbugs, swashing into and out of Valentia Street wharf seem to suit the place somehow. But of course you can reach the city by expressway. It's a shame that this dreaming peninsula should be cut in half by a thunderous traffic artery, though a necessary shame. This will carry you over Tarban Creek and the Gladesville Bridge, and very quickly into the city.

One is somewhat comforted by the lean elegance of the Gladesville Bridge. It gives the agreeable illusion that the road rushes up to the water's edge and takes off in a 305 metre leap with Olympic ease, landing like a butterfly and whisking away in a harmonious curve over Huntleys Point.

If by some magic, and to the consternation of motorists, we could stand on the bridge's topmost point, what would we see? To the east and south another bridge, the glamorous new Anzac Bridge, feeding the Western Distributor. The golden haze distorts it; from here its upperworks appear as two aerial teepees, suspended in frail webs of cable stays.

Between these bright diverse waterways and the Parramatta Road are streets and houses and houses and streets, heavy overbuilding sparsely freckled with the green of little reserves and sportsfields. Old suburbs these, with dreary Victorian schools and churches, the relics of light industry, war memorials – respectable suburbs only recently beginning to stir into redevelopment and imaginative real estate marketing.

Far more interesting to look up the Parramatta River, hurdling all the bays and headlands, the large and small bridges, and fancy that we can discern Homebush Bay.

There we would encounter a science fiction fantasy made real. A futuristic playground of domes and arches, glass and steel structures of intricate and inspired design, swooping and soaring in the midst of parks and gardens that seem to run on for ever, bounded by the sparkling waters of the river and the bay.

Two hundred years ago this area consisted of wetlands and dense woodlands. Much was reclaimed from the saltmarshes and the mangroves, only to become a dumping ground for Sydney's industrial and household rubbish. The waters of Homebush Bay and the Parramatta River degenerated into a lifeless sink of pollution.

This ecological disaster area has been transformed into a showpiece of regeneration and renewal. The process started slowly during the early 1980s when Homebush was identified as the appropriate location for the new showgrounds and large scale sports facilities. Bicentennial Park at Homebush was dedicated as a part of the 1988 celebrations.

For most people in Sydney, the first sign of major activity in the area was a forest of cranes on the skyline. Travellers on the sleek River Cats nosing up and down the Parramatta River observed the spectacular movement of soil and rubbish in reclamation and site preparation.

The Olympic complex is set in 400 hectares of Millenium Parklands, created from a massive effort in waste relocation as mountains of rubbish and rubble were terraced, drained, landscaped, capped and replanted with native shrubs and grasses. The propagation of native seeds was a triumph of research which provided large stocks of seeds for the replanting. Homebush Bay was dredged to remove the toxic sediments of decades of industrial and commercial activity.

The parklands intersect the main public space, the Olympic Plaza, by way of five east–west 'green fingers' of open space, each with a distinctive design to make a transition from urban to 'natural'. The northern or station finger has a grove of jacaranda and pear trees with cafés and stalls to create a cosmopolitan atmosphere. In contrast, the southern Boundary Creek finger is thickly planted with water gums and other wetland species.

During the Olympic preparations the Homebush skyline was dominated by the largest mobile crane in Australia, working on Stadium Australia. This is one of the largest outdoor venues in the world. With a capacity of 110,000 it dwarfs the Sydney Football Stadium.

Fourteen storeys high at the roof peak, the stadium is not fully enclosed, thereby permitting natural ventilation to save the grass from browning off and to provide cool conditions for competitors. The most distinctive feature of the stadium is the roof, three hectares of giant translucent tiles suspended from the main arches. The tiles allow natural light into the arena without allowing distracting shadows or shafts of direct sunlight onto the playing field.

The principles of innovation and energy efficiency have been applied to all the amazing arenas that have sprung into being for the Games. The Sydney International Aquatic Centre, described by the President of the International Olympic Committee, Juan Antonio Samaranch, as the best swimming pool he had ever seen, is constructed without columns to provide unimpeded views for up to 4,400 spectators. At the Olympic Village every permanent dwelling will have rooftop solar cells designed to provide all its own energy needs. The Olympic Village will thus be the largest solar-powered suburb in the world.

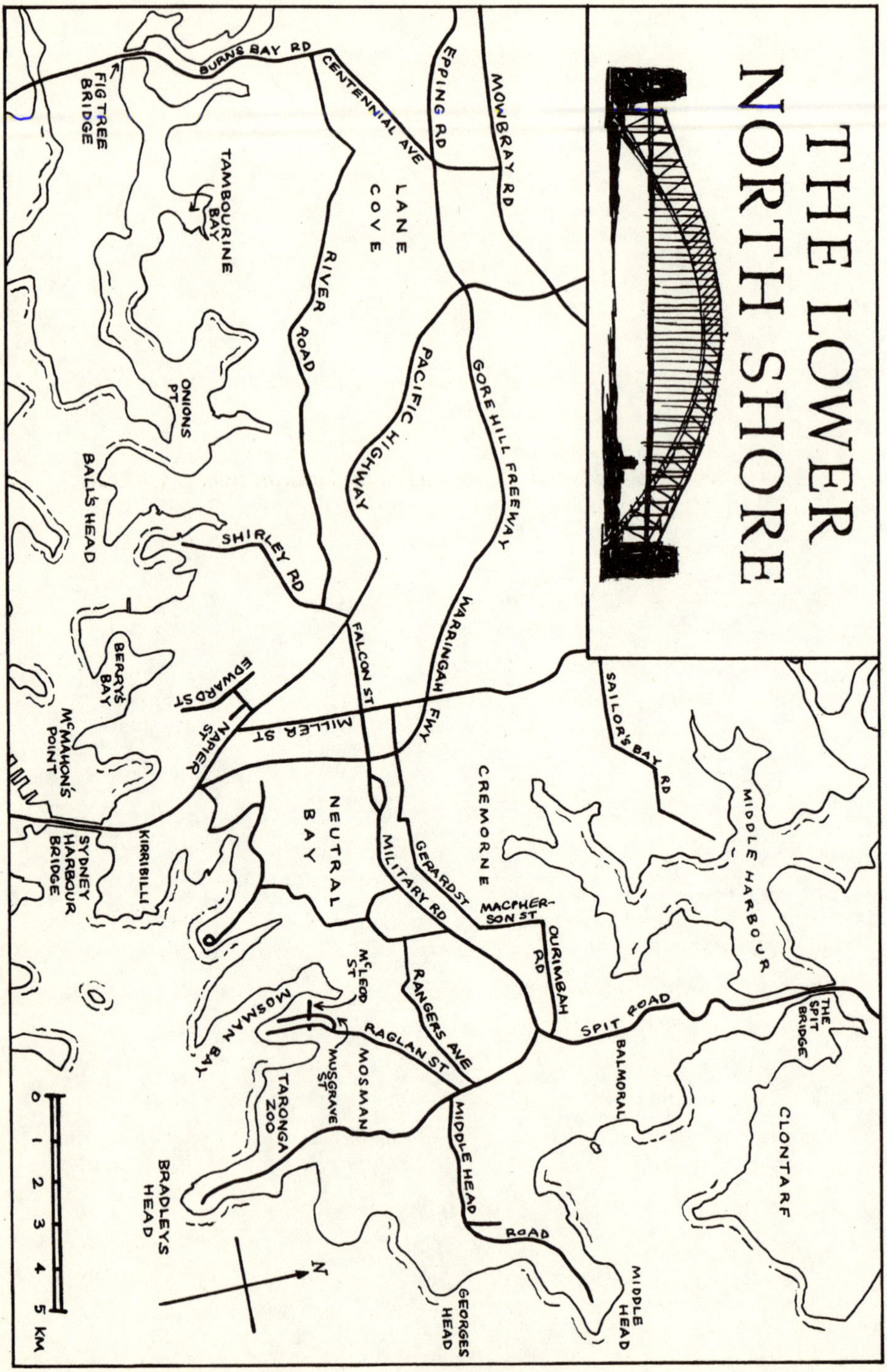
THE LOWER NORTH SHORE
BURNS BAY RD
FIG TREE BRIDGE
CENTENNIAL AVE
EPPING RD
MOWBRAY RD
TAMBOURINE BAY
LANE COVE
RIVER ROAD
PACIFIC HIGHWAY
GORE HILL FREEWAY
ONIONS PT
BALL'S HEAD
SHIRLEY RD
WARRINGAH FWY
FALCON ST
BERRY'S BAY
EDWARD ST
NAPIER ST
MILLER ST
McMAHON'S POINT
SAILOR'S BAY RD
CREMORNE
NEUTRAL BAY
SYDNEY HARBOUR BRIDGE
KIRRIBILLI
MILITARY RD
GERARD ST
MACPHERSON ST
OURIMBAH RD
MIDDLE HARBOUR
McLEOD ST
RANGERS AVE
MOSMAN BAY
RAGLAN ST
MUSGRAVE ST
MOSMAN
TARONGA ZOO
SPIT ROAD
THE SPIT BRIDGE
BALMORAL
CLONTARF
MIDDLE HEAD ROAD
BRADLEYS HEAD
GEORGES HEAD
MIDDLE HEAD
N
0 1 2 3 4 5 KM

CHAPTER 8
MIDDLE HEAD TO FIG TREE BRIDGE

Mosman, Ethel Turner land – hauling the guns to George's Head – Governor Brisbane meets Broomstick and Tarpot – when the larrikins went to Chowder – Taronga Park Zoo – Bradley's Head, guardian of the port – Oswald Brierly paints a wall – a tightrope across Long Bay – Ben Boyd and the cannibals – Kingsford-Smith puts Anderson Park on the map – quaint Kirribilli – old houses and churches in North Sydney – a forgotten scientist – Billy Blue who acted the goat to advantage – Blue's Point, and its history – Stone Age artists on Balls Head – the magical light of Sydney – millionaire Berry, a tycoon of the early days – Joseph Fidden, strong man of Lane Cove – Barnet Burns, a romance of the South Seas – the tragic tanner of Tanner's Creek.

TODAY we shall explore another part of 'across the water', from Middle Head to Fig Tree Bridge, which crosses the still tidal Lane Cove River to the Hunter's Hill/Woolwich peninsula. Along this northern shore of the main Harbour is a picturesque string of residential suburbs, with a pocket of light industry here and there. Their domestic architecture displays every style Sydney has ever employed, with the exception, I believe, of true Colonial Georgian.

On this spring day the northern shore is beautiful, its historic places scarcely altered, its maritime character emphasised by the many small boats flitting along its shores, the ferry wharves and boatsheds, the ferries themselves ceaselessly trundling back and forth like domesticated waterbugs.

Allow a generous half day for this expedition. A full day is better for you will wish to have lunch, wander in old graveyards, forage in antique shops, perhaps even swim in one of the many excellent public pools along the meandering shoreline. And then there is the native bush;

islets of it everywhere where one least expects it, lingering on in damp secluded gullies where possums and bandicoots still live, and the air is jocund with the cries of currawongs and magpies. 'Sydney or the Bush!' used to be the old warcry, but Sydney *and* the bush would be truer, for there is still so much of it on the North Shore.

It was settled much later than the south side, except of course, for oddikins like Billy Blue, who was living on Blue's Point before the Battle of Waterloo. And James Milson was farming on his point even earlier. His sons used to swim across the Harbour to Dawes Point, and in safety, for it is said sharks didn't come into Port Jackson until the whaling stations began tipping offal into the water.

But it was a long time before the Shore flew flags of smoke from kitchen fires. The first pictures show these deep sheltered coves crowned with small yellow beaches, all-year-round creeks splitting the green slopes above like white veins. Waterfalls are everywhere, rushing down the sandstone cliffs, for this was a well-watered land, and indeed even today from the air the whole terrain is marked with the sculptured forms of creekbeds, drained lagoons and old ponds.

The first Mosman photographs are of Archibald Mosman's old stone buildings long after he had left them, Ben Boyd's wharf and dam and his big house Craignathan. But in bush clearings there were slab huts under the turpentines and blue gums, and we have photographs of them as well; typical early settlers' photographs, with the family outside, men sitting and women standing. These people were post-splitters and firewood cutters. They always look fit, for theirs was a tranquil if laborious life, and they fed well according to the ideas of the day:

'Good beef and damper, of that you'll get enough.
While boiling in the bucket such a walloper of duff.'

We start our tour at Spit Junction, another of Sydney's whimsically-shaped squares; it is named Trafalgar. The junction is somewhat younger than the battle, however. Its first hotel was called the Inkerman which dates it correctly. Trams from North Sydney reached here in 1893; it was then already a sizeable market centre.

The village of Mosman lies to our south and east. Some people say that it ought to be called Mossman, but this is erroneous. Archibald Mosman himself was a sahib, son of Hugh, Deputy Lord-Lieutenant of Lanarkshire. Before arriving in Sydney in 1828, Archie and his twin brother George had made fortunes growing sugar in the West Indies. George became a grazier in northern New South Wales, but Archie decided to be a whaler. Whaling, as we have noted, was both lucrative and governmentally favoured.

When Mosman applied for a grant of four acres on Great Sirius Cove, it was granted, provided he spent £5000 on capital improvement. This was done by the wealthy young Scot, aided, so folklore says, by the labour of convicts assigned to him to build a 240 yard jetty, whaling station and his stone cottage orné, The Nest. Mosman's estate, by the time he sold out, extended all the way from the shore to Military Road between Cremorne and Spit Junction. He had become fabulously rich. At this time the Sydney whaling figures approximated £150,000 annually and accounted for more than half the total exports of the colony. (Mosman paid his whalemen 10/- per week, found.)

The whales, foundation of all this wealth, were the southern right whales, both timorous and slow, poor beasts. In pre-settlement days they came into the sheltered bays of Port Jackson to calve, even Mosman Bay. But fifty years of European settlement put an end to that.

Mosman sold out in 1839, so his connection with the suburb was very brief. Sadly, there is little to show nowadays of Mosman's whaling days. His old stone storehouse still stands. Locally called The Barn, it is the Boy Scouts' meeting place. Mosman's coat of arms also shows a blowing whale.

Archie Mosman later became a grazier in New England. In 1851 he persuaded the government to lay out a town on his home paddock. This is present-day Glen Innes. He died at Randwick in 1863, in the home built by Isaac Nathan, who had the assorted distinctions of being a friend of the poet Byron, Musical Historian to George IV, and the first man in Australia to be killed by a tram.

Mosman and his wife are buried in St Jude's graveyard at Randwick and the perpetual care of their monument (very nicely done, too) is the charge of Mosman Council.

Mosman's son, Hugh, went prospecting in Queensland in the 1870s with his black servant Jupiter Mosman, who was the discoverer of the fabulously rich goldfield of Charters Towers – 'piles of gold-spangled quartz, heaped in fantastic confusion'. There is a statue to Jupiter in Charters Towers but none to Hugh.

Mosman's beauty and its closeness, by sea, to the southern prestige suburbs made it obvious to many that it had a future. Ideas about this future varied. Mr J. J. C. Bradfield, builder of the Harbour Bridge, predicted in 1932: 'The City proper will become a New York in miniature, with skyscrapers exceeding 150 ft, while North Sydney and Mosman will emerge as a second Brooklyn, with property values equaling those of the city.' In later years, Mr L. J. Hooker, the real estate magnate, gave his opinion: 'Neutral Bay, Cremorne and Mosman will become a northside King's Cross.'

So far Mosman has resisted both dread fates with stubborn passion (while genteelly pretending none of it is happening, and getting on with pruning the bauhinia). What can one say of it at the present?

'It's Ethel Turner Land,' says one of our passengers, at whose school the beloved writer of *Seven Little Australians* has been enjoying a revival. And she hangs out of the car window counting cupolas.

You will never see so many and so diverse cupolas in another suburb. Copper-sheathed, shingled, carved stone, rough-casts with garlands of stucco ivy; with witch's hat roofs, gables, bell-towers, tarnished gilt roosters, dragon scales, flags; their residents owls, bats, dust and dried leaves, and sometimes, lucky, lucky children. It is true, these cupolas top Ethel Turner houses, with servants' quarters, huge willows for cubbies and swings, summerhouses with earwigs and tea on the lawn. Most of them are Edwardian, and date from Mosman's breaking away from North Sydney (1901) and becoming a municipality on its own. Then, as now, Mosman's population was largely middleclass. Nowadays it's professional also. It rates more lawyers, professors, architects and company directors on the electoral roll than any other suburb. Officers attached to the military and naval establishments built many large homes, and lesser ranks lived in rows of cottages, still existing. In fact, many of Mosman's residents are descended from garrison men of the 1870s and earlier.

Modern Mosman has an all-over mellowness. People haven't gimcracked-up the smaller cottages as in some other suburbs. The frequent renovations are done with taste and sympathy. Bradley's Head Road rambles away from Mosman Junction with the true old horse-era ramble of long gentle corners, curious gradings and turns that betray that once upon a time it avoided hillocks, large trees, and the corners of important people's estates. The Victorian high school stands on the site of an old market garden.

However, in the 1960s and 70s development was hurried, rude and greedy. Now and then at the end of some drowsy treelined street you catch a glimpse of an abrupt brick wall which has boxed in a dozen old dormer-windowed houses. At present it appears that replacement buildings are planned and erected with foresight and tender care.

'Too late,' laments a frail resident appparently held in one piece by very taut braces. 'For three generations my family looked at the Harbour, and then overnight there was nothing to see but a dirty big corn flake packet of red bricks with balconies stuck on it like wasp nests. Might as well be living in a well.'

From Spit Junction onwards, the sea is always on the left, with steep roads plunging down towards it. We turn towards it along Middle Head Road – more old houses, some of stone, and on the south the beginnings of Rawson Park and the vast military reserve which takes up almost all of George's Heights and Middle Head.

George's Head, only 6.4 kilometres by sea, east of the new town, was first fortified in 1801. Governor King's Battery, commanding the entrance to the main Harbour, was a source of much satisfaction to the little colony. What quaint conceit, one might think, to believe that the expanding republics of France and the United States might cast covetous eyes upon a remote speck of civilisation in the South Seas! But though remote, the speck was an Imperial outpost, and its officers regarded it as such. In those turbulent years Britain was always at war with someone, or in alliance with someone at war, and consequently the Colony of New South Wales was also at war and a legitimate object of attack. However, direct enemy action did not come until 1942.

People who lived across the water during World War II might recall 'the boom' – a barrage net stretched from Green Point, the northern cusp of Watson's Bay, to the Sow and Pigs reef, and thence to George's Head. The whole thing had a sheep-country air about it. Manly ferry chugs up to barrage and blows whistle. Little boat hurriedly undoes gate for ferry to pass, and immediately closes gate behind it before anything awful can get in.

Alas, two Japanese midget submarines succeeded in passing through the barrage net, it is thought concealed in the wake of the Manly ferry or other incoming vessel. Another was caught in the net and blew itself up. The one submarine which was able to surface and fire its torpedoes sank the *Kuttabul*, an old ferry then used by the Navy as a depot ship near Garden Island. Twenty men died in this catastrophe, the only Sydney Harbour casualties from enemy action.

In 1871 a previous invasion scare resulted in the extensive re-fortification of George's, Middle and Bradley's Heads. The enormous sum of £210,000 was spent on this ambitious project. Military Road, now the main highway from North Sydney to Spit Junction (Bradley's Head Road continues its original line) was constructed specifically for the fearful task of manhandling the guns to their sites.

The guns were built up with wood, so that they assumed equal diameters each end. After three months of incessant labour by 250 soldiers, during which about one-third were incapacitated by accident, the guns arrived at their destination and were placed in position 'Such a crop of broken and twisted limbs, sprains and severe flesh wounds were seldom if ever known before' lamented the *Sydney Morning Herald*.

We'll take a look at the massive fortifications still remaining when we visit Bradley's Head.

On George's Head was probably the first Aboriginal village in the colony. Governor Macquarie had established it with huts and gardens, 'and a most interesting and romantic road from the landing place to the village'. Like other governors, Macquarie could never comprehend the nature of the hunter–gatherer Aborigines. He appears to have concluded that they did not live in houses because they had none, so he built them some.

One of the last acts of his governorship was to throw a party for these sixteen families of Aborigines, at which he formally introduced them to his successor, Sir Thomas Brisbane. The valuable Bungaree, wearing his general's uniform and gorget embossed with his royal arms, an emu and a kangaroo, was the leader of these novel residents who were not at all interested in gardening or fishing with whitefella nets, and were baffled by floors and roofs. Nevertheless, long after Mosman was a prosperous settlement, this area was still officially called King Bungaree's Farm. Here we pause to ponder Bungaree's royal arms and their significant resemblance to our own.

It is not surprising to read that the Aborigines who greeted Governor-Elect Brisbane that day were announced as Onion, Ask-About, Pincher, Boatman and Tarpot, tags bestowed by white officers who could not pronounce their true mellifluous names. The ridiculous nicknames were always accepted cheerfully. Just the same, one longs to know what sobriquets the Aborigines bestowed on the stuffy self-important British gentlemen.

The formidable rockbound peninsulas, George's Head, Middle Head and Bradley's Head, were from early times fortified by both army and navy for the defence of the colony. Both these great establishments have now almost entirely withdrawn, and the headlands are under siege from powerful development corporations as well as the centre of undignified scuffles between state and federal governments. As Crown land these magnificent heights are surely the inalienable property of the nation and one hopes good sense will prevail.

As much of George's and Middle Heads has always been out of bounds to the civilian, the writer has visited only Middle Head, towering and windswept and scalped of bushland. The fort is gaunt and cold, a ponderous archaeological remnant of Imperial tradition. Shades of India and Africa! At stated times it is open to the public. Remember that although the above-ground structures are monumentally impressive, beneath your feet is another mysterious world – a network of tunnels, casemates, stairways, wells, dungeons for storing explosives. The British sapper, indefatigable descendant of Roman legionaries, has been at work in the sandstone.

The second army and navy obsession, that of constructing cubby-houses in any crevice or coign in cliffs, can best be observed from the Manly ferry. Astonishing how many of these lurking cement lairs, dens, lookouts, hideyholes can be discerned among the banksias and angophoras, probably built during the vigilant days of World War II, and still stoutly standing. What a challenge they will be to the archaeologists of the future! What purpose did these hutches have? Were they perhaps built by some unknown race? The questions are endless.

Down below Middle Head is delectable Balmoral, always called that though actually the bay is Hunter's Bay, named of course, for the governor. Balmoral and its environs is just about the most fetching place one could dwell in, all difficult leafy lanes, groves of trees, jacarandas, shady gardens approached through entrances on bizarre levels and perverse grades. Dead-ends abound, and there are empty bits here and there – perhaps leftover bits of Balmoral Park – where everything is smothered in blue draperies of vinca and morning glory. Coronation Avenue leads us into a little fishhook called Plunkett. We follow this up the hill because we want to see the view. The houses occupy arboreal gullies that once drained the severe heights above, and indeed still look somewhat ferny and mosquito-haunted.

These gullies (with others on the south side) used to be quite famous in the last century as the abode of hermits, rock-wallopers, or Jimmy Woodsers. Some occupied the decrepit shacks built for bushworkers on the original estates. Others lived under overhanging ledges and in gibbie-gunyahs or caves. These solitary men sometimes worked in gardens, or helped fishermen and oystermen. They valued their privacy to the extent that very few of their true names were ever known. So they are remembered as Antics, The Earl, Dublin Tom, Whaler Joe, Dirty Dan and Rock Lizard. Mosman Municipal Library has sketches of these picturesque shacks as well as the better-known 'camps' at Balmoral. It is difficult to say what in modern life equates with the latter. They comprised tents pitched in coveys amidst the scrub, sometimes with permanent occupants who worked in the city. We hear of sumptuous appointments, pianos, coloured drapings, carpets. Almost all the camps had an old seaman in charge who did the cooking and looked after things.

The camps were most popular during the seventies and eighties of last century, although the artists' camp, on the slope above Edwards Beach, was used for much longer than that. Among those who lived there were Julian Ashton, Arthur Streeton and Livingstone Hopkins (the cartoonist Hop).

Balmoral, presumably named after the Scottish castle, is a favourite bathing beach, with every necessary facility. Edwards Beach, on the other side of the sharp neb of Rocky Point, has a shark-proof enclosure and a rock pool. Both beaches are bordered by a wide green strip.

From our elevation we can see towards The Spit. Grotto Point with its tiny lighthouse is directly opposite, then beautiful Clontarf, once an Aboriginal corroboree ground, then a popular racecourse and pleasure garden, and now very high-priced real estate indeed. It was there, on a late summer day in 1868 that 'proudly floated the bravest flag the breeze kisses, the Royal Standard of England'. Clontarf was being visited by Queen Victoria's son, the Duke of Edinburgh, a weedy lad of unlovable disposition. Scarcely was His Royal Highness handed a cheque for the Sailors' Home than a fairly dotty Liverpool Irishman called H.J. O'Farrell took a pot shot at him. The Duke was not seriously hurt, and O'Farrell was hanged about a month later.

Clontarf, as well as Balmoral, had its hermits. Older residents can recall one who lived under an upturned boat near where the swimming pool is now.

The Spit Bridge is the bottleneck faced by the Manly and northbound traffic that swirls down the precipitous Spit Hill from Military Road. The unwinding view is a wonderful one, especially at sunset, when The Spit's myriad little boats are painted pink, and the polished water of Pearl Bay reflects dazzling windows from Beauty Point to Seaforth Bluff. For many years wagons, teams and all were ferried over the narrow channel on punts. Ponderous in weight and strength were those ox wagons, built like ships to withstand all the forces of nature and of time. They brought to Sydney timber, produce, fodder and lime from the shellbanks of Pittwater.

At a later date the punts started carrying motor vehicles and pedestrians, and after the tram service to Manly started about 1913, a specially-fitted punt occasionally ferried across a tram, not as a part of the passenger service, but to augment the existing Manly–Narrabeen tram fleet during surf carnivals and important football matches. The present bridge replaces a wooden one which stood until 1958. Its centre rises drawbridge-style to let boats pass under into the hundred bays and inlets of Middle Harbour which stretch beyond.

People still fish under the NO FISHING sign on the bridge, and no one pays attention. Low and sandy, The Spit is a villagey place of boatsheds, sailing, rowing and skiff clubs. It also has some of the best fish restaurants in Sydney.

On Seaforth Bluff are houses, some hanging five on the very edge of the scarp, others clinging like mussels to the rock. Cantilevered some, stilted others, with inclinators travelling up to the road, and shaky stairs angling down through bush to boatsheds.

From the high Mosman Ridge, we observe how surprisingly close Watson's Bay and Vaucluse Point really are. Beneath us Obelisk Bay and lovely Clifton Gardens beckon. They seem deserted, with only a few old men fishing from rocks or the little jetty. Chowder Bay Road will take us to both places and there is an easy walk around the foreshore. Clifton Gardens, the marine suburb that has arranged itself in a good-natured manner among the coral trees around Chowder Bay, pays no attention to the breakneck, winding roads; the fine houses perch where they will.

The spacious reserve is situated on the triangular drained tidal swamp so characteristic of Sydney parks. On this weekday it is deserted except for the fishermen and one skindiver porpoising around the netted pool. Everything is sparkling clean: the sand swept; the grass mowed, the immense bushy trees looking good for another hundred years. The whole area is amusingly like a Victorian watering place. Its ghosts are all long-skirted with veils and mushroom hats; moustached papas with rolled up trousers paddling along the little beach; children with sailor suits with buckets and spades; hokey pokey men; German bands and Italian organ grinders.

This is a true picture, for Clifton Gardens was once a kind of colonial Blackpool, where one went to have fun at the seaside but never entered the water. Early photographs show an extraordinary number of buildings, a large dance hall, a circular swimming pool with a tall diving tower from which show-off chaps in baggy cotton swimsuits swandived, a jetty, and a tidy row of bathing huts along the shoreline. Surprisingly, mixed bathing was allowed.

There is nothing now but the wide beautiful green, majestic coral and flame trees, and the somnolence of a sunny afternoon. Only the sea and the magpies break the sheltered silence.

The vale was one of the old whaling grants made about 1831, but it was never used for this purpose. Six hectares were drained and cultivated by Thomas Graham of the Botanic Gardens. Here he had a large orchard and garden where he succeeded in acclimatising many European plants. Access was, of course, by sea. After Graham's time, the grant was bought by a retired American whaler, Captain Cliffe, who also cultivated the heights above. He sold fresh water and vegetables to the many American whalers that anchored in Chowder Bay. The name of the latter was bestowed by these seamen who made chowder of the oysters and cockles, which abounded.

As a watering place, Clifton Gardens was ruined by its popularity with the louts of the 'pushes', and their equally ferocious "donahs". A song of the 'nineties runs: 'He put a rock in the heel of a sock/And went down the bay to Chowder.' Aside from a little trampling of respectable picnics, and wholesale arson of straw boaters, the ordinary citizen was not molested. Most of the riots which finally closed Clifton Gardens were civil warfare between rival pushes. Here is a description of a boss larrikin. His clothes were ornamented 'coster fashion with pearl buttons. He had red parrakeet boots all silk and embroidery, and decorated with rows of silver bells which jangled as he walked. He had his photo inlaid on the toe of one boot, and his donah's picture on the other. His queer little hat was sacred. To knock it off was to challenge him to war. Formidable fighter as he was, his donah was yet more feared. When she got properly going, no one, not even a policeman, would attempt to quieten her.'

On Sunday Clifton Gardens is crowded colourfully with the new visitors whose enthusiasm for it has caused residents to rename it Little Sicily. Once again ice-cream sellers wander among tents full of wine-drinking singers, and family parties sitting European-style around camp tables, with Granny at the head in a comfortable chair. Fathers and uncles play scrums on the grass. The Australian-born children are all in the pool.

To the right, an easy bush track goes around Chowder Head to Bradley's Head. This large peninsula was named for young Lieutenant William Bradley, who landed there with Captain Hunter about two days after the flag was raised at Sydney Cove on January 26, 1788. Natives thronging the rocky point pointed out to the sailors the best place to land. Their name for the peninsula was Burrogy.

William Bradley subsequently had a notable naval career. A gifted marine cartographer, he served in many distant parts of the world, and left a fascinating journal about most of them. One is astonished to learn that in 1814 he was sentenced to death for attempting to defraud His Majesty's Mails. At the time he was a Rear-Admiral of the Blue, and fifty-seven years old. Narrowly missing a fourteen-year transportation (the customary reprieve from the death sentence) to New South Wales, he was allowed to flee to France, where he died in 1833.

Taronga Zoological Park covers some 30 hectares on the western side of Bradley's Head. From 1880 the Zoo had been sited on the old Billygoat Swamp in Moore Park. Just before World War I, work began on the new Zoological Gardens and in 1916 the animals were shifted by chartered ferry to their new home. Jessie the elephant walked from Moore Park to the Quay, where the civilised creature boarded a ferry, remaining placid until the moment came for disembarking. Zoo records comment: 'A pontoon slipped slightly under Jessie's tread. She drew back and had to be severely spoken to by her keeper before she finally tiptoed across the pontoon.' Jessie survived at Taronga until 1939. She had been a gift from the King of Siam (Thailand) in the 1880s.

My emphatic opinion is that it is best to visit the Zoo by ferry, when your feet are in tiptop condition and your head is not full of a million other impressions. The ferry leaves Circular Quay at brief intervals and is an agreeable little trip. At the Taronga Bay terminal you can hop onto a cable car which whizzes over apes and crocodiles and deposits you near the front entrance. Taronga Zoo is noted for its gardens, which are very fine and its view, which is dazzling, but most of all for the unique native animals. As much as one detests that word unique, it is the only one for these strange, fascinating survivors from an ancient world.

The Nocturnal House is well suited to Australia's night creatures. Here the inhabitants have had their cycle gradually reversed. Artificial lighting during the night simulates day, and during viewing hours the light is that of a moonlight night. The first two weeks the Nocturnal House was open more than 40,000 voyeurs filed underground to watch wombats, pouched mice, goggle-eyed cuscuses and the delicate little striped numbats go about their normal life.

Most children wonder what these animals eat. Many native birds and animals have weird diets; they're gourmets, one might say. The Zoo has wandering staff members who go off every day for casuarina nuts for the cockatoos, or grasshoppers and cockroaches for the lyrebirds. A platypus eats worms, about a kilo a day, and the rare numbat delights in a special kind of termite. These specialised dainties are the difficulty – finding forty-two bales of hay weekly for the elephants is simple.

The rest of Bradley's Head is called Ashton Park. The entire area is an animal and bird sanctuary. You may therefore startle a wandering bandicoot as you walk, spot possums in the low gum branches or a blue-tongue lizard dozing on a flat rock.

Bradley's Head is still satisfactorily wild and romantic, in spite of the excellent road and walking tracks. Wildflowers grow there, small hard nubbins on the end of long stalks, bottlebrush bursting into flame on twigtips, and the banksia laden with bristling 'bad banksia men'. Anyone who has ever read May Gibbs's children's books never fails to think of the cobs as such.

Long before you reach the point, where stands the mast of HMAS *Sydney*, you come across bits of old masonry, retaining walls, scraps of grassy ruins apparently from an older world. These remains are from the first fortifications of 1841. They were much in demand as background for the dashing early photographers who posed their intrepid crinolined womenfolk against them in the same way as their English contemporaries tried to drape a shattered Roman column with some chubby contadina. It was no cop getting to Bradley's Head then. You went by small boat – 'tremendous squall from the south ... torrents of rain ... large hailstones ... muttonchops soon fried on forked sticks ... crackle of campfire ... various cries of animals, less harmonious than elsewhere'. Other photographers struggled overland – 'High broken ground ... mosquitoes, also battalions of light infantry [fleas] ... a few steps bring one from the depth of bush to the verge of the precipice, another step would precipitate him into the fearful gulph that yawns beneath!'

Not all the Bradley's Head fortifications are on the point. Look to the east side of the road and you will see a forbidding rifle gallery, and above it massive cannon in gunpits. They command the Heads. Children ride these grim old brutes – relics of an endangered past. Rustless and dully shining, their prime condition is a consequence of the energetic tidy-up of Harbour foreshores in preparation for Olympic visitors.

Some distance from the point, we descend overgrown stone steps to a sandy beach, quite anonymous, with grassy patches and flat rock ledges slapped by clear water. A delightful little beach, it remains quite natural, with a broken boat's scant skeleton cast up on the rocks not far away. Once all the beaches were like this, wonderful places for Aborigines and children to wander, and for us to discover still in existence.

Sitting in the wind-combed cutty-grass, we look straight across to the half-exposed Bottle and Glass Rocks on the near cusp of Vaucluse Bay. They were named in earliest days by the Harbour's watermen and indeed did once resemble a bottle and two wine glasses. (A watercolour of them done in 1888 by Fletcher Watson is in the Mitchell Library.) Sydney folklore variously says that the rocks were belted down into a heap of boulders either by a French warship or the guns of Bradley's Head during target practice. Above the reef shows the big white tower above Hermit Bay, and then the huge hollow of Rose Bay.

Here comes a cold southerly puff. Like a child skipping stones over the water, it lofts little vaporous willy-willies before it. So we return to the car and drive along to the point, where an American visitor is already standing on what she describes as a monstrous round military mystery. It is part of the 1871 fortifications, when three gunpits, a powder magazine and other stone buildings were erected. We join the lady upon the structure, which is made of cyclopean blocks of stone. A Moreton Bay fig has grown into its side, its extensive complex of naked roots melding into the stone in a Daliesque manner. It is exactly like a melted elephant in texture, colour and shape.

From our high perch on the gun emplacement we look straight northeast to the severe brow of South Head. Before the garrison's time the signal station and lighthouse were surrounded by dense bush and scrub. The promontory was charred to the bone by a bushfire in 1868, and never recovered.

Some think that Sydney looks its most ravishing from here. It sounds its best, anyway. All the earsplitting chirrups, grindings and bellows from its groves of macadam have faded into a plaintive murmur. The Opera House seems only a stone's throw away across the narrow sparkling water. Behind us are the sunshot woods, before us very clear green water washing around a tiny white lighthouse and jetty.

The *Sydney's* mast (it is correctly called her fighting-top) is painted blue-grey and in apple-pie order. It commemorates the sinking of the German cruiser *Emden* in 1914. The *Emden*, a rogue vessel based in a Chinese treaty port, had sunk a tremendous amount of merchant shipping in the Pacific and Indian Oceans, and no doubt it was with enthusiasm that HMAS *Sydney* peeled off from a convoy and went after her. The *Emden* was forced to beach on one of the Cocos Islands and surrendered. It was the first time a vessel of the Royal Australian Navy had engaged an enemy in battle.

Tradition says that this was a gentleman's battle, and that the *Emden's* captain and crew were taken on board the *Sydney* with courtesy and respect. Not the way the personnel of the defenceless merchant ships had been treated, according to the few survivors. On the other hand, tradition has also preserved the longstanding tale that the German party left behind on Cocos were hunted down and killed by that island group's giant tree-climbing coconut crabs. A horrible story.

HMAS *Sydney* was retired and sold for scrap to Japan in 1931.

The stone pillar which stands isolated just ahead is the nautical mile marker. The other end is the martello tower on Pinchgut. The column is historic in itself; it is from the Doric facade of the George Street post office. Not Isaac Nichols' first one in lower George Street, but that office which was used for many years until the building of the

GPO in Martin Place.

Though the bush on Bradley's Head appears luxuriously tangled and undisturbed, it is in fact a century's regrowth after two hectares were leased to a coalmining company in 1895 and cleared as bald as the top of Middle Head. The previous year, coal had been discovered at neighbouring Cremorne Point, though at immense depths. Geological indications were that the seam continued below Bradley's Head. Drilling was already underway when Mosman residents rose in their well-dressed wrath and stopped the whole project. The vision of a colliery on both sides of heavenly Mosman Bay was too much. The richly varied bush on present day Bradley's Head shows how well the earth can reclothe itself when left alone.

To our right is Athol Bay, long associated with the navy. Several jetties and mooring dolphins remind us that these are naval waters.

Mosman Bay itself, especially after whaling petered out in 1851, has long been associated with interesting ships. *Rattlesnake*, *Beagle* and *Fly* were docked and repaired there, and HMS *Bramble*, astonishingly, was deliberately sunk in order to kill her plague of cockroaches. During World War II both the *Queen Mary* and the *Queen Elizabeth* moored there to receive and disembark troops.

High on the ridge behind Athol Bay stands the oldfashioned reminder of a merrier age, Athol Hall. Once there were a number of buildings there, for Athol Bay was a notorious harbourside playground. Like Clifton Gardens it was eventually closed down. Athol Hall appears from old photographs to be the last of the three or four 'dancing saloons' which became famous for high-kicking, boozy good times. Only a few years ago the verandahed and shingle-roofed old entertainment building was renovated, and is now going great guns with wedding receptions and the odd choice lunch. Athol Hall has one of the sweetest views of Sydney city that you can imagine, and the picnic grounds sloping greenly to the ramshackle jetty and the sparkling bay are perfect for an al fresco feast. Though you will have to share the crusts with the kookaburras.

Small paddlewheel steamers used to ply to this jetty in its high days, and one traveller has recorded an indignant protest at being carried past the anchored hulk *Vermont*, a home for destitute boys. 'Although the Lord's Day, the rigging was festooned with the boys' washing, unmentionables included, and even worse, the destitute boys made rude signals at the lady passengers.'

Nothing like that now. Sunshine, peace, and a chortle or two from a magpie with his eye on your dessert.

We drive back along Bradley's Head Road, leaving it above the Zoo to explore the hilly roads and admire the charming homes in old, half-tamed gullies which lead down to Sirius Park, a green dab with a netted swimming pool. Aside from cicadas, there is silence on those bright bushy slopes. This is a lovely secluded area. The crabbed lanes dodge around big old trees and walls hung with swathes of bougainvillea. They are never far from the lisping sea.

Coming north up Musgrave Street, we turn left into McLeod Street and then immediately right into a sickle-shaped street called Badham. On the south side was Archibald Mosman's home, The Nest, demolished in the early 1920s. Watching carefully on the north side of the street (which follows faithfully the original zig-zag track from the water) we spot in the rock face the ponderous ringbolt Mosman used to support the whaling station's signalling mast.

While we drive north towards Military Road at the top of the ridge, let us recall the most interesting occupant of Mosman's The Nest. This was the Corkonian Richard Hayes Harnett, a lifelong yachting enthusiast, whose sailing about the Harbour gave him a shrewd knowledge of areas likely to appreciate in value. His first purchase in 1859 was the original Mosman grant. He tried to turn the old whaling station into a holiday resort – picnics, pigeon shooting, coconut shies, lovers' lanes and Crowe's Celebrated Quadrille Band. He ran two ferries to and fro, at threepence a time. The venture was unsuccessful, and he had to relinquish the property. Twelve years later he repurchased it.

His faith that the North Shore would become a twin city to Sydney must have seemed fantastic to his contemporaries. However, his dealing in immense tracts of land from Lane Cove to Mosman was entirely successful. Harnett was the compleat businessman. He built roads, and ran early ferry and horse bus services. He often gave land to schools and churches, and was a liberal supporter of sporting and civic bodies. In a word, this early Victorian fully realised the importance of amenities in the development of unbroken land. Fortunately Harnett lived into the age of photography, and so we know him as a man with a firm, meditative face, all straight lines and intelligent eyes beneath a silvery rooster's crest.

The growth of Mosman as a town can be attributed almost solely to Harnett, and his son R. H. junior, who was Mosman's first mayor. Some of Harnett's advertisements to entice visitors and prospective settlers to Mosman showed an amusing knowledge of human nature. Without actually committing himself, he implied that somewhere in Mosman's lost gullies was buried the loot from an early bank robbery, as well as the hijacked payroll of a British warship. Bait for the guileless? Not at all. Harnett was merely publicising well-known Mosman folktales which still crop up from time to time. Harnett was the founding father of the North Shore Ferry Co. in the early 1870s. This company became Sydney Ferries Ltd, which ran an immensely profitable business until the Harbour Bridge was opened in 1932.

Reid Park, a characteristic, drained salt-fen, sits at the top of Great Sirius Cove. The latter, with its smaller twin, Little Sirius Cove, join to become the broader Mosman Bay (Mosman's Bay, it was in the beginning). In Great Sirius Cove, HMS *Sirius* was careened in 1789 for repairs after her epic journey to the Cape of Good Hope to collect stores for the starving newborn settlement.

During the period that the ship was careened, two members of the crew were lost in the bush for three days, and on another occasion Midshipman Francis Hill, during a short walk in the woods, vanished, never to be seen again, though the ship's guns were fired at four-hourly intervals for several days. The *Sirius* set off after her refit for Norfolk Island where she was wrecked without loss of life in March 1790.

Rangers Avenue runs to the left from Avenue Road. We follow this dog-legged street till we come to Spofforth Street. On the corner stood for several decades a 'baronial Elizabethan mansion', a landmark from Vaucluse to Balmain. It was built in 1844 by Oswald Bloxsome, who bought the estate of almost twenty hectares in which it stood, for £400 . The bell-towered stone house stood in an English garden, cared for by imported Bavarian gardeners. Bloxsome is credited with bringing the first English thrushes and skylarks to Sydney. The nightingales would not acclimatise. Almost every notable Sydney visitor was a guest at The Rangers, including the Duke of Edinburgh, Huxley the naturalist and George V as a young midshipman.

Conrad Martens has left us a fairylike sketch of The Rangers, gabled and ivy-covered, sailing on a green sea of deciduous trees. After its demolition in 1914 much of its skilfully-worked stone was used in walls and other structures around Mosman, and it is still possible to spot elderly Mosman cottages with roofs patterned with the distinctive shingle-shaped red and blue terracotta tiles which once embellished Bloxsome's great house. One wonders what happened to the many works of art incorporated in its structure, such as the large sculptures illustrating the *Canterbury Tales*.

We know the deplorable end of Oswald Brierly's famous fresco. Brierly was a celebrated marine artist (he ended as a knight, and Marine Painter to Queen Victoria). There is also a street named for him, although misspelled, just down the road from Rangers Avenue. The painting was done on the spur of the moment. Oswald Brierly, who had just returned from Captain Owen Stanley's 1848 exploratory voyage to New Guinea and northern Australia, had been telling dinner guests at The Rangers of a terrifying squall through which Stanley's ship *Rattlesnake* had passed off the coasts of Timor.

'I'll show you what it was like!' he shouted, and seizing a burned stick from the fire 'began the picture on the wall, in great strokes stormy as the gale and free as the water'. This picture was later finished by the artist in charcoal, crayon, and colour distemper. It was a work of elemental vigour, occupying the whole northern wall of the dining room and measuring 18 feet by 12 feet. The ship seemed to be sailing down into the room. Years afterwards, it is told, an old sea captain who saw it bawled agitatedly: 'Why the hell don't they let the braces go?' When the house was demolished, the wall was removed in one piece and clamped in iron. But this effort to save the fresco was unsuccessful, and the famous picture crumbled away in a junkyard at Crow's Nest.

Many of Brierly's marine paintings remain in Australia. The Art Gallery of New South Wales owns several, and some may be seen in the Mitchell Library.

The back streets between Cremorne Junction and Long Bay in the north and Cremorne proper in the south, are unmistakably ex-working class; small neat standardised villas of brick and weatherboard, their identically pitched roofs zig-zagging down the hills towards the sea. There is bitty development everywhere; great cream brick towers, all their balconies gaping greedily at the Harbour or northward across Cammeray and Primrose Park.

On the Middle Harbour side, where there are some admirable homes, there is still folklore to be heard about 'the Australian Blondin', Harry L'Estrange, who in 1877 walked across Long Bay between

Cammeray and Northbridge on a tightrope stretched from cliff to cliff. The distance was 450 metres and the rope over 100 metres above the water. L'Estrange, an expert businessman, hired twenty-one ferries to carry the crowds. Eight thousand customers attended.

Following Murdoch Street left from Military Road, we drive down the quaint narrow peninsula of Cremorne, to find ourselves surprisingly close to Pinchgut and Garden Island. This is Robertsons Point, named for the London family Robertson. Their patriarch, James, brought out his large family in 1816. He had waiting for him a post as serviceman in the Parramatta Observatory erected at Parramatta by the astronomically minded Governor Thomas Brisbane. It is said that Brisbane bestowed the grant of this picturesque peninsula upon James in recognition of his skill.

In 1853 Robertson sold the peninsula to James Milson of Milson's Point. Milson leased some of the land to two theatrical promoters, who cleared the bushy ridge, laid down tracks and ambitious gardens. They built a jetty and enlisted the ready co-operation of the ferry company which ran vessels at half-hourly intervals to what was to become one of the most notorious resorts for 'brazen riot and bacchanalia' Sydney has ever boasted. This dubious place was called Cremorne after the famous and equally scandalous Cremorne Gardens of Regency London. Anyway, Cremorne lasted only six years. It was closed, the gardens were demolished, and the Milson land subdivided, with the Crown's proviso that water frontage 30 metres deep and almost two kilometres long should be public property. This is the present green strip running along the east side of Shell Cove.

Any of the streets leading west from Murdoch Street will take us on an agreeably roundabout tour of Neutral Bay. Like Mosman it is a place of sudden roads, which rush uphill in erratic hops, or nervously trace a temperature chart about the countryside. In this old suburb roads are mostly leafy. Neutral Bay's special tree is the camphor laurel (*Cinnamomum*) which produces commercial camphor, but in this south-facing marine suburb was probably planted for windbreaks. The name Neutral Bay was given by Governor Phillip, who directed that all foreign ships should anchor there. He feared that convicts would abscond in foreign whalers and other wanderers, so he wanted such ships kept at a distance.

Turn left from Murdoch Street into Bannerman Street, driving south down Wycombe Road and into engaging Kurraba Road, which is the major of whole adders' nest of self-willed little byways that wiggle around the heads of Neutral Bay and Careening Cove. You can get lost a dozen times in ten minutes, until reversing out of brief jacaranda-hung lanes becomes a habit of life. There are some pretty recherché dwellings here, more modern than the cupola'ed beauties of Mosman, but in the same way hanging above the blue sea, with overgrown gardens pulled about their ears. Some are late Victorian, some Edwardian, and even though units have crept in, the architecture doesn't seem as brutal as it is in Cremorne. Kurraba Road actually begins at the end of Kurraba Point, where there's a small tously reserve called Hodgson's Lookout. It is the original road which wound up from the landing place. Halfway up the peninsula there's a little ferry wharf with independence and personality.

Let us sit here on the warm stones of the retaining wall and recall Ben Boyd, whaler, dreamer, con man and main course at a cannibal feast. Long before Ben Boyd there came an unfamous Alfred Thrupp, a free settler who had the luck to wed Sarah Piper shortly after he arrived from London in 1814. Sarah, the daughter of Naval Officer Captain Piper, was returning from her finishing school in England. This was in Captain Piper's lordly days of wealth and hospitality. He was able, without any trouble whatsoever, to toss his new son-in-law a 300 hectare grant at Neutral Bay.

Though Thrupp never worked or cleared his land, and the grant was listed among Piper's own effects after his ruin, the name Thrupp's Acres persisted for decades. A stone cottage built on the property in 1826, and having no connection whatever with Thrupp, was called Thrupp's Cottage for the best part of a century. It was one of the eight cottages in the Neutral Bay of 1863. Bushfire was a constant terror to these settlers of the wild woods. We recall the great one of 1826 that wiped out James Milson's farmhouse and Edward Wollstonecraft's first cottage, the Crow's Nest, which gave its name to the present North Shore suburb. In the early 1870s a fearful fire swept the North Shore from St Thomas's graveyard to Middle Head. Here is a picture of the very spot where we sit.

'The paddocks around the only houses in Neutral Bay made a firebreak, but each residence had blankets etc. covering the dry shingle roofs . . . kept wet by passing up buckets of water. Here along the narrow track, [now Kurraba Road] snakes, opossums, native cats, bandicoots ... were going for their lives. Along this lucky firebreak there came, with a willing gang of helpers, Major Tunks, first Mayor of St Leonards, a fine burly fellow of splendid physique. With an axe on his shoulder he gave his commands ... and worked with a will until the fire had burned to the water's edge.'

Following the path of the snakes, native cats and Mayor Tunks towards the north and west, we pass Thrupp Street, and then Ben Boyd Road. On the corner of this important artery is a colourful and unusual little memorial to the adventurer Benjamin Boyd. It depicts his yacht *Wanderer*, described in a Sydney newspaper as 'armed to the teeth ... fitted up in a most splendid manner', which arrived in 1842. One of the *Wanderer's* passengers was the painter, Oswald Brierly.

Four trading vessels accompanied the *Wanderer*, as well as a gale of gossip from Melbourne, where Boyd had stayed for a while before coming north. A Scotsman by birth and stockbroker by training, he was reputedly a wealthy aristocrat. In fact the money supposed to be his own was £200,000 invested by London speculators in the Royal Bank of Australia, which he had formed three years before.

In person he was supposed to be remarkably handsome but his portrait shows him with a spiky arrogant nose and an icy stare. He had both business acumen and an authoritative personality; five years after his arrival, Governor Gipps said that he was one of the country's most powerful squatters, owning or leasing almost a million hectares of land. Part of this was in the Riverina and the Monaro, and reliable tradition states that these huge pastoral holdings were worked by slave labour imported by Boyd from the Pacific Islands. He was, in short, blackbirder as well as banker. These slaves worked 'for sixpence a week, a Kilmanock cap and shirt, and indifferent rations'. Boyd's ambitious whaling schemes at Twofold Bay, where he erected two towns, East Boyd and Boyd Town, adorned by a lighthouse, a Gothic church and an Elizabethan hotel, are fascinating, but our concern is with his wool-washing establishment at Neutral Bay. This, with his tall verandahed residence, Craignathan, stores, wharf and dam, were near the spot now occupied by Neutral Bay's Hayes Street wharf.

Ben Boyd, like so many others, crashed in the great depression of the late 1840s. He sailed off to make another fortune on the Californian goldfields, but failed. In 1851 he was on his way back to Australia, but on the Solomon Islands disappeared on a hunting expedition. It seems certain that he ended in the cooking pots. He was then fifty-six. The *Wanderer* continued on her homeward voyage, and was wrecked at the entrance of Port Macquarie without loss of life. Her bell is not far away from Ben Boyd's old territory on Thrupp's Acres. It hangs in the foyer of the Royal Sydney Yacht Squadron's premises on Wudyong Point across the bay from Kurraba Point.

Kurraba Road angles steeply down along the fringe of Anderson Park, another reclaimed tidal swamp of placid beauty. Anderson Park had its finest hour on July 17, 1934 when Charles Kingsford-Smith took delivery of the Lockheed Altair he had had shipped to Sydney by the tourist liner *Mariposa*. Smithy, being publicity-minded, had asked for the aircraft to be landed on Circular Quay East. He would then wheel it to Macquarie Street and take off for Mascot for the beginning of the Melbourne Centenary Air Race, for which she had been expressly bought. Understandably, permission was refused.

The story is best told by Kingsford-Smith's co-pilot, Gordon Taylor. 'The plane was slung over the side of the ship and put on a barge. The barge was towed to Neutral Bay and the plane was wheeled ashore. In those days there were no trees there. We put the tail of the aircraft as near the road as possible. I knew she would only just take off. We took off from the end of the park and we had nothing to spare. The wheels just left the ground as we took off.'

A photograph of Anderson Park just before this feat of airmanship shows it as solid humanity from Kurraba Road to Clark Road. Kurraba Road now rushes away to meet Alfred Street on the east of the roaring complex, the Warringah Expressway. It is much better for us to continue along Clark Road across the head of Careening Cove and into Kirribilli, which is largely Milson country. The little reserve, Milson Park, was once the mouth of Rainbow Creek, which rose near the foot of the MLC building in North Sydney, and cascaded in a series of waterfalls into Careening Cove. This cove was for a long time known as Slaughterhouse Bay. James Milson's slaughterhouse was there, presided over by an elderly Aboriginal caretaker called Tarpot.

Local tradition says that Milson's slaughterhouse was built of salvaged timber thrown up from the wreck of the immigrant ship *Dunbar* at South Head in 1857. Every Saturday could be seen a kite's tail of little boats from the settlers along the foreshores, bobbing into

Slaughterhouse Bay to pick up the week's meat, much of which would go into pickle. Tarpot on his own behalf would have collected bottles of rock oysters in brine. These were bought very cheaply, and eaten on the long row home.

This slender bay is singularly sheltered, walled in by cliffs and towering home units; the homes are mostly working class dolls' houses though they are now being converted into costly townhouses. A passing resident says that Careening Cove was never favoured by the wealthy because 'Milson Park used to be a rubbish tip'. In such ways is the character of a district determined.

By continuing from McDougall Street into Elamang Avenue, we can drive around for a leisurely look at the very old, tiny suburb of Kirribilli, which to my mind has less personality than North Sydney, but has elegance and much historical interest. Many old houses survive among homely terraces embellished with impressive ironwork. John, one of James Milson's sons, built No. 6 and No. 24 in Winslow Street. Though one is stone and the other timber, they both boast comical little balconied gables. Another son, James, built a cottage which is now part of Loreto Convent; the latter in itself is worth looking at, with its Georgian copper tower of intricate design.

Basically the district is Victorian, the architecture often gingerbreaded, inconvenient and sentimental. The houses are frequently close to the street, just a few feet back, in the archaic way. Often gardens are below street level, for the topography is immensely rocky and irregular. Vines spill down rock faces, and flights of stone stairs appear in unexpected places.

The most important building, Admiralty House on Kirribilli Point, is also one of the most attractive. Externally it exhibits all the simple charm of a classic colonial mansion. It was built in 1845–46 by the Collector of Customs, Lieutenant-Colonel J. G. N. Gibbes. The house, originally called Wotonga, had a succession of distinguished owners, including Lieutenant-Colonel George Barney, who built Paddington Barracks and constructed Circular Quay. Wotonga was bought in 1885 by the New South Wales Government as a residence for admirals of the British fleet. Twelve admirals resided there until 1913. For many years stately Admiralty House has been the Sydney residence of the Governor-General.

Next door is Kirribilli House. Built in 1885 by a rich merchant,

A. F. Feez, it plainly shows the changes in architectural tastes, which the decades had wrought. With its twin gables and scalloped bargeboards, it is completely Victorian. Fortunately it has an agreeably peekable fence, and one can have a good squiz at its manicured gardens and soothing air of stability and peace. It is kept as the Sydney residence for the Prime Minister. You may get a better look at both these houses from a ferry.

If we continue down this tranquil dead-end street we come to the Lady Gowrie Lookout, which makes an effort to be completely vertical. Its steps and stairs go down to clear green water lapping against stone embankments and a little jetty. There are plenty of warm sheltered seats, surprisingly tucked away behind banks of hibiscus and cassia so that you can't see the sea.

On the way towards the Harbour Bridge, with an increasing number of highrise buildings appearing at every turn, we spot the first block of flats ever constructed on the North Shore, No. 1 Waruda Street. It was built in 1908 by the owner of Carbine, the celebrated racehorse. Nearby is a tiny waterfront reserve locally called The Dingle, and one does wonder if this odd name commemorates the house of the same name. The latter was an iron pre-fab with scalloped roof and tiny-paned windows, and was brought out from England about 1844 by a pair of honeymooners called Riley. Conrad Martens has left us a picture of it, three feet above cloudy green water, with a dinghy tethered to the wall like a cow.

Kirribilli was probably Sydney's earliest victim of haphazard, greedy development. From the sea its ruined profile is that of a broken comb. A great shame, for it is a quaint, deliciously situated place.

Now duck under the Bridge, for we are going to visit Bradfield Park. The Harbour Tunnel roars underground very close to this spot, but you would not know it.

In Bradfield Park we may sit in the sunshine on grass which is always green, even on days of liquefying heat. This is Milson's Point, once precipitous and rocky, and a painful drag for ferry passengers toiling up from the wharves. Farmer Milson's dwelling, the Milk House, was near the northeast pylon. In 1814 his family had a great fright when the vessel *Three Bees*, carrying kegs of gunpowder and with its cannon loaded, caught fire at her berth in Sydney Cove. The lines were cut, and as the *Gazette* says, 'Providence in its mercy decreed that the ship began to drift towards the north shore, her guns firing indiscriminately'. The large Milson family, at whom the guns were pointing took cover, but luckily only one ball landed near their home. The *Three Bees* burned to the water's edge.

Two photogenic historical objects to be seen close by are another column from the second GPO (the Martin Place building is the third one) and the prow of the HMAS *Sydney*, the mast of which we have already seen on Bradley's Head.

On the western side of the point lies Lavender Bay, its waters easing like oil over thumbnail beaches. The sweet Aboriginal name for this bay is Quiberie. Early settlers called it Hulk Bay, because of the hulks moored there to serve as barracks for convicts working on stone-cutting and lime-burning. George Lavender, for whom the bay is now named, was a boatswain on one of those hulks. Ships watered from the perennial stream which ran into the head of the bay. The casks were lashed into covies, like a raft, and towed out to vessels waiting to depart.

It is thought that the last of this stream is the drizzle just below Christ Church in Walker Street. In fact, a keen eye can detect the water-worn flat stones of a cascade in the grounds of this church. My advice, now that we've reached this point, is to wander around Lavender Bay and North Sydney by yourself, perhaps beginning by going up Alfred Street, teetering above narrow diagonal streets leading to the water.

It's not difficult to imagine how the point looked before the Bridge swept it away. For example, in the 1890s the little Gothic Congregational Church in Alfred Street once commanded some of the finest views in all Sydney. Although it now has nothing to look at, spare it more than a glance as you pass by; it is an endearingly frivolous little building with sandstock brick walls and a somewhat cockeyed steeple.

Already we have noticed the fantastic cellular growth of North Sydney. The place seems to erupt from the blue calyx of the Harbour. It is an unusual and diverting place to explore on foot. Some streets present a comic debate between extremes in architecture – a thirty metre frontage of Modern Carminative next door to a grand terrace as fine as those in Elizabeth Bay. Adjacent will be another terrace, yellow with age, slam-bang on the footpath. As in the houses of Balmain, these workmen's terraces display a wide range of architectural idiosyncrasies, including hooded gables, which I have not seen elsewhere in Sydney.

Two important churches should not be missed. First, St Thomas's in Church Street. The plan of this substantial church was the last work by architect Edmund Blacket before his sudden death in 1883. Construction was carried out by his sons, Arthur and Cyril, and the church was open for worship in 1884. It was actually built over and outside of the first St Thomas's, a small cosy square-towered building designed (and built, some say) by Conrad Martens. Services thus have never been interrupted on this site since 1843. The older church was demolished from within and the ruins carried out through the western door of the present church. The east window is superb. It is dedicated to the first long-serving rector of the first St Thomas's, William Branwhite Clarke.

This frail, almost forgotten man was both parson and geologist. Coming to Australia for his health in 1839, he spent a brief period as headmaster of the King's School, Parramatta. When he was appointed to St Thomas's his parish covered almost 600 square kilometres. He describes his church as having whitewashed walls, hanging kerosene lamps, and a harmonium. As he stood at the door to farewell evening worshippers, he said, their hurricane lamps vanished into the pitch-black valleys like stars into infinity.

He made many geological explorations of New South Wales, and although not the first discoverer of gold, did discover it in a number of places from 1841 to 1845. He was forbidden by Governor Gipps to publicise his discoveries, for fear of insurrection in the large convict population. He accurately predicted, from geological observations, existence of large fields in the Ballarat district and also in New Zealand. He was almost equally accurate in his estimations of New South Wales's coalfields. Branwhite Clarke was honoured both in Europe and Australia for his scientific work, and at his death in 1878 was acknowledged as the founder of scientific thought in Australia. It was his collection of fossils, bought by the State Government for £7,000 after his death, that was destroyed when the Garden Palace burned in 1882.

St Thomas's drowses today in a lovely rest park. It is indeed a hard-working parish church, but it seems in half a dream. The park commemorates those pioneer people buried in the original St Thomas's graveyard. Such historic names! Major Ovens, Owen Stanley, Ellis Bent, Edward Wollstonecraft, Conrad Martens, William Lithgow, founder of the town of that name. Family names of great significance, Barney, Milson, Holtermann and of course that wonderful man Branwhite Clarke himself.

The second Victorian church to be seen is St Francis Xavier's in Mackenzie Street. The structure (1881) is good in itself, but the church is memorable for two remarkable art works, the first a symbolic stained-glass back wall, 300 metres of brilliantly dramatic modern craftsmanship. The second work of art is much older, an adorable series of Stations of the Cross in wood. One could swear they were Black Forest folk art, and indeed they were carved by the German master Josef Dettlinger about a century ago.

Few of the good old houses remain. Bernard Otto Holtermann's home, Holtermann's Tower, was incorporated into Shore, as Sydney Church of England Grammar School is popularly known, as long ago as 1889. The mansion really did have a tower almost twenty-five metres high, and I believe it is still used as a trig station. Local tradition maintains that the only way into the tower is through the headmaster's bedroom. Holtermann, a German member of the Star of Hope Gold Mining Company, is the man who struck gold at Hill End. Here the company turned up that fantastic nugget now known as the Holtermann Nugget. (In Shore's library is a stained-glass window showing Holtermann with the nugget.) It took one horse and twenty men all their time to get it above ground. Its incredible proportions are as follows: its length was nearly 1.5 metres; its width 70 centimetres; its average thickness 10 centimetres; its weight 285 kilograms.

Holtermann died rather young, but we are indebted to him for the magnificent series of photographs he took from his tower. He was one of the world's eminent photographers in the wet-plate era.

One of my favourites is Don Bank (No. 1 Napier Street). Poor little thing, it is jammed between a high wall and an office block – the oldest building in North Sydney. This farmhouse was built about 1820, a rare example of vernacular timber slab construction, with cedar joinery. It is a particularly interesting community museum. It is thought to have been built for a member of Edward Wollstonecraft's family. Wollstonecraft, a cousin of Mary Wollstonecraft Godwin, the writer of *Frankenstein* and wife of Shelley, gave his name to the nearby suburb. We shall learn a little about him when we get there.

The Priory, Colonel Barney's house, is still standing, but it's unrecognisable. Nearby in Edward Street (after Wollstonecraft) is the site of Conrad Martens's home. The cat's cradle of roads below Martens's site are very old, ambling and indolent. They are bordered by midget houses, quite charming. One of these streets is Euroka, where Henry Lawson used to live. It's a wide sunny road, which dips under the railway. Henry's house, No. 31, is a semi, with an exceedingly narrow frontage. Henry wouldn't recognise it in its present cheerful colours. Just above Euroka Street is my favourite lane in North Sydney, Ancrum Street, with falling fences and frangipani. It's crumbling to pieces, but retains a homely dignity. The houses are incredibly small, definitely for miniature people. Blue Berry's Bay flashes between their peaked roofs like light through a shutter.

North Sydney is a great place for lunch, so many small restaurants and cafés. But perhaps you would rather get sandwiches and coffee in containers and visit a lost park, Watt Park, at the head of Lavender Bay. There's scarcely ever a soul there, except in the dusk, when you sometimes meet dogs taking owners for walks. Here in October, jacarandas weep purple in the deep glen which on the hottest day seems dim and moistly green. The railway line runs along the south side. It once serviced the decrepit Lavender Bay wharf, but is now only a siding. Its banks are overgrown with flowering convolvulus, lantana, and tall fennel that is full of little birds chomping on the dry seeds.

An airy mansion called Masalou once dominated the Miller Street Ridge. Built by Francis Lord, a contemporary of Milson, Berry and Wollstonecraft, it has been incorporated into the Catholic girls' college, Monte Sant' Angelo. Double-storeyed and columned in the late colonial style, it is visible from the main gates.

Diving into Blue's Point Road, we are very nearly back in the nineteenth century once more. St Peter's on the right is the oldest Presbyterian Church still in use in Sydney. It was built in 1865, and the handsome manse was added six years later. What a scallywag of a road this is! It's suitably named for the gammoning, flamboyant old tike, Billy Blue, who so tickled Governor Macquarie's sense of humour that he dubbed him the Old Commodore and bestowed upon him 32 hectares of this desirable nib of land.

Billy Blue, described as a Jamaican Negro, was sentenced to seven years transportation at the Kent Assizes in October 1796. He always claimed that he had been in Quebec when General Wolfe was killed and was in Virginia with Lord Cornwallis as an Army scout. But he could have been lying. At his death in 1834, it was generally believed he was one hundred years old. So also states the entertaining Blue Family Bible, now in the Mitchell Library.

Billy had a genius for acting the goat for the gentry; he seems to have got away with all kinds of impudence. His passengers frequently did the rowing on his ferryboat service from Dawes Point to Blue's Point. They would then pay him for his return journey. He always carried a sack on his shoulder and wheedled food, beer or clothing from passengers and passersby. He married at seventy (so he said) and produced 'a small helpless family', among them the daughters who married Lavender of the Bay, and French of the Forest.

The Old Commodore Hotel was established about 1848 by one of Billy's sons. His stone house still stands in Commodore Crescent. The shop next door was once part of the inn, in George Lavender's time, and they say you may see the words 'Spirituous Liquors' under the paint on one of the inside walls.

The bush track from the point was there from 1817, when Billy took possession officially. But the present road was laid down in the 1850s under the direction of Colonel Barney. Verandah posts once used for hitching, sandstone kerbing, a horse trough, flat-faced cottages of the most venerable type remind us that Blue's Point Road belongs to an age gone by, the era of the teamster and horseman. We are told of a teamsters' camp under a solitary fig tree on the point and the sparkle of campfires like beacons, 'flickering like heliographs as the men danced around them, heel and toe like Russian seamen. They were a type no longer seen, huge men in canvas duds, speaking strange English, for they came from Cornwall and Cromarty, and oft times from Bohemia; strong as bears they was.'

A wagoners' road, therefore, as the Old Commodore was a wagoners' tavern, Blue's Point Road rollicks up the ridge, baulking at corners, canting where it feels like it. Starveling lanes wander off on the west. (On the east the roads are much more respectable, with many old homes now converted into flats and guesthouses.) But the western lanes end above hazy pearly Berry's Bay, with an enormous view up the Parramatta River and a sunset at the end of it.

At the end of Blue's Point Road is a little joyful park with swings, slides, a few supine bodies in the grass, one of them with roast beef face partly shielded by an expensive brief case. The Aboriginal cliff is directly behind the park, fig trees growing along it, vines tumbling over. The Blue's Point Tower, having been built with regard for its environment, does not look entirely out of place. On the contrary, it is solemn and imperious, rising from a ruffle of greenery. The Harbour is before us, with the Opera House below it, just a stone's throw away, it seems. The city has hidden its gorgon face behind a grimy, faintly sparkling veil; the only sound is of a train tearing over the Bridge. Worn convict-hewn stone steps go down to the water, launches and yachts tilt at their moorings. In this hot still bay, sheltered from the westerlies, so near to Sydney, and yet so rustic, Billy Blue (and after him, Susannah Lavender) lived in a stone house beside an orchard.

Around the low cliffs to the east, Henry Lawson Avenue runs around to the fetching little McMahon's Point wharf. Steps lead up to Warung Street and its tall Edwardian houses. The changes effected in McMahon's Point by developers have been cautious and well mannered. The cliffs and drop downs, the rocky, idiosyncratic nature of the entire peninsula have been respected; new houses snuggle and old ones present cleaner but unaltered faces to the twisting streets. Resident action was firm from the beginning.

'No one wants to stop progress. But why does progress have to be redevelopment instead of development? Sydney's still floating in a sea of scrub, big and all as it is. Let 'em develop that, and for people instead of big business. It's a bloody awful time for *pro bono publico*, never you doubt it,' says a longtime resident.

Well, as Billy Blue used to enjoin passersby 150 years ago, 'Go, go, my child! True blue for ever! Never strike the flag!'

Union Street, at the top of the promontory, marks the boundary of Billy Blue's grant. We turn west, driving along Woolcott Street, which skirts Waverton Park at the head of Berry's Bay. Woolcott Street takes us into Balls Head Road. Balls Head is the first of the north shore peninsulas to demonstrate the characteristic club shape to be seen along the north bank of the Lane Cove River. Their extremities must surely have been tied islands, joined to the mainland by sandspits.

The western view from such places as McMahon's Point or unimpeded high spots in Wollstonecraft or North Sydney (few indeed, alas) almost never appears on postcards, yet it is surely one of the grandest and most significant you could find. This extraordinarily ragged, deep-bitten, complicated Top End of the Harbour hides itself behind so many knobs, elbows, capelets and blunt peninsulas that its enormous extent cannot be guessed. Yet it is the origin of Port Jackson itself. The huge area of the Sydney Harbour basin was carved out by the Parramatta and Lane Cove Rivers, officially separated on modern maps at Onions Point but carrying a common load of brown silt into the harbour after heavy rain. This magnificent Top End is the major water road to the 2000 Olympics, as it leads via the Parramatta River to Homebush Bay.

Balls Head, an impressive eminence and nature reserve, was named for Lieutenant Henry Lidgbird Ball, the energetic young commander of the tender *Supply* of the First Fleet. (Mt Lidgbird and Ball's Pyramid at Lord Howe Island are also named for this officer.) Ball successfully took the toy-sized *Supply* to Batavia (Jakarta) for provisions, after the loss of the *Sirius* on Norfolk Island.

Balls Head is thought to be the richest repository of Aboriginal relics on this side of the Harbour. But it is not all that easy to find them. If you look up above the road just at the entrance to the drive which loops through the reserve, you will notice a fenced group of scribings, a man and a whale. Further study of this rock will show other, fainter carvings, fish, spears and boomerangs. More interesting drawings are in a cave reached by a roughish track from the tidal swimming pool on the east. Here are fish pictures, which are done, so it is said, by holding the fish against the wall and stencilling an outline by spraying with the pigment held in the mouth. Axe-grinding grooves are plentiful throughout the bush.

Balls Head Bay waters are among the deepest in the Harbour, nearly 40 metres in some places. HMAS *Waterhen* operates on the western side, so much of this shore is a prohibited area. Here until fairly recent times was a large coal storage facility, with mountains of coal, winches and waiting coal-burning steamers, but that is now closed. On the east, perfectly situated on circular, sheltered Berry's Bay is the National Maritime Museum Shipyard.

We look right across to Goat Island, Balmain, Miller's Point, the immense city floating in its spectral cumulus of smog and bushfire smoke. Across Balls Head Bay is Berry Island, thickly wooded and connected by a thin green nexus of lawn to its own peninsula. Beyond this is Gore Cove, most graceful and serpentine of coves, its glassy water marked with the beetle tracks of launches.

In spite of the industrial air of this part of the Harbour, the eastern shore of Gore Cove sliced into stark sandstone shelves to accommodate the Shell Oil tanks, it is marvellously beautiful – like Turner's 'Thames', but under a different light. For Sydney's is a morning light, blithe, blissful, a touch hallucinatory. It fills one with lingering wistfulness, for like all other youthful things it seems doomed to change and die. But it scarcely ever does. Occasionally in mid-May, when abruptly summer is blown out, a chill seaweed-coloured sky will throw over the landscape a Danish or Canadian tinge. And sometimes in drought, when all is bleached and wan with heat, and

> *The monstrous continent of air floats back*
> *Coloured with rotting sunlight*

there is a strong sense of Spain or Sicily in the trembling glare of afternoon. But this is fleeting.

'Here is the light of the Hesperides' garden which answers the imprecise cry of the artist's soul' said the artist Julian Ashton, probably with his nose on the canvas, for he was in his later years almost blind. Dreamlike then, in this morning light, swim the bays, headlands, roads dipping into the sea, wharves and ferries and, far away up the Lane Cove valley, mirage-like gilded cities which we know are the unremarkable suburbs of North Ryde, Boronia Park and Artarmon.

Much of the land to the north was owned by the partners Alexander Berry and Edward Wollstonecraft. Of the pair, Berry was the more daring businessman. This Fifeshire doctor arrived in Sydney in 1808. He was then twenty-seven, owned his own ship, and had cargo to sell – almost 21,200 gallons of spirits. In that year spirits were priced in Sydney at fifty shillings a gallon.

In spite of his cargo, Berry was an ardent advocate of temperance. A letter to his brother seethes: 'This district of Shoalhaven has lost its character and is considered the abode of drunken butchers and drunken coopers. Damn all drunkards – we must get rid of them and in all clearing leases you must insist that selling spirits or drunkenness will vitiate their leases.'

Berry also traded in timber, spars, salted hides, whale oil and grain. In 1810 he took into partnership Edward Wollstonecraft who brought as a dowry to the partnership a letter from the Colonial Office which directed Governor Macquarie to bestow upon him and Berry a grant of nearly five thousand hectares. Most of this was around the Shoalhaven River in the Illawarra district (around the present town of Berry) where it is said Berry lived like a petty chieftain among one hundred assigned convicts.

Wollstonecraft, who became a director of the Bank of Australia and was on several government advisory bodies, was delicate and died in early middle age. He built the cottage Crow's Nest after which the suburb was named. It was next door to St Thomas's Church and commanded an eagle's eye view. Berry used this cottage, much enlarged and renovated, after Edward's death. Berry married his friend's sister, Elizabeth, who is supposed to have borne a notable resemblance to their aunt the tragic Mary Wollstonecraft who died at the birth of Mary, Shelley's second wife.

Alexander lived to be ninety-two. At his death in 1873 his estate was valued at 2.5 million pounds. He is one of those pioneers commemorated in St Thomas's rest park, North Sydney.

An icy brain and a masterly reading of road signs will get you on to the River Road, which bends and wriggles like a river itself until it reaches Bridge Street and runs into Burns Bay Road. As we travel the River Road we are traversing the harbourside municipality of Lane Cove, a mere fragment of the old Lane Cove which once encompassed Gordon, Greenwich, Roseville and many other modern suburbs. To our near south is Greenwich peninsula, a mixture of shoaling units, and respectable elderly houses. There is also Northwood, and lots of greensward. Northwood is just across the water from Onions Point on the end of the Hunter's Hill–Woolwich district.

The extreme tip of Onions Point (named for a merchant who owned land there in the 1830s) is washed by the Lane Cove and Parramatta Rivers. It is thought that the first naval chartmakers did not realise that the water on the other side of the Woolwich peninsula was a river and this is the explanation of the Lane Cove's curious name.

Lane Cove seems to have been christened very early in Sydney's history. The first mention of it is in William Bradley's journal, February 2, 1788, during the course of Captain Hunter's survey of the upper harbour. During a later visit to the river in August 1788, Bradley records an extraordinary incident when James Keltie, the sailing-master of the *Sirius*, shot a fish in the boughs of a high tree. It was, at the time in the claws of a large hawk. The earliest watercolours of the Lane Cove River are by Lieutenant Bradley; bosky islets and bent-legged capes swimming like woolly frogs in a smudge of Prussian blue.

This original Lane Cove was associated mostly with timber-getting.

The bushmen were often emancipees, for Alexander Harris tells us that there 'was a general disinclination to work with a free migrant'. The men brawled, grogged and worked very hard. They lived rough in bush clearings. One tells us: 'All we had to sleep on was a dog.' The endless North Shore woodlands retreated before their invasion. They split posts, cut firewood, palings for fences, shingles for Sydney's roofs. They felled cedar and mahogany for builders and cabinetmakers, and squared logs for joists and foundations. The river was their highway. (Even in 1840 when the district had one thousand inhabitants, there was no government road.)

Their locally-built boats came down the Lane Cove River on every tide – these are described as 2.5 to 3 tonne vessels, stowed with top-heavy loads of wood, propelled by oars, but sometimes helped along by a large bough stuck up to catch the wind, or a blanket sail. Alexander Harris notes that 'one chap had his jacket with a stick passed through the arms for want of a sail'.

One of these Lane Cove bushmen was Joseph Fidden of Fidden's Wharf, Killara, a Birmingham gunsmith who arrived in Sydney in 1801 on a seven-year sentence. Governor Macquarie granted Fidden almost twenty hectares of this remote but accessible reach of the Lane Cove River, and in 1821 he took possession. But it is not as a farmer but as a boatman that Fidden dominates the folklore of the river. Harris, the observant traveller to whom we are so much indebted for his descriptions of Sydney in the 1820s, describes Fidden, then the best-known river boatman: '[he was] certainly two-fifths of his own height, which could have been little beyond five feet, across the shoulders. Yet every tide did he make a trip to Sydney, pulling heavy oars with three tons of wood in the boat besides loading and unloading; two trips up and down … about forty-six miles, and that not all at once, but just going day and night as the tide served. When he got home he usually set to work chopping wood till he wanted to load and when loaded started again. Thus he kept on day or night for weeks together.'

When Harris met him, Fidden would have been nearly sixty. He also ferried fruit and farm women to Sydney, his passengers taking an oil lamp to light themselves home along the bush tracks. Joe Fidden died at the age of ninety-three, and is buried in Camperdown Cemetery.

This early Lane Cove was the butt of many scandalised remarks from Sydney. It was the abode of murderers, the resort of villains, its hard-labouring settlers 'a herd of the most flagitious banditti on earth'. Even Joe Fidden is accused of having a still among his peach trees, so that his farm 'was a social centre'. It is certain that this is a district rich in extraordinary characters.

Provost-Marshal William Gore, described by one of his ex-friends as 'the greatest Swindler, the most absolute Thief and Cheat', held land along the Greenwich peninsula. He is recalled by Gore Cove, the haven for oil tankers; the suburb of Artarmon, the name of his house; and Gore Hill, now a landmark because of its TV towers. Gore was a fearfully peppery old yahoo. He was noted for abrasive treatment of convicts, loyalty to Governor Bligh in his ruin, and, somewhat heroically, seventy years of unalloyed inebriation. He died at eighty.

Gore finally crashed over the hasty shooting of a soldier who had been ordered to cut grass for fodder near Gore's property. Poor Gore tried to commit suicide, went bankrupt and died in disgrace, and there is a weird tale in the Harnett records that when Richard Harnett leased these lands he found the leaden coffins of Gore, his wife and daughter reposing on trestles in the middle of a paddock. Gore had apparently believed this curious lack of interment would keep the family grant intact. Harnett 'gave decent burial to these relics of a pioneer family'.

Tambourine Bay is supposed to have been the camp of a semi-retired Cyprian called Tambourine Nell, or Sal, who had wearied of keeping 'a sailors' home' at Dawes Point. This is a fetching bay, with a mint-green foreshore and a long rivulet of bushy reserve which trickles down from River Road.

The western shore is dominated by the boys' school, St Ignatius College. The estate Riverview was developed by Emmanuel Josephsen, a wealthy gentleman with good taste and a wife with a genius for landscaping and gardening. Some of Mrs Josephsen's work, notably in the rock garden, still remains. Harnett, who bought the Josephsen estate, sold it to the Jesuit order for £4,500 in 1878 (profit, £1,100). The distinctive four-storeyed stone building was erected eleven years later, le dernier cri in academic buildings, and lighted by electricity. In the first years the pupils either rowed to school – some still do – or tramped across fields. Christopher Brennan the scholar and poet was one of these. He was dux of the college in 1886.

The heart of Riverview is the exceptionally beautiful Dalton Memorial chapel, built in 1910 to commemorate the founder, Father J.

Dalton. 'None of his pupils could kick a football further than he'. Riverview Observatory was established in 1908 by an Irish Jesuit, Father E. F. Pigot. It is still one of the better seismological observatories in the world.

The imposing Riverview complex is bordered on the west by Burns Bay, once called Murderer's or Murdering Bay from an untidy Jack-the-Ripper kind of crime. Three people with similar names have been traditionally attached to Burns Bay; Barnet Burns, Terence Byrne or Burn, and Captain George Burn who wanted to open a whaling station in Lane Cove, was thwarted by the barks and screams of William Gore, and died leaving a widow who had written the first novel published on the Australian mainland. This lady Burn was Anna Maria; her novel was *The Guardian*, published in 1838 and dedicated to Bulwer Lytton.

Terence Byrne, a short Irish convict with a cast in his blue left eye, is undoubtedly the Burn of the Bay. In 1827, by then a ticket-of-leave man, he squatted on the western side of the Bay, probably near the boundary of the present-day Burns Bay Reserve. Simultaneously he applied for a grant of 'this small portion'. He was one of the unlucky ones. Five years later the authorities were still waffling about it, though by then Byrne had 7.5 acres under cultivation and had cleared a good deal. A year later he was informed that he would be allowed to apply for purchase of land not exceeding 10 acres, the price being five shillings per acre. But Byrne seems to have been rightly huffed about this, refused to purchase, walked off and vanished into history.

Barnet Burns, another person after whom the Bay is supposed to have been named, was in fact granted a small plot of land for an orchard at the head of Tambourine Bay. It does not appear that he ever worked it before sailing off to his novel and romantic career in New Zealand. In 1829 Burns voyaged to New Zealand on a brig chartered by the Sydney flax-dealers, Montefiore and Co. In later days Burns wrote a melodramatic pamphlet which tells how he was captured by the Maoris, made to witness cannibal feasts and was forced to be tattooed. New Zealand historical records indicate that he voluntarily became a North Island tribe's *pakeha*, that is resident white man who would interpret and barter on their behalf with whalers, timber-getters and flax merchants like Montefiore.

Undoubtedly these venturesome *pakeha* were both courageous and self-reliant, for they were often completely alone in a darkly savage land racked by inter-tribal warfare. Like many another *pakeha*, Burns was loved and cherished by his tribe, and given the chief's daughter as a prize. During this time his entire body was tattooed, it is said at his own request, paying the tattooer with a musket. The process was so long and exquisitely painful that Burns must surely have made up his mind to remain in New Zealand as one of the tribe. The Maoris evidently thought so, for they made him the chief of a large *hapu* or sub-clan.

Burns continued to act successfully as agent for his firm in Sydney. However, after a number of years, he became homesick, and bidding a painful and eternal farewell to his wife and children, he took ship to Sydney, received a sympathetic settlement from his employer, and went on to England. Naturally enough his remarkable appearance caused a sensation wherever he went. Tradition says that he capitalised on this by becoming an exhibit in a raree-show.

The first tanner of Tanner's Creek which runs into Burns Bay, was Charles Fay, sentenced to life transportation for 'machine-breaking'. A victim of the agricultural depression following the Napoleonic wars, this Hampshire youth was accused of being one of three hundred persons who 'tumultuously assembled and ... feloniously and wilfully pulled down, demolished and destroyed several machines ... for the purpose of casting iron'. Fay pleaded not guilty, but a witness deposed: 'Some of them said the factory was ruining everybody ... they were shaking the gates ... I saw Fay making a blow at the base of the left pillar with his pickaxe.'

The prisoners, we are told, were 'fine young men, and most of them shed bitter tears as they were told that they must abandon forever the land of their birth'.

The tanner's young wife, as detailed in probably the saddest letter still in our historical archives, died within a few months. 'You may depend upon it, Charles, you was never out of her thoughts night or day. She travelled miles if anyone had a letter to know if any one had seen you. She never sit down to a meal. But she was talking about you in the night, she would sit up in her bed and cry to God ... She is no more in this life, she departed the second of May and the doctor Said she broke her heart.'

Charles Fay did not remarry for seven years. In his Lane Cove days he is described as sober, honest and industrious.

The Lane Cove River now meanders away to west and north, vanishing from our sight into the bushland of Lane Cove National Park. It is navigable by small craft for about eight kilometres above Fig Tree Bridge, which we now approach.

Fig Tree Bridge connects Linley Point with the Hunters Hill peninsula. Let us halt at the adorable old house Carisbrook at the side of Burns Bay Road. A sandstone mansion of the 1860s, it has been restored to pristine beauty, furnished in period, and is now open as a historical museum and example of old Lane Cove architecture. Here we may sit in the oldfashioned garden, very well maintained by the Lane Cove Council, and rest awhile, as other travellers rested a hundred years ago.

THE SOUTH-EASTERN SUBURBS

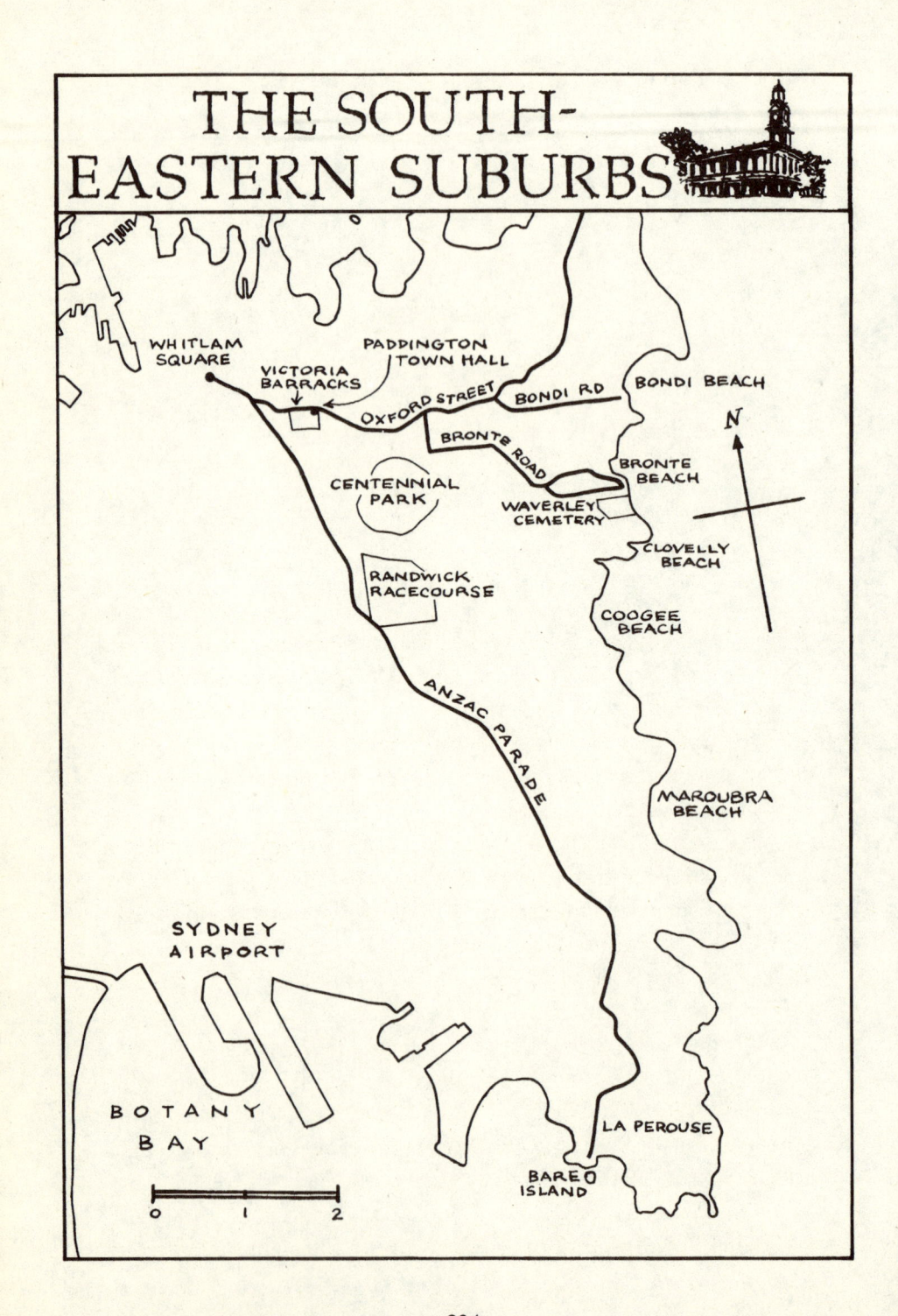

CHAPTER 9

HERE WE BEGAN

Sent away people's country – the rescue of Typhoidville – the trials of Victoria Barracks – the renaissance of Paddington – off to the secret south – the battle of Centennial Park – they're racing at Randwick – the loyal citizens' ball – one poet in another's grave – curious Mr Matra – Simeon Lord's woollen mill – old graves, new ways – Kingsford-Smith Airport – we visit an old fort and consider Captain Cook.

TODAY we are going to Botany Bay, where in truth it all began. If in April 1770, Captain James Cook had succeeded in making a landing at Wollongong, instead of being beaten back by fierce surf, the history of the first Australian settlement would probably have been quite different, and the name Botany Bay never a synonym for exile and an inhuman penal system.

Again, if Captain Phillip had not sensibly decided to overrule his specific instructions to found the new colony at Botany Bay, or had not so speedily found 'the finest harbour in the world' as in his jubilation he described Port Jackson, Sydney might today be a small village on Botany Bay, a ruined or failed town that had far more desperate struggles than were destined to be its lot on more generous shores.

Botany Bay has a haunting sound. It is said that the English gipsies, always likely candidates for a seven-year stretch, called it *bitcheno padlengreskey tem*, 'sent away people's country'. Yet no convicts ever lived there except small parties sent from Sydney to break stones, lay roads or, much later, build the dam for the Botany waterworks.

On this expedition there's plenty of walking to do, here and there, so best take a cab to Oxford Street, at least to the point where it joins

Taylor Square. The square is a nightmare knot of busy roads, pockets of which seem permanently inhabited by dazed harmless winos. Within the cab there is the customary brisk discussion about the exuberant heads of hair all winos seem to have, but no resolution is reached.

Oxford Street, the oldest part of Old South Head Road, used to be populous, busy, cheaper than Town, the very-nearly city shopping area for the once industrial suburbs round about. It's sleazy now, though hard to say why. Still, it's internationally famous for gay pride, gay clothing and bookshops and the Gay and Lesbian Mardi Gras parade.

Underneath it survives the remains of Busby's Bore which first brought water as far as Hyde Park. The ancient tunnel is sealed and partly filled in, so Oxford Street won't collapse under the taxi wheels just now. However, yet another tunnel runs under this street – probably the first efficient sewer to drain what was practically Typhoidville. It debouched in rather dreadful style near Bondi Beach. A formidable structure for its era, circa 1889, it was spacious enough for drainage inspectors to travel along it in canoes.

The Victoria Barracks are only five minutes drive away. The massive wall looms starkly upon our right. Truly a stupendous wall. In some places its foundations go down more than nine metres; the soldier builders despaired of finding firm footing for the masonry. One might ask why Governor Bourke chose to construct such a significant complex of buildings in a wasteland of rocky reefs and shifting sand dunes.

It was elevated, a necessity for imperial buildings, which had to give an impression they were keeping an eye on even the humblest. The barracks, in their original state, had a commanding view to Botany Bay and over Port Jackson. There was also a certain urgency in Governor Bourke's mind. Not only was the old George Street Barracks falling down, but the populace was constantly complaining about convicts, transportation, prisons, leg irons. These things, carped respectable residents, gave Sydney a déclassé look, and they'd had enough. Governor Bourke, who detested the entire transportation system, was known to agree. The time for the cessation of transportation had almost come. Nevertheless the cost of building so huge a project as Victoria Barracks necessitated free labour, so the Governor acted quickly.

Even today Victoria Barracks are considered to be one of the finest examples of British imperial barracks; what a majestic sight they must have been when surrounded only by 'the saddest heath, the most melancholy swamps', and rolling downland of hills so sandy that 'a stranger might imagine them to be snow-capped'.

Victoria Barracks, which, in spite of the name, are Regency-style, were designed by capable George Barney who also built Fort Denison, (Pinchgut) and reconstructed Circular Quay. The work took seven years, 1841 to 1848, and was carried out by convict gangs under the supervision of free masons and carpenters. The first regiment to occupy the new barracks was the 11th (North Devonshire) Regiment of Foot, many of whose senior officers had fought at Waterloo. These were the soldiers who 'were cured of complaint at their remove to the sandhills' by being detailed off to build a kilometre of fortress-like wall.

Visitors may wander into the parade ground at any time, and I recommend your doing so. The natural megalomania of the Victorians ran wild when they were given unlimited space and plentiful forced labour. From the grassy expanse of the parade ground the 225 metre length of the main building is awesome. In this structure the private soldiers lived with their families, in cramped quarters where, as one of them recorded 'you cannot turn about without skinning your arse'. They had a lean time on their miserable pay. Punishment for infringement of regulations was savage, the army lash being much heavier than that used on convicts.

Wives wove cabbage tree hats and sold them outside the barracks wall, and the soldiers' children hawked mutton pies, pickled oysters and 'pottles of aperient native plums' in the street. A certain ailment must have been endemic, for the wives also made a variety of syrup from the fruit of the Moreton Bay fig trees, reputed to 'move a cannonball'. Water came from wells, often polluted. Later households fetched their water from the standpipe that still survives outside the barracks wall.

British regiments dreaded being sent to any of the Australian settlements, so fearfully remote from Home. Many deserters became convicts, and many emancipated convicts became soldiers in the false hope of a better life. Soldiers suffered greatly from boredom. One of them records 'naught to do but guard nobs or chase bushrangers'.

The barracks dominated Paddington from the beginning. A mushroom village sprang up on the north side of South Head Road, most of the houses being small timber pre-fabs from England. They were imported complete with readycut iron roofs, window frames and doors, and boxes of nails to do the job with. Though some of these houses are supposed to have survived the late Victorian development which gave Paddington most of its present terrace houses, I've never yet found one. There's a row of stone houses in Underwood Street that predate even the barracks, and among other elderly houses to which the residents will be happy to direct you, there is in Ormond Street enchanting Juniper Hall (circa 1820) built as a family home by the likeable gin distiller Robert Cooper. He was another emancipated convict who made good. His crimes were minor – he had smuggled wine and silk from France – his colonial achievements mighty. A perfectly enormous man, he was called Robert the Large, and not just because his was a family of twenty-eight children, in which achievement he was assisted by three wives. Like several successful emancipists he was a philanthropist, interested in many charities. He founded Sydney College, which later became Sydney Grammar School.

Robert's stunningly large family is the reason why Juniper Hall exists today; the house was so big it was easier to preserve than demolish. The National Trust acquired the property in the 1980s, and the house is splendidly restored, a gem of wealthy Georgian domestic architecture.

After its well-to-do townhouse days, Paddington fell upon grim, cockroachy, even criminal times. From these it was rescued after World War II by the intellectual, the artistic, and those Johnny-come-latelies, the fashionable, who have restored many dilapidated terraces with good taste, courage, and ruinous amounts of money. Today Paddington is a chauvinistic village, a showplace of folk architecture, mad-hatter shops, good galleries and excellent restaurants and craft markets. Several of the curly leafy streets will make you smile, they are so charming. The pampered expensive terraces are pretty to the point of romanticism, especially the three-storey houses, tall and skinny, with parapets, finials and amazing chimneypots. These 'grand' terraces, though they predated Federation by three decades, were originally painted Federation colours, charcoal, pine green, and chocolate; their lavish iron lace was black. But life is more lightsome nowadays, and the tall houses preen in palest pastels, their lace white, rose, aqua. Look closely at this iron lace, for it was in Paddington, we are told, that the revered English designs first became unfashionable, and waratahs, lyrebird tails, palms and even emus began to appear in railings and front gates.

Several roads lead to Botany Bay, but we have decided to travel

Anzac Parade which joins Moore Park Road on the southern side of Victoria Barracks. But first let us take to the air. Come now, straight up into the blue. To the west and southwest, to the north, behind us, lies a tremendous city, overbuilt, one feels, to explosion point. We see signs of light industry, even medium industry, but mostly high and low residential development, the everlasting rectangular unit blocks that have cursed Sydney ever since vertical living took over from horizontal. Nevertheless, here and there is a time warp, a huddle of carrot-red roofs, or a few nice old houses cowering together against the oncoming tide.

But that is not all. To the south, at our very feet as it were, is the vastest green grassland, speckled with little ponds and rivulets, groves of trees and meandering roads. It is the most unexpected sight, and we cannot wait to descend to earth and join the horse riders and cyclists who appear and vanish among the greenery. This wide-open heart of Sydney must surely have its own boundaries, but it seems to go on for ever, via Randwick Racecourse and Pagewood and Eastlakes, and after that in little jumps and spurts to Botany Bay.

Anzac Parade runs through the west side of this oasis, Moore Park. It is a gracious highway, its north and south lanes divided by trees and banks of flags. Moore Park was once part of the Sydney Common, and the road very nearly follows the track from the barracks used by the soldiers who did much of the leveling and reclamation. The common was for many years a wild and somewhat uncanny place. Here settlers grazed goats and cows, gentlemen ventured with swan-shooting parties, and paupers and wanderers, grown farouche with solitariness, set up hidden wurleys among the reeds and spinneys. The first portion to be reclaimed was the Cricket Ground No. 1, levelled and laid out by the soldiers.

Cricket is described as 'a noble obsession' with the early settlers. 'Your milkboy sets his can down, in open day, for the vegetable lad to have only just one ball at it with a turnip, and old women are continually seen scolding because their legs have, quite accidentally, of course, been treated as a set of stumps.'

Moore Park is, so to speak, the cheering, ball-bashing side of the old common. We note Sydney Girls High and Sydney Boys High schools to our right, and to our left cricket, soccer and rugby grounds, hockey and netball fields; tennis courts; major football and cricket stadia; the impressive Moore Park Golf Course; and, where the old Agricultural Showground used to be, Fox Film Studios.

This side of the common is not always green as it is today. Sometimes in summer it is as yellow as a quince. The grizzling winds which whip up small puffs of sand tell us the reason – the topsoil is so thin you can spit through it. Just a handspan or so down are the intractable dunes which once extended from here to Botany Bay.

To our immediate left is Centennial Park, also sited on the old common, though this area was not sand dunes but a spongy marshland, the Lachlan Swamps. These were named not for Macquarie, but for his only child.

As we know, these swamps, via the Busby's Bore, supplied Sydney with water from 1825 to 1886. They were a haven for wildfowl, eels and freshwater mussels, and were visited by kangaroo and wallaby, as we have learned from the Aboriginal middens in the area.

This is a quiet, harmonious place; the voice of the city is muted, birds are sleepy, reeds hiss around the manmade ponds. We drive around the circular Grand Parade, which was constructed by relief workers during the great crash of the 1890s. It is bordered by Norfolk Island pines and Fort Jackson figs, for exotic trees do not thrive here.

On the northern side of the Grand Parade is the sandstone pavilion that houses the 1901 Commonwealth Stone, a six-sided slab of granite that lay under the table where Queen Victoria signed the Act that made Australia a federation of six states. One can imagine how this historic stone will feature in the January 2001 celebrations.

It is scarcely-known that we owe Centennial Park's existence to the jolly Dick Whittington of Victorian Sydney, Charles Moore, three times Mayor, and a doughty one. It was Moore who threw Sydney's most spectacular party – the Citizens' Ball to honour the youthful Duke of Edinburgh in the summer of 1868. As there was no building large enough to shelter the three thousand odd 'better-class' guests his Worship proposed to invite, he built one in Hyde Park. It was, he bragged, the largest wooden structure in the world, though somewhat bombastic in design. The ballroom was seventy-three metres long and thirty metres wide, and in its centre a fountain gushed into an artificial lakelet. Three other fountains disposed among the dancers 'breathed forth as from Elysium Mr E.H. O'Neill's choice colonial perfumes. Mr O'Neill's druggist's establishment in King Street is well-known to all refined ladies and gentlemen.'

The supper room was of almost equal proportions. The band of

HMS *Galatea* played schottisches and galops, and the prince proved himself a graceful and indefatigable dancer. 'The ladies, sweet angels, were gowned in the height of Home fashion by Messrs Hordern, Farmer and David Jones.'

Not invited to the splendid affair were the prince's relatives, the family of Sydney's late Chief of Police, William Augustus Miles, an illegitimate son of Prince Alfred's great-uncle, William IV. His royal blood is cryptically indicated on his tombstone in Camperdown Cemetery:

> ... the beating heart with cultivated mind
> Which thousands might have blessed
> Sank into death unmourned.

The government of the day had, in the high-handed, non-consultative way of most governments, sold off some of the common to land investors. One conjectures that the residential areas of Randwick, Kensington and Zetland originated in this manner. But Mayor Moore, rummaging through old documents, discovered that the common had long ago been granted to the people of Sydney. He dug out the grant, and the Corporation of the City of Sydney laid claim to the common, both sold and unsold. The government was aghast, but Charles Moore was immovable. After noisy wrangling and litigation, the government conceded the title as far as the unsold land was concerned, and the common became 'a great national property', a complex of parks, semi-wilderness, lakes and golf links.

Centennial Park was opened on the first hundred-year anniversary of the founding of the colony, that is, January 26, 1888. It was a bright clear day, and on the 'hills and flats of the erstwhile Lachlan Swamps was ... an assemblage almost as multifarious as the multitude of Hannibal'. Popular Governor Carrington did the honours, and the enormous crowd was formally admitted to full and free possession.

Mayor Moore left the landscaping to others more competent in that field, but he asked that the great green space should remain 'a countryside in the midst of a city'.

The premier of the time, Sir Henry Parkes, suggested that Centennial Park should also contain a noble pantheon where the city's great could be enshrined after death. Fortunately that did not come about.

Centennial Park is a great place for dogs and children, a jumping, running wild, tree-climbing place, with mud to slosh in and swamps that squelch. The park covers almost 200 hectares but seems even larger; they say there are 8 kilometres of iron picket fence, but the terrain is so irregular that mostly you don't guess a fence is there. In someone's good phrase, there's a variety of countryside here. Naturalist Vincent Serventy has called the park 'a great outdoor laboratory where more and more people are studying ecology, the way Nature works'. The lakes still provide secluded breeding spots for waterbirds, and forty-three species have been logged as nesting there.

And now, off to Botany Bay, still following Anzac Parade. Of course there are other routes, other roads, to the coast. A portion of the first has actually survived. Described in 1813 as wretched in the extreme, so lonely 'that one might suppose he was travelling through the deserts of Arabia', this remnant, now named O'Riordan Street, the disagreeable entrance to Sydney from the airport, may not be lonely, but is still wretched. Mayor Moore would not have put up with it for a moment.

A better road was laid down in 1833. The irresistible gossip Lieutenant-Colonel G. C. Mundy writing in 1845 says, 'There is a pretty good turnpike road, besides innumerable tracks for equestrians across the stunted scrublands.' A memoir of 1858 gives further directions: 'Set out from Pitt Street, in a coat of rose-tinted China silk and a broad ribbon with fringed ends for a necktie. Up George Street we bowled along, a row of hansom cabs bound for ... dear old Botany, grim old Botany, of which our English childhood heard so much and formed ideas so false.'

Both Mundy and the rose pink person travelled on what is now the Bunnerong Road, which leads straight to La Perouse. Horse buses also used this route 'pitching and rolling like a trawler in a southerly buster'.

The horror of being a horse in colonial days!

But here we are in sight of Randwick Racecourse. Sydney racing is almost as old as Sydney itself, and we remember that, among other titles, Hyde Park was called the Racecourse long before the first official race meeting was held there in October 1810. The Sydney Turf Club was formed in 1825, and held race meetings both at Parramatta and a new course at Grose Farm, approximately where Sydney University now stands. The Turf Club operated, usually under vice-regal patronage, until 1840, when an Australian Race Committee was formed. (It appears to be the direct ancestor of the Australian Jockey Club which was founded two years later and continues in full vigour today.) The Australian Race

Committee superintended the building of a track at Homebush, on already cleared, level land owned by William Charles Wentworth.

The extreme enthusiasm of the public is amusingly described in the *Sydney Herald's* report of the first general race meeting in March 1841, at the fine new course. 'About eight o'clock immense numbers of carts, well loaded with passengers, were to be seen ... moving to the scene of action. About 11 o'clock gigs and carriages of every description appeared, together with some thousands of equestrians and pedestrians, the latter plodding along the road in the broiling sun to Homebush.' Other racegoers used the river steamers, which cruelly landed them at Kissing Point at low water, so that they had to wade to shore, and then 'trudge over three miles of boggy flats to get to the course, nearly the whole distance of which they were over shoes in mud'.

The Homebush Racecourse, which was fully equipped with large training stables and spelling paddocks, operated for seventeen years. The Randwick course seems to have been used for racing since 1860, though it was not officially opened until 1862. For nearly half a century afterwards, the old Homebush track was still used for training, but in 1906 the government bought the land for the State Abattoirs. The complex of stockyards, saleyards and administrative offices was among the biggest in the world. Today Homebush Bay is the stunning site for the Sydney 2000 Olympics.

Anzac Parade runs past the buildings of the University of New South Wales, built on the site of the long defunct Kensington Racecourse. Though devoid of dreaming spires, it is a lively university, instituted in 1949 and expanding in all ways ever since. Its academic emphasis is on technology. The campus also houses the National Institute of Dramatic Art (NIDA) which trains theatre performers and producers.

As we drive southwards along this road we move parallel to a magnificent coastline. Easy enough to take a look at it. Any easterly street will do. Perhaps we should turn a little north as well, for it's the right thing to start with Bondi.

Surely Bondi is the word most overseas people remember when they think of Australia, the Greater Hawaii, the hedonist land of sun, sea, flies and sportsmen. And I'd be willing to bet they mispronounce it. Still vivid in my mind is the bright day I landed in Australia, when, wanting to visit the beach which for years had symbolised Sydney, I climbed on a tram and asked the conductor for a ticket to Bondee. At his shaming snort of laughter, I added conciliatively, 'But if you're not going there, Coogee will do.' Naturally I pronounced Coogee with a hard G, and this led to further snorts.

'Bondi is the most famous 1000 metres of sand in Australia,' they say, and rightly so, in my opinion. The beach itself is a sweep of half-moon (indeed almost three-quarter moon) pale sand with a deep belt of surf. If you approach Australia by air from the east, this oceanic bite in the cliffs is almost the first thing you note. Certainly Bondi Bay encloses several famous surf beaches, but Bondi Beach itself is the queen.

Locals say that Bondi has the beach and is cool, but Bondi Junction has the shops and isn't cool. This is so, though the renaissance of both strand and supporting suburb has marched ahead in irresolute fits and starts for at least three decades. For example, when I first saw it, the beach was awesome, but the suburb was downright eerie. I felt I had time-travelled to 1935, an Enid Blyton summerland of sandy feet, ugly boarding houses, wet 'cozzies' and peeling noses. Any moment I expected to see the Famous Five buying ice cream cones from the van playing 'Greensleeves'. Long ago some criminal had rooted out every tree; the enormous expanse from Bondi Junction to Dover Heights was almost solid red tile roof, all hipped, all trembling under a mirage-like stratum of reflected heat. The whole place was like a supine sacrifice to the sun, pegged out, helpless, hopeless.

Even the sunlight seemed harsher cadmium yellow, and the endless roofs, set in place by some golem who knew no angle but one, sent up a fierce shimmer. Boys with surfboards and hair of bitter gold, produced dangerously with washing machine detergent, wandered through the stunned air, beautiful with youth and no knowledge they'd be bald before thirty.

But stay! Waverley Council has now done great things with trees. Street trees, yes, little groves shading green spaces, leafy blobs struggling in the narrow half-kilometre-long strip of park that separates the advancing army of home unit buildings from the promenade. Why did they allow this assertive row of unit blocks to rise along the beachfront, a jungle of nearly identical buildings nearly identical brick, and design? Their balconies form positively horizontal lines, and their height is such that construction on the gentle slope behind must get higher and higher to permit the residents to catch a glimpse of sea.

There has been a good deal of carelessness, greed, and heartless development here. An example is the northern horn of Bondi Bay, Ben Buckler (a corruption of Ben Becula, one of Governor Macquarie's names). The point is a tumble of fallen cliff and boulders as big as locomotives that came crashing in during great storm years ago. A small green plateau once crowned it, where stood buildings connected with the old sewage outfall workings. Now, sewage gone somewhere else, the plateau is crammed with four-storeyed unit blocks, square windows in square walls, many flat roofed, and black flat roofs at that. They are so close together, so neat, so dumb that they might as well be packet groceries lined up in a kitchen cupboard. Humans shouldn't be treated like this, and neither should Ben Buckler.

But the wave of fashion is sweeping towards Bondi, as it swept towards Paddington, turning a slum of criminal repute into astronomically priced real estate. A realtor says, 'Bondi is only a few kilometres from the GPO, after all, we call it outer inner city. The middleclass are moving in, knocking down the old liver brick bungalows with the autumn toned carpets, and building the latest and glassiest. The climate is wonderful, there's always a sea breeze, and we're close to racing and surfing. Don't knock it. European migrants have always loved it. We have many Greek families and businesses here and at Maroubra.'

If you're visiting in winter you might be lucky enough to view the heroic initiation ceremony of the Bergs (Bondi Icebergs Club). Its men's only clubhouse is just above the southerly public baths. Initiates hurl blocks of ice into the water and swim among them. If you whinge or drop dead with a heart attack you're out. Usually only ten per cent of the aspirants pass the test.

As we travel south we observe a series of attractive parks and reserves following the coast. It was not always like this. 'Sand dunes and wildflowers of dazzling orders' recorded Mrs Louisa Anne Meredith, who went everywhere and never ran out of quill pens 'little shanties built by folk who shoot or fish. There are rumoured to be tracks through this wilderness tramped out by the native Blackfellow, and a tradition that they traded stone tools with visitors to Botany Bay.'

It is true that in earlier times what were termed 'workshops' were found around Coogee and Tamarama, very like the Neolithic flint quarries of Europe, where ancient man fashioned and sharpened spear heads and axes.

Aside from a few stone scribings, which Waverley Council has regrooved and protected as far as possible, little is known about the people of this coast who did, however, speak a variant of the Cadigal language. They were one of the very few tribes – at least observed by Europeans – who wore a kind of poncho of animal skin, and decorated their bodies and hair with flowers and shells. But alas, they are but a distant memory.

These ancient dunes extended past Nelson Bay and the now prosperous suburb of Bronte. Between Bronte and the narrow squinch of Clovelly Bay is Waverley Cemetery, historically interesting. Its matchless situation, which must cause property investors to weep, makes the mourning angels and shattered pillars seem all the sadder, standing as they do against sapphire sky and an intermittent glitter of leaping surf. Twilight tours of this old cemetery are quite memorable. Here, amid other remembered names, we can find Henry Lawson, strangely buried in the poet Henry Kendall's grave. How did this extraordinary thing happen? The tubercular Kendall died in 1882; Lawson, that drunken and yet unforgettable man in 1922.

His mother Louisa, who married the Norwegian goldminer Peter Larsen (a name later changed to Lawson) was a prototype feminist, a difficult, prickly creature, insatiable for justice and self-realisation, who expectedly achieved neither. She was a great admirer of Kendall, and when she brought her family to Sydney in the year after the poet's death, she went to Waverley to visit his grave. 'Oh, disgrace!' she cried. 'It is sunken, covered with rusty tins, wild grass, decayed flowers. Delicate spirit of Kendall, forgive us!' Somehow this penniless woman contrived to save enough money to buy the ground around the Kendall grave so that there would be space for a memorial.

At a later date, after a comic war between rival committees, Kendall's remains were moved to a commanding site on top of a hill in Waverley Cemetery. The vacated grave thus belonged to the Lawson family, so there Henry was interred. His sense of irony would surely have been tickled.

As we move inland again, the flattening of the land becomes increasingly visible. The downland market gardens that the ever present Chinese cultivated have been levelled, the duck and swan marshes drained. Small settlements have merged into working class villages. Matraville is such a one, still in the 1930s or so it appears, with an ardently patriotic inception. It was the first of the 'garden settlements' devised by Sydney's residents for returned soldiers. Almost all streets have names of battles in which the first AIF participated. By 1923 sixty homes had been built, mostly by voluntary labour. But somehow Matraville did not flourish, and none of those little cottages, so well meant, exists today. Caught in a time warp as it is, too far from Sydney and potential employment, it bears nevertheless a name of great historical importance.

It was named for Sir Joseph Banks's shady, axe-grinding chum, James Matra (his real name appears to have been Magra or McGraw) who sailed with Banks and Cook in the *Endeavour*. Matra was a member of an American colonist family which remained loyal to the Crown during the Revolution, consequently being skinned of its possessions. Matra spent the rest of his life being 'a ruined Loyalist' and getting some useful friends and jobs because of it.

Because of this enigmatic man, though indirectly, Sydney was born a distant daughter of the American Revolution. For many years England had disposed of her criminals by transportation to the American colonies, but after the latter declared their independence there was nowhere to send these wretched felons. In insupportable numbers they were crowded into prison hulks. Meantime, James Matra had discussed with Banks a plan for recompensing dispossessed American loyalists by settling them on the New South Wales coast at Botany Bay. With Banks's encouragement, Matra drafted a proposal to the British Government. Banks brought his own version of the draft to the attention of Lord Sydney, who was in charge of colonial affairs. Others had had similar ideas. However, it appears to have been Matra's plan which Lord Sydney adopted, not with the intention of resettling impoverished Americans, but to the sole end of getting rid of 'the ever-increasing hordes of brutes' in the woeful prison hulks.

The rest, as we know, is history. Matra himself never saw New South Wales again. He spent the last years of his life as a British consul in Morocco.

From Matraville it is a short drive back to Anzac Parade, which loops through Botany Bay National Park, overlooking queer little Bare Island and giving a fine view of almost everything for those who don't wish to get out of the car and walk. But a walk is well worthwhile; here is probably the most historic spot in Australia.

Captain Cook did not land here but across the bay, directly opposite Bare Island, on the southerly horn of Botany Bay, now called Kurnell. Near Kurnell, on a Sunday afternoon, April 27, 1770, the *Endeavour* was anchored. Cook, Banks, Solander, the Tahitian Tupia and others, were rowed ashore. 'Jump out, Isaac!' Cook is supposed to have called to the boat's midshipman. Thus the young boy, Cook's nephew by marriage, who became the distinguished ancient, Admiral Smith, was probably the first white man to set foot on the east coast of the mainland.

Still, Cook's expedition did examine and chart the opposite shore. The wealth of wild flowers and foliage unknown to the *Endeavour's* naturalists was eagerly noted, drawn, and described, so the name, which replaced a temporary one of Stingray Bay, began its famous career. It is known internationally not however for flowers, or even convicts, but for wool, and for that we are indebted, as we shall see, to the emancipée Simeon Lord, who had the grand house in Macquarie Place.

The Botany Bay National Park comprises 436 hectares, and includes the wetlands at Kurnell as well as the ancient north shoreline, now almost lost behind the immense reclamations of Port Botany, but delineated by Foreshore and Botany Roads.

This southern gateway of Sydney differs so greatly from the north, with its radiant entanglements of sea and land, precipitous boundaries and once impassable uplands, that one can scarcely believe both belong to the same country. In spite of the modest houses, the tidy streets, it is still heathland. The land has flattened out, withdrawn itself, so that one feels the earth is but shallowly marked with mankind's small scratchings and scribblings.

In spite of the science fiction city of Port Botany, the cyclopean installations devoted to bulk liquid storage, giant cranes and oil tanks, the place is still wild, bright with everything tossing and glittering before a fresh wind which stitches the shirt to the ribs. Sand oozes up between the grass roots, trees have a permanent cant before the wind, seagulls rise and fall above the rough water like willy-willies of torn white paper. You can feel very strongly the Aboriginal character of Australia, the profound indifference to the stranger which gave the early settlers such psychic unease. Give Botany Bay half a chance, one feels, and it would blow down the factories, submerge the rows of demure mousy houses, steal back the reclamations, and flood the droplet lakes that curve in a chain through the Lakes Golf Course until the whole bayside became a water meadow once more.

Like the people of Lieutenant-Colonel Mundy's time, hundreds of riders (but riders in cars) go to Botany Bay on Sunday, to snuff this fierce wind and enjoy the sights. On a small green flat, within a safety fence, the Snake Man handles tiger snakes, adders, a red-sequined black snake. He's a herpetologist, collects snakes for zoos everywhere, and he knows exactly what he's doing every moment. The snake shows have gone on here since 1919. Before that the Chinese market gardeners working round about trapped snakes for medicine.

Sometimes the local Aborigines demonstrate boomerang throwing, and the soft voiced women and children sell artefacts made of shells. They live in pleasant cottages, but it was not always like that at 'La Per', as they call their home. 'We had corrugated iron shacks. So hot you'd cook in summer. No bath, no toilet. That was in Mission days. But then the Housing Commission took over, and we had good times.'

The old worndown suburb retains many historic sites. Thus it is a nostalgic, fascinating place to spend a few hours. The stone watchtower standing solitary upon its green hillock was built to the order of Macquarie in 1821. Here soldiers watched for suspicious vessels carrying foreign flags, and a customs officer watched for smugglers. The exciseman slept on the top floor, in an owl's nest reached only by a ladder, and we are told that at least one officer's children came and slept there, too. But they were not allowed to run freely around the shores 'because of the escaped convicts in the mangrove swamps'. The rugged Norfolk pine near the watchtower was planted by Governor Darling.

The La Perouse monument was erected to honour the lost French navigator in 1829, by the son of another famous Pacific explorer, Louis de Bougainville. Visiting French warships usually arrange for a little ceremony at this lone monolith, and it is local belief that the tiny plot of land surrounding this and the nearby grave of Pere Receveur is French.

'Yeah, the Government gave it to France, just like the Scotch Government gave the bit around Macquarie's grave to Australia.'

Pere Receveur was an accomplished naturalist. He died on February 17, 1788, probably only a few weeks before the two well-equipped ships of La Perouse were wrecked (it is believed) in the New Hebrides, with total loss of life. No relics of the expedition were discovered until 1826. The Comte de la Perouse, whose journal is witty and coarse, was an experienced captain who read Shakespeare and idolised James Cook. He was sent forth to explore the Pacific by another and more unlikely Cook admirer, Louis XVI, destined to lose his head in the French Revolution.

By an extraordinary coincidence, La Perouse reached Botany Bay just six days after Phillip, though at first heavy weather prevented *La Boussole* and *L'Astrolabe* from entering. The ships actually anchored on January 26 when, as we know, the First Fleet was just leaving Botany Bay for Sydney Cove. It is said that Phillip turned pale when he saw the ships, fearing that they were Dutch, come to dispute the founding of a British Colony in New Holland. Then, his remarkably sharp eyes having distinguished the strangers' colours, he 'grunted and shut his trap'.

The two commanders did not meet, but Phillip's officers visited the French ships, feasting on the bountiful fish of Botany Bay, prepared by superior French methods. On a single day the French sailors, using a seine, had caught 'nearly 2000 light-horsemen'. This is the old name for our snapper.

La Perouse's ships remained six weeks, the crew making repairs and rebuilding longboats damaged in the expedition's fatal encounter with hostile natives at Samoa. They also planted a garden at Frenchman's Bay, before sailing away never to be seen again by Europeans.

The first important settler at Botany Bay was Simeon Lord, who arrived as a young convict in the Second Fleet, and survived to 'become a merchant whose stores and factories were the largest in the antipodes, one whose vessels were as well known to the whales of the Antarctic as to the shroffs of Bombay'. He was already a wealthy emancipist when he established a fulling mill at Botany in 1815. It was built near a strong stream which ran his machinery for him. The mill's site is marked by Mill Pond Road which runs into Botany Road on the eastern side of Sydney Airport. In later years the woollen goods produced at Lord's mill were regarded as comparable with the best English. When he began manufacturing, however, he produced 'coarse cloths, blankets and flannels' which were dyed with extracts from Botany Bay's abundance of native flora. Most of Lord's cloth went to the government. The agreed price was two shillings and sixpence per yard, plus two pounds of soap and ten pounds of copper for every 100 yards he delivered.

Other wool-scouring firms followed Lord's, and Botany became so identified with the production of high quality wool that the word

'Botany' is still applied to fine merino wool, and is as familiar in other countries as it is in Australia.

When Busby's Bore proved inadequate for Sydney and the Botany Waterworks were being planned, some 30 hectares of Lord's original grant were resumed, and the stream flowing into Lord's convict-built dam intercepted. His dwelling and works were demolished about 1856. Simeon himself had died in 1840. If he'd been still alive, one might confidently predict, Sydney would have gone hang for its water supply, for a more accomplished charmer of governors and getter of his own way never existed.

For many years, until the Nepean system of water supply was in use, the old engine house at Botany pumped water to the Crown Street reservoir. Here the city reticulation system took over. Now, in those days before telephones, how did the Botany crew know when the Crown Street reservoir was full? A standpipe was placed near Victoria Barracks. By telescope it was visible from the top windows of the Botany engine house. If it overflowed, they stopped pumping.

The ghost of Simeon Lord will nudge us momentarily when we visit the serene Botany Cemetery. For there is Simeon's headstone, clean and repaired, along with nearly one thousand others, many of which, like Simeon Lord's, had originally been erected in the old Devonshire Street (or Sandhills) graveyard, and moved to Botany when the Central Railway Station was constructed on the site. John Cadman, the one-eyed boatman of Cadman's Cottage, is there too, and Barnett Levey, the theatrical pioneer, and many others of familiar name and career.

Part of Simeon's land was resumed once more in 1947 to provide expansion for the Airport. The flatness of La Perouse and Botany protects them from topographical over domination by the airport on their western side. But the sky rolls with intermittent thunders of jets boring into and out of Mascot like glittering wasps.

Despite the astonishing reclamations that have been engineered to provide the Airport with more runway or more administrative space, there does not seem to have been the usual warfare over its site. It was chosen by Nigel Love, veteran airman of World War I, and managing director of the newly formed Australian Aircraft and Engineering Company. He searched Sydney extensively for a suitable airfield site before he found one that 'was aeronautically a winner'. This comprised 160 hectares of flat, drained swampland, used as a fattening paddock for the nearby abattoir. The Botany residents called it 'the bullock paddock'. Love obtained a cheap lease of the grazing ground in 1919. Only a few months later the first of the airfield's many famous visitors flew in – Sir Ross Smith, who had flown a Vickers Vimy from England.

In 1921 the Commonwealth purchased 65 hectares of this land for use as an airport, and in 1924 the first regular flights between Sydney and Melbourne and Adelaide began. Ten years later Qantas began its schedule of overseas flights.

The Laperouse museum, which opens every day, is crowded with 'group bookings' from tourist buses, so we wander down to restless Congwong Bay. There's a nude beach around here somewhere, but perhaps the wind is too bitter for its habitués. What misery must have awaited the hundreds of evicted, unemployed families that fled here during the Great Depression, people utterly without resources in those days before social welfare worth the name. 'We lived in shacks of hammered-out kerosene tins, bits of sacking, driftwood. One fellow had half of a wrecked boat with a bedspread over the open part. The women cooked outside of course; it was like the Stone Age. No running water. What we had were running wild kids; even if they were half starved it was like a perpetual picnic for them. We called it Happy Valley; it went on for years. There were flies and ticks and sandflies, they were the worst. Raised big welts, festered. Who would ever think a big wealthy city like Sydney would come to that?'

These people lived on the parsimonious food ration tickets handed out by the government, but survived because of the generosity of neighbours only slightly less poor than themselves.

'The Aborigines shared all the fish they caught. Oysters, crabs, rabbits, they were wonderful. The Chinese market blokes would drive over with a cart full of vegetables; they were pretty good at doctoring, too. And of course the charities did what they could. But it was hard, harder than you can think.'

Nearly all this peninsula seems to be golf links, celebrated courses too. Both Henry Head and the Cape Banks Fort are quite heavily fortified, the latter being the main coastal defence system for Sydney's back door. But it's a long walk (though on excellent track and road) to inspect guns, so we choose to see Bare Island instead. A wooden causeway connects the islet with the mainland and shakes with every wave. The sea runs, spills off long platforms of rock. Constantly turbulent, it comes through the gates of the Bay with a headstrong rush.

Bare Island has a curiously archaic look; I don't know if this is intrinsic, or is borrowed from one's memories of European islets tethered to the land by rickety causeways or stone roads awash in a hissing tide. But there's something here reminiscent of Tintagel in Cornwall, a wild solitariness, rough bright sea, a strong feeling that the past is nearby, separated from us by the thinnest integument.

Gulls screech around us as we cross the causeway; handsome lousy birds with manic eyes and feet pink as clover. With them are two or three little shearwaters, the flock bird that was one of the species Captain Cook observed upon squally autumn seas in 1770, and took heart, knowing that these birds do not fish far from their breeding grounds. 'Indeed, we cannot be far from it,' said Cook, of the invisible land to port.

We can hardly believe that this queer little fort was ever taken seriously. It was erected in 1885 to defend Botany Bay and the southern approaches to Sydney. Against whom? It is hard to imagine. We can only remember that in this year the colony was feeling its oats, for it had just sent a contingent to aid the British then working their way up the Nile to rescue gallant Gordon. The death of General Gordon threw Sydney into a hysteria of imperial patriotism; in sixty days a troop was readied to sail off in the *Iberia* and the *Australasian* amidst 'a brilliant and exciting spectacle'. The little Sudan contingent was Australia's first military offering to the motherland. It did not see active service, but the effect on the colony was stimulating. The Bare Island Fort is quaint evidence of this efflorescence of national sentiment.

Sheltered behind the high, fortified walls, we find sandstone buildings flooded with light. Incredibly, we overhear from the scrambling, peering tourists constant references to convicts – 'This is where they kept them when they landed from England. That's where they flogged them, tied up to that big hook in the wall. That stone pit must be the punishment cell.' Of course no convicts were ever imprisoned here. The fort was occupied by a permanent artillery garrison until it was taken over as a war veterans' home. The returned soldiers were, in their turn, shifted in 1963 to comfortable modern quarters at Narrabeen.

The barracks house a small but interesting historical museum. It is a lovingly-kept repository of Cook, Phillip and La Perouse mementoes, uniforms, weapons, natural history specimens, Aboriginal artefacts, pictures and records of old Randwick (Sydney's first formally proclaimed municipality) and all kinds of other slightly irrelevant treasures. It is open on Saturdays and Sundays and there are guided tours for a small fee. Kids are always impressed by one of the big guns, an 18-tonne Armstrong, so lovingly restored and polished you'd think it had never fired a shot in anger. (It never did.) But it points out to sea in a most satisfyingly threatening manner.

Outside the museum is a wide stone verandah, where I recall the old soldiers snoozing in the sun. The white-walled courtyard with its embrasures and high gateway inscribed V.R. 1885 is extraordinarily warm and quiet.

But outside the barracks, up on the walls, the wicked wind catches us again, sweeping through the heads like an enemy, bustling about the mysterious curving passages of the fort, sending dry leaves, grass and an occasional gull feather spiralling around the massive circular gun emplacements. The fort is in perfect order, still of military cleanliness. Nothing is ruinous, but grassy earth has banked up against some of the exterior walls, so that the structure appears to be emerging from a rath.

Phillip did right not to plant his settlement here. One feels that the wind blows always, Antarctic chill upon its breath. Treeless hills, combed grass, the sea's shoaly run towards the Kurnell sandhills – all speak of a habit of climate severer than that of Port Jackson. Even the ocean beyond the heads is unlike that seen from Sydney. Here is a Hokusai seascape, with sharp edged waves and a colour like agate.

Chilled to the bone, we climb down to a sheltered grassy hollow near the causeway and sit beside the huge barrel of a surviving gun. We think of the *Endeavour*, 32 metres long – her lubberly high-built stern something like a galleon's. And we think of Captain Cook

> *... drawing thin lines across*
> *The last seas' uncut book.*

The father of Australia, as his admirer Arthur Phillip was father of Australia's first and largest city, remains an enigmatic figure. Thoughtful, immensely practical, he was also an intensely private man. Except in rare instances, his words drop like clinkers. 'Yesterday,' says he, 'being Christmas Day, the People were none of the soberest.' (We know from the Banks journals that all hands were abominably sloshed except the Captain and two or three others.) James Boswell found Cook to be 'a plain sensible man with an uncommon attention to veracity ... a grave, steady man'. When Boswell met him, Cook was accompanied by his wife, 'a decent plump Englishwoman'. (Curiously, Sydney has a memorial to Mrs Cook at Caringbah.)

Cook's voyage to the Pacific was not in the nature of an *embarquement pour Cythere*. It was a scientific expedition, primarily to observe the transit of Venus, and was carried out with notable success. In Cook's secret instructions, the Admiralty directed him to search for the fabled continent of which Marco Polo seems to have been the first to speak – Terra Australis Incognita. In 1578 the explorer Martin Frobisher thus described it: 'A great firme land, lying under and aboute the south pole, being in many places a fruitful soyle ... it is included almost by a parallel, passing at 40' in south latitudes yet in some places it reacheth into the sea with greate promontories, even unto the tropicke Capricornus. Onley these partes are best knowen, as over against Capo d'bona speranza where the Portingales see popingayes commonly of a wonderful greatnes, and againe it is knowen at the south side of the straight of Magellanus and is called Terra del Fuego ... '

Did Cook realise that he had charted and claimed for England part of this Pacific ghostland? We know that he did not. Not even the popingayes gave him a clue. Day after day Banks shot cockatoos, rosellas and lorikeets, all varieties he had never seen. The skins were preserved as specimens, and Cook and crew ate parrot pie daily until they sailed away on May 6, 1770 for the undiscovered Great Barrier Reef and nearly fatal disaster.

Seventeen and a half years later, on a boiling hot January day, eleven ships straggled into Botany Bay. They were eight months out from Spithead, and several of them carried 'live lumber'. The commander of this adventurous little fleet, Captain Arthur Phillip, used Cook's chart to enter the bay. Thus, as a child of Aquarius, Sydney began.

ACKNOWLEDGEMENTS

'Flag Raising Ceremony, 1788', 'Sydney, 1803', 'George Street, c. 1880' and 'Circular Quay, 1873' from the Mitchell Library, State Library of NSW.

'The Rocks, c. 1900' from the Archive Office of NSW.

'Botanic Gardens entrance', 'Mosman Cupola', 'Argyle Cut', 'Macquarie Street', 'Macquarie Lighthouse', 'Durham Hall', 'the Clyde Bank' and 'the Victoria Barracks' from John Callanan.

'Mosman Bay': Jason Busch, 'Sydney Harbour': David Moore and 'Lord Nelson Hotel': Greg Hard from Wildlight Photographic Agency

'Row of terraced houses': Gary Lewis, 'The Gap': Rob Jung and 'View from Observatory Hill': Jeffrey C. Drewitz from the Photo Library of Australia.

'Bondi Beach': Craig Lamotte and 'the Opera House': Craig Lamotte from the Australian Picture Library

INDEX

Admiralty House, Kirribilli Point	217-18
Ady Street, Hunters Hill	189
Agar Steps, Miller's Point	30, 60
Airport, Sydney	251-2
Albert Street, Sydney	15, 17
Albion Brewery	90
Albion Street, Surry Hills	90
Alfred Street, Sydney	15
Alfred Street, North Sydney	216, 219
Ancrum Street, North Sydney	222
Anderson, Charles ('Bony')	182-3
Anderson, James	152
Anderson Park, Neutral Bay	216
Anzac Bridge	165
Anzac Parade	239, 242, 243, 247
Aquarium, Darling Harbour	162
Aquinas Academy, The Rocks	45
Archibald Fountain, Hyde Park	122
Argyle Cut, The Rocks	26, 27, 55, 56, 64, 82, 86
Argyle Place, Miller's Point	56, 57
Argyle Steps, The Rocks	55, 64
Argyle Stores, The Rocks	27
Argyle Street, The Rocks	24, 26, 33, 55, 58, 65
The Ark, Kent Street	60, 171
Art Gallery, Sydney	70, 117-18
Art Gallery Road, Sydney	115
Artarmon	229
Arthur, George	186
Ashton, Julian	226
Ashton Park, Mosman	206
Associated Trade Unions	93
Athol Bay	209
Athol Hall, Mosman	208
Australian Gas Light Company	3
Australian newspaper, former	84, 146
Australian Jockey Club	242-3
Australian Race Committee	242, 243
Australian Subscription Library, George Street	93
Ball, Henry Lidgbird	225
Balls Head	225
Balls Head Bay	225
Balls Head Road, Waverton	224
Balmain	169, 170, 172-80
Balmain, William	178
Balmain Colliery	173
Balmoral	201-2
Bank of Australia	20-1
Bank of New South Wales	13-14, 20
Banks, Joseph	247, 248, 255
Bannerman Street, Cremorne	214
Bare Island	247-8, 252-3
Bare Island Fort	253
Bare Island Museum	253-4
Barnet, James	15
Barney, George	15-16, 56, 107-8, 217, 221, 223, 237
Barton, Edmund	29, 32, 51
Bathurst Street, Sydney	87, 97, 99
Beagle, the	34
Becke, Louis	184-5
Ben Boyd Road, Neutral Bay	215
Ben Buckler	245
Bennelong Point	5, 18, 19
Bent Street, Sydney	70
Berry, Alexander	226-7
Berry Island	225
Berry's Bay	223, 224
Bicentennial Park, Homebush	191
Bigge, J.T.	73, 84, 91, 134
Birchgrove House, Balmain	169
Bishopscourt, Darling Point	138
Black Dog tavern, The Rocks	53
Blacket, Arthur	220
Blacket, Cyril	220
Blacket, Edmund	17, 49, 57, 89, 90, 138, 143, 150, 166, 174-5, 220
Blacket, Sara	17
Blackwattle Bay	158, 165, 166-7
Blaxcell, Garnham	75
Bligh, William	47, 48, 74, 105, 112, 163, 229
Bligh Street, Sydney	10
Blore, Edward	18
Bloxsome, Oswald	211
Blue, Billy	196, 222-3, 224
Blue Berry's Bay	222
Blue's Point 196,	223
Blue's Point Road, North Sydney	222, 223
Blue's Point Tower, North Sydney	223
Bohemia, E.J.	84
Bondi	243-5
Bondi Bay	244, 245
Bondi Beach	244
Bondi Junction	244
Boswell, James	255
Botanic Gardens	7, 9, 69, 70-3
Botany	250-2
Botany Bay	235, 239, 242, 247, 248-54, 255
Botany Bay National Park	247, 248
Botany Cemetery	251
Botany Road, Botany	248
Botany Waterworks	251
Bottle and Glass Rocks, Vaucluse Bay	207
Bourke, Richard	91, 184, 188, 236
Bowes, Dr	4-5
Bowman, James	76, 164, 166
Boyd, Benjamin (Ben)	214, 215-16
Bradfield, J.J.C.	62-3, 198
Bradfield Park, Milson's Point	218
Bradley, William	205, 227

Bradley's Head	200, 201, 205, 206-9	Clarence Street, Sydney	51
Bradley's Head Road, Mosman	198, 210	Clark Road, Neutral Bay	216
Brennan, Christopher	229	Clarke, William Branwhite	71, 173, 220, 221
Brickfield Hill, Sydney	97-100	Clifton Gardens	203-5
Bridge Stairs, The Rocks	64	climate, Sydney	46
Bridge Street, Sydney	8, 10, 40, 46-8	Clontarf	202-3
Brierly, Oswald	212, 215	Clune, Frank	115
Brisbane, Thomas	78, 200, 213	Clyde Bank, Dawes Point	29, 57
Broughton, William Grant	90	Cockatoo Dockyards	184
Brown's Lane, Hunters Hill	189	Cockatoo Island	183-5
bubonic plague	54-5	Cockle Bay	158, 160, 172
Bungaree	93, 109, 200	Collins, David	4
Bunnerong Road	242	Commodore Crescent, McMahon's Point	223
Burn, Anna Maria	230	Concord	187
Burns, Barnet	230-1	Congregational Church, North Sydney	219
Burns Bay	230, 231	Congregational Church, Balmain	176
Burns Bay Reserve	230	Conservatorium of Music	73
Burns Bay Road, Lane Cove	227	Container Terminal, Johnston's Bay	175
Busby, John	86	convicts	4-5, 8, 23, 24, 56, 76, 81-2, 98, 107, 128, 134, 145, 181, 184, 185, 237
Busby's Bore (Sydney water supply)	86-7, 236, 240, 251	Coogee	244
Byrne, Terence	230	Cook, James	2, 235, 248, 250, 253, 254
Cadigal tribe	93, 100, 139, 246	Cooper, Robert	238
Cadman, John	25, 32, 251	Coronation Avenue, Mosman	201
Cadman's Cottage, The Rocks	25, 32, 251	Cottage of Content hotel, Bourke Street	116
Cahill Expressway	7, 20, 22, 70, 104, 115	Cowper, Charles	78
Cambridge Street, The Rocks	54, 64	Cowper's Wharf Roadway, Woolloomooloo	116
Cameron, Ewen Wallace	174	Craignathan, Mosman	196
Camp Cove	150-1	Crane Place, Sydney	20
Campbell, John	49	The Crane and Wheel shop, Sydney	20
Campbell, Robert	29, 31, 33-4, 48, 49, 66, 111, 112	Cremorne	212, 213
Campbell, Robert Jnr	29, 34, 36	Crick, W.P.	78
Campbell's Bond Stores, Circular Quay	33	Crowley, Catherine	145
Campbell's Cove, The Rocks	31	Crows Nest	214, 227
Campbell's Wharf, The Rocks	29, 33	Cumberland Street, The Rocks	43, 44, 51, 63, 64
Camperdown Cemetery	241	Cunningham, Allan	72
Cape Banks Fort, La Perouse	252	Cunningham, Peter	109
Captain Cook Graving Dock, Garden Island	108	Cureton, Edward	12
Careening Cove	214, 216	Customs House, Sydney	7, 15
Carisbrook, Hunters Hill	232	Cutty Sark	35, 36
Carrington, Earl	241	Dalton, J.	230
Carthona, Darling Point	131, 137-8	Dalton Memorial Chapel, Riverview	230
Cathedral Street, Woolloomooloo	112	Darling, Ralph	84, 140, 146, 147, 157, 249
Cattle Point (Bennelong Point)	5	Darling Harbour	16, 30, 31, 35, 100, 157-63
Centennial Hall, Town Hall	94	Darling Point	131, 137
Centennial Park	86, 240, 241-2	Darling Street, Balmain	172, 173-5
Centrepoint, Sydney	122-3	Darlinghurst Courthouse	136
Childs, Joseph	183	Darlinghurst Gaol	134-5
Chisholm, Caroline	83	Darlinghurst Ridge	128, 132, 136
Chowder Bay	203, 204	Darlinghurst Road, King's Cross	128, 129, 136
Chowder Bay Road, Mosman	203	Darwin, Charles	34
Chowder Head	205	Davis, Sam	136-7
Church Hill, Sydney	44, 45	Davis, William	45
Church Street, North Sydney	220	Dawes, William	30-1, 36-7, 61
Circular Quay	1, 3, 4, 7, 13, 14-17, 19, 20-1, 32-6, 55, 56, 108, 237	Dawes Battery	12, 28, 30, 39, 53, 57
		Dawes Point	5, 16, 22-3, 30, 63, 69
		Dawes Point Park	30

de Bougainville, Louis	249
Depression, 1840s 89, 90, 252; 1930s 63, 64	
Dibbs, George	189
Dickens's Pond, Haymarket	99
The Dingle, Kirribilli	218
Dixson, William	74
Dobell, William	27
Dodd, Henry	72
The Domain	7, 113-14, 118-20
Domain Baths	112-14
Don Bank, North Sydney	221
Dorman Long and Co.	63
Dossers' Alley, The Domain	114-15
Double Bay	138-9
Downes, Thomas	120
Downshire Steps, Dawes Point	30
Druitt Street, Sydney	96
Drummoyne	185-6
Duff Reserve, Point Piper	139
Dunbar House, Watson's Bay	150
Dunbar	152, 216-17
Edward Street, North Sydney	221-2
Edwards Beach	202
El Alamein Fountain, Kings Cross	129
Elamang Avenue, Kirribilli	217
Elizabeth Bay	131-3
Elizabeth Bay House	131-3
Elizabeth Street, Sydney	87, 88
Emu hotel, George Street	93
Entertainment Centre, Haymarket	31, 160, 162, 164
Erskine Street, Sydney	171
Essex Street, The Rocks	20, 43-4
Euroka Street, North Sydney	222
Ewenton, Balmain	174
Fairfax, John	42, 79
Family Colonisation Society	83
Farm Cove	9, 103-6, 109
Fay, Charles	231-2
Feez, A.F.	218
Female Orphans' Asylum, Parramatta	46-7
Ferry Road, Hunters Hill	190
Fidden, Joseph	228, 229
Fidden's Wharf, Killara	228
Fig Tree Baths, Woolloomooloo	112-13
Fig Tree Bridge	188, 195, 232
Fig Tree House, Hunters Hill	188, 190
First Fleet	7, 11-12, 250
First Fleet Park, The Rocks	23, 52
Fish Market, Pyrmont	165
FitzRoy, C.A.	184
Fitzroy Dry Dock, Cockatoo Island	184
flag/flagstaff, first	3, 12, 24
Flagstaff Hill, Miller's Point	30, 61
Fleet Steps, The Domain	104
Foreshore Road, Botany	248
Fort Denison, see Pinchgut Island	
Fort Macquarie, Sydney	18
Fort Phillip, Dawes Point	30, 61, 62
Fox Film Studios, Moore Park	240
Fraser, Charles	72
Frobisher, Martin	255
gallows, The Rocks	43, 44
The Gap, Watson's Bay	148, 151-2
garden, first	109
Garden Island	108-9
Garden Palace, see Palace Garden	
Garibaldi Inn, Hunters Hill	189
Garrison Church, see Holy Trinity, Miller's Point	
General Post Office, Sydney	15
George (Governor Macquarie's servant)	105-6
George III, King	45, 119
George Street	20, 23, 24, 27, 39-42, 44, 66, 88-9, 91-100
George Street Barracks	50, 53, 171, 236
George Street Gaol	184
George Street North	20, 23, 27, 28, 98
George's Head	199-200, 201
George's Heights	199
Ghost, Bathsheba	77
Gibbes, J.G.N.	217
Gilchrist, John	178-9
Gipps, George	107, 183, 184, 185, 187
Gladesville Bridge	190
Gladstone Avenue, Hunters Hill	189
Gladstone Hotel, Hunters Hill	189-90
Glebe	166
Glebe Island	163
Glebe Point	166
Glendinning, Balmain	175
Glenmore Hotel, The Rocks	64
Globe Street, The Rocks	20, 23
Gloucester Street, The Rocks	43
Gloucester Walk, The Rocks	27, 28, 31
Glover, Thomas	60
Goat Island	180-2, 184
Godley, Charlotte	28
Godwin, Mary Wollstonecraft	221
Gold Fields House, Sydney	20
The Golden Cob hotel, The Rocks	44
Goossens, Eugene	19
Gore, William	229, 230
Gore Cove	225-6, 229
Gore Hill	229
Government House, first	8-9, 46, 72
Government House, Parramatta	61, 62, 106
Government House, present	17, 18
Government Shipyard, The Rocks	27
Grafton Street, Balmain	175
Graham, Thomas	204
Great Balloon Catastrophe	119
Great North Road, Five Dock	186
Great Sirius Cove	197, 211
Great Synagogue, Sydney	88

Greenway, Francis	12, 62, 73, 79, 80-1, 84, 91, 134, 148	International Exhibition, first	71, 161
		Iron Cove	185
Greenwich	227	Iron Cove Bridge	185
Griffiths, Albert	26, 29, 34-5	Jacky Palmer's farm, see Woolloomooloo	
Grose, Francis	104	Jeanneret Street, Hunters Hill	189
Grosvenor Street, Sydney	44, 46, 49	Jewish Museum, Darlinghurst	136
Guilfoyle, Michael	139	Johnson, Richard	10
Hangman's Hill, The Rocks	43	Josephsen, Emmanuel	229
Harbour Bridge, see Sydney Harbour Bridge		Joubert, Didier	169, 188
Harbour Tunnel	218	Joubert, Jules	188
Harbourside Festival Marketplace	161-2	Joubert, Numa	190
Hardwick, John	50, 179	Juniper Hall, Paddington	238
Hargrave, Lawrence	141	Justice and Police Museum, Sydney	17
Harnett, Richard Hayes	210-11, 229	Kelly, Ned	17
Harnett, Richard Hayes Jnr	211	Keltie, James	227
Harrington Lane, The Rocks	26, 66	Kemp, Charles	42, 79
Harrington Street, The Rocks	23, 31, 43, 44, 52, 66	Kendall, Henry	246
		Kendall Lane, The Rocks	26
Harris, Alexander	47, 50, 53-4, 227	Kennedy, Edmund	84
Harry's Caffè de Wheels, Woolloomooloo	116	Kent Street, Sydney	58, 59-60, 171, 172
Hayes, Henry Browne	143, 144-5	King, Alexander	75
Hayes Street wharf, Neutral Bay	215	King, Mrs P.G.	46, 47, 110-11
Haymarket	99	King, Philip Gidley	3, 44, 46-7, 143
Hayson, Tom	159	King, Phillip Parker	109
Hen and Chicken Bay	186	King Bungaree's Farm (Mosman)	200
Henrietta Villa, Point Piper	140, 141	King George V Memorial Park, The Rocks	27
Henry Head, La Perouse	252	King's Cross	126, 127, 128-31, 136
Henry Lawson Avenue, McMahon's Point	224	Kingsford-Smith, Charles	216
Hero of Waterloo hotel, Miller's Point	57	Kirribilli	216-18
Hickson Road, Miller's Point	31, 58, 171	Kirribilli House	218
Hodgson's Lookout, Neutral Bay	214	Knatchbull, John	135
Holtermann, Bernard Otto	221	Kokera Street, Hunters Hill	189
Holtermann's Tower, North Sydney	221	Kuring-gai tribe	93
Holy Trinity, Miller's Point (The Garrison Church)	55, 56-7	Kurnell	248
		Kurraba Road, Neutral Bay	214, 215, 216
Homebush	191	La Perouse	32, 242, 249, 251
Homebush Bay	190-2	La Perouse, J.F. de	2, 249-50
Homebush Racecourse	243	La Perouse monument	249
hospital, first	23, 76	Laperouse Museum	252
Howe, George	41-2	Lady Gowrie Lookout, Kirribilli	218
Howe, Robert	41	Lambert, George	114
Hughes, John Terry	90	Lancer Barracks, Parramatta	61
Hulk Bay	219	Lands Department, Sydney	10, 15
Hume, James	89	Lane, Timothy	56, 82
Humphries, Barry	94	Lane Cove	227-9
Hunt, Horbury	142-3	Lane Cove River	187, 195, 224, 225, 227, 228, 232
Hunter, John	3, 7-8, 11, 45, 98, 128, 205, 227	Lane Cove National Park	232
		Lang, John Dunmore	41, 45, 50, 58, 108
Hunter Street, Sydney	10	Lang, J.T.	63, 120
Hunters Hill	187-90, 232	Lang Park, Sydney	28, 49, 50
Huxley, Thomas	34, 133, 211	Larra, James	88
Hyde Park	6, 84, 85-7, 122, 240	Lavender, George	219, 223
Hyde Park Barracks	56, 79-83	Lavender, Susannah	224
Hyde Park Scent Bottle	87, 88	Lavender Bay	219, 222
Illoura Reserve, Balmain	172	Law Courts	120
immigrants	82-3	Lawson, Bertha	114
Inkerman hotel, Spit Junction	196	Lawson, Henry	14, 114, 115, 222, 246
Innisfree, Hunters Hill	189		

Lawson, Louisa	246
Leighton, Jack	57, 59
L'Estrange, Harry	213
Levey, Barnett	251
Lewis, Mortimer	60, 61
lighting, first street	13
Lindesay, Darling Point	131, 138
Linley Point	232
Little House Under the Hill hotel, Woolloomooloo	116
Little Sirius Cove	211
Loftus Street, Sydney	3, 4, 7, 8
Lord, Francis	222
Lord, Simeon	13, 66, 248, 250-1
Lord Nelson hotel	58
Love, Nigel	251-2
Lowe, Robert	135-6
Lower Fort Street, Dawes Point	28, 29-30, 57
Lumberyard, Bridge Street	47, 82
Lyndhurst, Glebe	164
Macarthur, Elizabeth	24
Macarthur, John	24, 41, 48, 92, 164
McCredie, George	54-5
McDougall Street, Kirribilli	217
Mackennal, Bertram	70
McKenzie, Henry	174
Mackenzie Street, North Sydney	221
MacLeay, Alexander	132-3
MacLeay, William John	133
MacLeay, William Sharp	132-3
Macleay Street, Potts Point	129, 132
McLeod Street, Mosman	210
McMahon's Point	224
Maconochie, Alexander	182-3
Macquarie, Elizabeth	9, 72, 104-6
Macquarie, Lachlan	8, 12, 40, 47, 69, 78, 81, 82, 84, 85, 91, 105, 106, 109, 112, 121, 126, 134, 157, 158, 172, 200, 236, 249
Macquarie, Lachlan Jnr	106, 133
Macquarie Lighthouse, South Head	12, 147-9, 153
Macquarie Place, Sydney	7, 11, 12-13
Macquarie Street, Sydney	17, 20, 69-79, 106
Macquarie Trust	106
Macquarie's Wall, Botanic Gardens	72
McRae, George	96
Maigre, Pierre	119-20
Man-o'War jetty, Farm Cove	104
Man-o'War Steps, Farm Cove	104
Maritime Museum, Darling Harbour	162-3
Maritime Museum Shipyard, Waverton	225
Market Street, Sydney	10, 96
markets: George Street 21; Market Street	96
Marsden, Samuel	10, 44, 47, 90
Martens, Conrad	16, 132, 211, 218, 220, 222
Masalou, North Sydney	222
Matra, James	247
Matraville	247
Melocco, Peter	121-2
Meredith, Louisa Anne	134, 245
Metcalfe Bond, The Rocks	31
Middle Head	199, 200, 201
Middle Head Road, Mosman	198
Miklouho-Maclay, Nicolaus	150
Miles, William Augustus	241
Military Hospital, Miller's Point	60-1
Military Road, Mosman	210
The Milk House, Milson's Point	218
Mill Pond Road, Botany	250
Millenium Parklands, Homebush Bay	191
Miller Street, North Sydney	222
Miller's Point	55-62, 171
Milson, James	196, 213, 214, 216, 218
Milson, James Jnr	217
Milson, John	217
Milson Park, Kirribilli	216, 217
Milson's Point	63, 218-19
Milton Terrace, The Rocks	29
Mint, Sydney	79
Mint Museum, Sydney	79
Mitchell, David Scott	29, 51-2, 74
Mitchell, Thomas	137-8
Mitchell Library	29, 51, 52, 65, 69, 74, 122
monorail	160
Monte Sant' Angelo college, North Sydney	222
Montez, Lola	34
Moore, Charles	104, 240-1
Moore, Jerry	93
Moore Park	239-40
Moore Park Golf Course	239
Moore Park Road	239
Moore's Bookshop, Sydney	93
Moore's Steps, Sydney	20
Mort, Thomas Sutcliffe	90, 138, 139, 159, 176-7, 179-80
Mort Bay	175, 179
Mort Bay Park	175, 180
Mort's Dock	175, 176, 179, 180
Mosman	196-201, 209, 210-12
Mosman, Archibald	196-7, 310
Mosman, George	196-7
Mosman, Hugh	197
Mosman, Jupiter	197
Mosman Bay	209, 211
Mrs Macquarie's Chair, Domain	9, 104, 106, 108
Mrs Macquarie's Road, Sydney	104-5
Mundey, Jack	32-3, 130
Mundy, G.C.	21, 152-3, 154, 242, 249
Murdoch Street, Cremorne	213, 214
Murphy, Jeremiah	13
Museum of Contemporary Art, Sydney	23, 25
Museum of Sydney, Phillip Street	9
Musgrave Street, Mosman	210
Napier Street, North Sydney	221

Natatorium, Sydney	113	Phillip, Arthur	2-3, 4, 6, 7, 9, 11, 22, 23, 24, 32, 40, 70, 72, 85, 93, 103, 108, 109, 110, 137, 150, 178, 180, 213, 235, 250, 254-5
Nathan, Isaac	197		
National Institute of Dramatic Art (NIDA)	243		
National Trust	32, 57, 88, 138, 175, 238	Phillip Street, Sydney	17
The Nest, Mosman	210	Pigot, E.F.	230
Neutral Bay	213, 214-16	Pinchgut Island	18, 106-8, 237
New South Head Road	142, 147	Piper, John	139-41, 214
New South Wales Swimming Association	113	Piper, Sarah	214
newspaper, first	41	Pitt Street, Sydney	10, 113
Nichols, Isaac	40-1, 208	Plunkett Road, Mosman	201
Nielsen, Juanita	130	Point Piper	139-41
Nightingale, Florence	77	Police Boys' Club	116
Noah's Ark, Kent Street, see the Ark		Police Office, Market Street	96-7
Norfolk Island	182-3, 185	population, Sydney	41, 97
North Shore Ferry Co.	211	Port Botany	157-8, 248
North Sydney	219-24	Port Jackson	4, 254
Northwood	227	post office, first	40
Obelisk Bay	203	Powerhouse Museum, Ultimo	161
Observatory, Sydney	30, 56, 62	Prince Albert Road, Sydney	120
Observatory Park, Miller's Point	55, 57, 59-60, 61, 64	Princes Street, The Rocks	28, 50, 51, 63
		The Priory, North Sydney	221
Ocean Avenue, Double Bay	139	'Pure Marinos'	47-8, 92
The Octagon, Darling Point	138	Putland, Mary	48, 105
O'Flynn, Jeremiah	45	Pyrmont	158, 160, 163-4
Okey, William	136-7	Pyrmont Bridge, old	160, 165
Old Burial Ground, George Street	92-3	Queen Victoria Building	94-6
Old Commodore Hotel, McMahon's Point	223	Queen's Square, Sydney	83-4
Old Moore's Almanac	93	Ragged School, The Rocks	66
Old Nat (Natorium), Sydney	113	Randwick Racecourse	242
Olympic Park, Homebush Bay	191-2	The Rangers, Mosman	211-12
O'Neill, E.H.	240	Rangers Avenue, Mosman	211, 212
Onions Point	187, 225, 227	Rawson Park, Mosman	198
Onslow Place, Elizabeth Bay	132	Receveur, Pere	249
Opera House, Sydney	5, 15, 17, 19-20, 27, 208	Redman's Court, Sydney	42
Ormond Street, Paddington	238	Regent Hotel, Sydney	21
Osburn, Lucy	77	Reiby, Mary	8, 13, 27, 65-6, 188, 190
Overseas Terminal, The Rocks	19, 29	Reiby, Thomas	65-6
Oxford Street, Sydney	235, 236	Reiby Place, Sydney	65-6
Oxley, John	84	Reiby Street, Hunters Hill	188
Paddington	237-8	Reid Park, Mosman	211
Palace Garden (formerly Garden Palace), Botanic Gardens	70-1, 161	research station, first biological	150
		Reynolds, William	52-3
Palisade Hotel, Miller's Point	58	Reynolds Cottages, The Rocks	52
Palmer, John (Jacky)	104, 110, 111, 112, 115	Richmond Terrace, Sydney	120
Parbury Bond, Miller's Point	58	Richmond Villa, Miller's Point	60
Park Hyatt Hotel, The Rocks	31	River Road, Wollstonecraft	227
Parkes, Henry	32, 62, 77, 78, 175, 241	Riverview	229-30
Parliament House, Sydney	77-8	Riverview Observatory	230
Parramatta River	187, 191, 225, 227	Robertson, George	52, 114
Parramatta Road	61	Robertson, James	213
Passy, Hunters Hill	189	Robertsons Point	213
Passy Avenue, Hunters Hill	189	Robinson, Michael Massey	78
Paterson, William	40	Robinson's Hot and Cold Sea Water Baths, The Domain	114
Payne, Bryant	146		
Peacock's Point, Balmain	172	Rocks, High	27, 28, 29, 51
Pearl Bay	203	The Rocks	20, 22, 25-33, 51-7, 65-6
Peck, B.C.	119	Rocks Push	26

Roden's Lane, Miller's Point	59	Smith, Ross	252
Rose Bay	141-3	Snapper Island	183
Rouse, James	159	Solomon, 'Sudden'	20, 42
Rowe, Thomas	88	South Head	12, 208
Royal Australian College of General Practitioners	79	Southwell, Daniel	39
		Sow and Pigs reef	151
Rozelle Bay	165, 166	Spectacle Island	183
The Rum Corps	47-8	The Spit	203
Rum Hospital, Sydney	75-7, 79, 85, 145, 164	Spit Bridge	203
Rum Rebellion	47-8, 105	Spit Junction	196
Rushcutters Bay	133, 136, 137	Spofforth Street, Mosman	211
Sacred Heart school, Rose Bay	142	Spring Racing Carnival	85-6
St Andrew's Cathedral	89, 90-1	Spring Row/Sergeant Major's Row	40, 42
St Andrew's Cathedral School	91	Stadium Australia, Olympic Park, Homebush Bay	191-2
St Andrew's Congregational Church, Balmain	176		
St Francis Xavier's, North Sydney	221	Star City Casino, Pyrmont	160, 163
St Ignatius College, Riverview	229	State Archives Office, The Rocks	23
St James, King Street	80, 83, 84-5	State Library of New South Wales	52, 74, 74
St John's, Parramatta	45, 61	Stingray Bay	248
St Joseph's College, Hunters Hill	190	'Suez Canal', George Street, Sydney	66
St Mark's, Darling Point	138	Supply, HMS	4, 39, 225
St Mary's, Balmain	174	Sussex Street, Sydney	171, 172
St Mary's Cathedral, Sydney	120-2	Swan hotel, Sydney	93
St Patrick's, Church Hill	45	swimming pool, first indoor	113
St Patrick's Girls' School, Church Hill	45	Sydney, Lord	4, 40, 247
St Peter's, Watson's Bay	150	Sydney, origins of	1-2, 4
St Peter's Presbyterian Church, North Sydney	222	Sydney Church of England Grammar School (Shore), North Sydney	221
St Philip's (earlier Phillips), Church Hill	45, 49-50	Sydney Cove	4, 5-6, 7, 11, 15, 110
		Sydney Cove Redevelopment Authority	33, 54
St Thomas's, North Sydney	220	Sydney Free Library	93
St Vincent's College, Darling Point	131	Sydney Gazette	21, 41, 44, 75, 76, 85, 92, 219
Samuels, Joseph	43-4	Sydney Harbour Bridge	18-19, 27, 28, 30, 62-4
Sandhills (Devonshire Street Cemetery)	92	Sydney Herald/Sydney Morning Herald	42, 78, 79, 120, 243
Saturday Evening Post	53		
Sawdrey, Alexander	128	Sydney Hospital, Macquarie Street	75-7, 85, 164,
School of Industry for Indigent Girls, Sydney	70	see also Rum Hospital	
Scotch Row, Miller's Point	58	Sydney International Aquatic Centre, Olympic Park, Homebush Bay	192
Scots Church, Church Hill 45,	50		
Scott, James	4	Sydney, HMAS	208, 219
Seaforth Bluff	203	Sydney Square, George Street	91
Second Fleet	23-4, 149	Sydney Tower, Centrepoint	122-3
Serventy, Vincent	242	Sydney Turf Club	242
sewerage system	87-8	Tambourine Bay	229
S.H. Ervin Gallery of Australian Art and Architecture	61	Tank Stream	6, 8, 10-11, 16, 20, 21, 110
		Tanner's Creek	231
Shakespeare Memorial Library	74	Tarpeian Rock, Sydney	20
Shakespeare Place, Sydney	70	Tarpeian Way, Sydney	17, 18
Sheer Hulk hotel, The Rocks	53-4	Taylor, Gordon	216
Shell Cove	213	Taylor Square, Darlinghurst	236
Signal Station, Vaucluse	149	Telephone Exchange, Sydney	20
Simonetti, Achille	70	Tench, Watkin	46, 107, 149
Sirius, HMS	4, 7, 11-12, 104, 108, 211, 225, 227	terrace houses, first	60
Sirius Park, Mosman	210	Terry, Sam	90
Slessor, Kenneth	127	Thermopylae	35-6
Smith, Ann	5, 36	Therry, Joseph	121
Smith, Henry Gilbert	138	Thornton, George	87

Thrupp, Alfred	214
Thrupp Street, Neutral Bay	215
Thrupp's Acres, Neutral Bay	214, 216
Thrupp's Cottage, Neutral Bay	214
Toronga Zoological Park, Mosman	205-6
Town Hall, Sydney	93-4
Tunks, Major	215
Tyrrell, James	52
Underwood Street, Sydney	20
Underwood Street, Paddington	238
Union Street, Waverton	224
University of New South Wales	243
University of Sydney	52
Upper Fort Street, Miller's Point	28
Valentia Street, Hunters Hill	190
Vaucluse	143-6
Vaucluse Bay	207
Vaucluse House, Vaucluse	143-4, 145, 146
Verge, John	132, 164
Victoria Barracks	50-1, 236-8
Victoria Street, King's Cross	129, 130
Villa Maria Church, Hunters Hill	190
Viret Street, Hunters Hill	189
Walsh Bay	30, 58, 60
Ward, Frederick	185
Wardell, Robert	84, 146
Waruda Street, Kirribilli	218
Warung Street, McMahon's Point	224
Watch House, Balmain	175
water supply, first, see Busby's Bore	86
Waterman's Cottage, Balmain	174
Watson, Fletcher	207
Watson, J.F.	76
Watson, Robert	148
Watson, HMAS	153-4
Watson Road, Miller's Point	65
Watson's Bay	149-52
Watt Park, North Sydney	222
Watts, John	61
Waverley Cemetery	246
Waverley Council	244, 246
Waverton	224
Waverton Park	224
Wells, Billy	58
Wentworth, D'Arcy	75, 76, 85, 145, 164
Wentworth, William Charles	84, 85, 106, 142, 144, 145-7, 243
Wentworth Park	99, 164
Wharf House, The Rocks	31, 33
White, John	178
William Street, Sydney	127
Wilson, Hardy	79
windmill, first	128
Windmill Street, Miller's Point	57-8
Wishing Tree, Botanic Gardens	72
Wollstonecraft	227
Wollstonecraft, Edward	214, 220, 221, 226, 227
Wollstonecraft, Mary	227
Wolseley Road, Point Piper	139
Womerah tribe	110
Woolcott Street, Waverton	224
Woollahra House, Point Piper	141
Woolloomooloo	7, 110-12, 115-16
Woolloomooloo Bay	104, 108
Woolloomooloo Hill	110
Woolloomooloo House	111-12
Wotonga, Kirribilli	217
Wran, Neville	159
Wudyong Point, Kirribilli	216
Wybalena, Hunters Hill	189
Wycombe Road, Neutral Bay	214
York Street, Sydney	50
Young Princess hotel, The Rocks	54, 57